You're close to g̶e̶t̶t̶i̶n̶g̶ a better computer

HIGH-STREET SHOPS and computer retailers may have great deals on the latest PCs, but they can't sell you the best computer you'll ever own: the one you'll build yourself. When you decide to choose the PC's components yourself, you're making sure that you get exactly the PC you need to do exactly the job you want it to.

It's not just which components you choose to buy, however, but also what you leave out. While most manufacturers offer deals on complete systems, you may be able to reuse kit from an old PC, such as the monitor, keyboard and mouse, which will save you money.

Building a PC from scratch is also a great learning process. By the time you've finished, you'll know everything about how a PC is put together. Should you have a problem in the future, this in-depth knowledge will be invaluable, as you'll know exactly how to take your computer apart, fix it and put it back together again.

Finally, many people believe that building your own PC isn't the cost-saving exercise that it once was. While PCs from manufacturers may be cheaper overall, however, they generally come with lower-quality components. Pick the best kit yourself and, pound for pound, you'll end up with a better-value computer.

In this book, you'll find everything you need to know about building a PC, from choosing the right components and operating system to fitting everything inside the case. Essential skills and troubleshooting information will help make sure that your build goes smoothly. We've also included a bonus project, where you can learn how to build a power-efficient, environmentally friendly PC.

And of course, you'll also get the enormous satisfaction that comes from building your own PC.

Happy building!

David Ludlow, Editor
david_ludlow@dennis.co.uk

BUILD A BETTER PC

Contents

Chapter 1
ESSENTIALS
Find out what you'll need before you start building a PC and learn some key skills.

PC builder's toolkit	6
Your workspace	8
Essential skills	10
Finding and installing drivers	12

Chapter 2
CHOOSING AN OPERATING SYSTEM
Find out which operating system is best for you.

Windows Vista	16
Windows XP	18
Linux	20

Chapter 3
CHOOSING YOUR HARDWARE
We explain what to look for when choosing components and suggest some ideal combinations.

Components explained	24
Budget PC	30
Mid-range PC	32
High-end PC	34
Extreme PC	36
Media Center PC	38
Mini PC	40
Essential peripherals	42

Chapter 4
BUILDING YOUR PC
Everything you need to know to go from a pile of components sitting on a desk to a complete working computer.

Taking the case apart	50
Installing the power supply	52
Installing the motherboard	54
Installing an Intel processor	58
Installing an AMD processor	59
Installing memory	60
Fitting the internal cables	62
Installing a hard disk	64
Installing an optical drive	66
Installing a graphics card	68
Installing expansion cards	70
Putting the case back together	72

Chapter 5
BUILDING AN ATOM PC
We show you how to build a capable, environmentally friendly PC for just £225.

Building a power-efficient computer	76

Chapter 6
INTO THE BIOS
Follow our step-by-step guide to the BIOS and take control of how your computer operates.

Into the BIOS	82
How to edit the BIOS	83

Chapter 7
INSTALLING AN OPERATING SYSTEM

From the initial configuration screens to installing drivers, we show you how to install an OS.

How to install Windows Vista	90
How to improve Media Center	94
How to install Windows XP	98
How to install Ubuntu Linux	102

Chapter 8
NEW PC ESSENTIALS

Once your computer is up and running, you'll need some applications to complete the perfect build. We've picked the best free software around.

OpenOffice.org 3	108
AVG Anti-Virus Free Edition	109
Paint.NET	109
Picasa 3	110
CDBurnerXP	110
Free Download Manager	111
Freebyte Backup	111
ExtractNow	111
VLC media player	111
Saving power with your new PC	112
Making an image of your hard disk	118

Chapter 9
TROUBLESHOOTING

If you've run into problems, don't panic – our tips and tricks will soon get your PC running smoothly.

Troubleshooting hardware problems	124
Troubleshooting Windows	128
Testing memory	134
Testing your hard disk	136
Testing your new PC for heat	138
Testing your processor	140

JARGON BUSTER

Glossary	142

All the buzzwords and technology explained.

BUILD A BETTER PC 3

CHAPTER 1
ESSENTIALS

BEFORE YOU RUSH out and buy the bits for your new computer, there are some essential things that you need to know. Here, we'll show you what tools you'll require, the kind of workspace you should work on, the skills that you'll need and how to download the latest drivers for your new kit.

IN THIS CHAPTER

PC builder's toolkit	6
Your workspace	8
Essential skills	10
Finding and installing drivers	12

BUILD A BETTER PC

CHAPTER 1
ESSENTIALS

PC builder's

ESSENTIAL TOOLS	
No 2 crosshead screwdriver	£1.50
Long-nose pliers	£4.50
Multi-head screwdriver	£9
Total	**£15**
www.screwfix.com	

OPTIONAL TOOLS	
Torch	£6
Cable ties	£3
www.screwfix.com	
4GB flash drive	£9
www.pcnextday.co.uk	
Thermal paste	£3
Anti-static wristband	£3
www.lambda-tek.com/componentshop	
Total	**£24**
TOTAL AMOUNT	**£39**

CAREFUL PREPARATION IS the key to every successful build, and the very first step is to get together the basic tools for the job. Over the next two pages, we'll show you how to put together a PC builder's toolkit that costs just a few pounds, but contains a range of hardware and software, which you can use again and again to tackle any build or future upgrade project with confidence.

WHAT YOU'LL GET WITH YOUR KIT
When you buy the components for your new PC, they will include a number of essential items. Your motherboard manual will have details of your motherboard's specifications and features, and an explanation of its ports and connectors. It'll also give you help with BIOS options and updates, and talk you through any bundled utility programs.

Your motherboard's box will contain all the data cables that you'll need to connect your hard disks and optical drives. There will be more cables than you need, so keep the other ones spare for future upgrades. Check the box carefully for any additional ports, such as rear-mounted USB, FireWire and eSATA. These will be easy to fit and your motherboard's manual will explain how.

Your case should have a manual that tells you how to take it apart and how to fit your components inside. Your case will generally ship with the screws that you'll need to fit your motherboard and other peripherals. If your case requires hard disks and optical drives to be fitted on runners, look for these in an accessory box either inside the packaging or the case itself.

If you're installing a graphics card, look inside its box carefully. Here you'll probably find DVI-to-VGA adaptors, which you'll need if you have a monitor with analogue inputs only; Molex-to-PCI Express power adaptors, which you'll need if your power supply doesn't have the necessary power connector; and, if your card supports it, DVI-to-HDMI adaptors. In the case of ATI graphics cards, this last item is really important. You have to use the ATI DVI-to-HDMI adaptor in order to get the sound working correctly; a standard adaptor will only deliver the picture.

Look inside all the component boxes for driver CDs. You can use these to get your hardware installed, although it's best to follow our guide on downloading the latest drivers on page 12 before you start building.

OPERATING THEATRE
A computer is useless without an operating system, so make sure that you've got your Windows or Linux disc handy before you begin building your computer.

A Windows install CD is made by Microsoft, bears a holographic Microsoft logo and has all the files needed to install the operating system. You can also use this CD to recover damaged Windows installations if you have trouble later on.

Your software box should also contain the licence key that you'll need to install Windows. You'll need this key when you install your operating system and if you ever have to reinstall Windows or contact Microsoft for support. It's critical, therefore, that you keep this key somewhere safe; without it, you'll need to buy a new copy of the software. Our complete guide to installing Windows Vista (page 90) and Windows XP (page 98) explains everything.

You will have to create a Linux installation CD before you build your computer. This is easy to do, and our guide to installing Ubuntu Linux on page 102 explains everything you need to know.

SAVE IT FOR LATER
When you build your PC, you'll find that you may be left with some spare parts, such as blanking plates for expansion cards and extra drive rails for more hard disks. We recommend that you keep these parts somewhere safe, as you may need them should you decide to upgrade your computer in the future. It's also worth keeping any spare screws, as you never know when they'll come in handy.

TOOL UP
Building a PC isn't a particularly complicated procedure, and you'll only need a few tools to complete the job successfully. The picture on the right shows you the most common tools that you'll need, and you shouldn't need anything more specialised. Our guide to essential building skills on page 10 will show you how to use these tools, and our guide to your workspace on page 8 shows you the kind of area in which you should work.

BUILD A BETTER PC

toolkit

RECOMMENDED Hardware tools

MULTI-HEAD SCREWDRIVER A ratchet or electric screwdriver with a wide range of fitments should cover anything that a standard crosshead screwdriver can't. Choose one with a range of hex sockets that includes at least 5, 6 and 7mm sizes.

CABLE TIES (not pictured) Great for tidying the inside of your PC, or to clip groups of wires or loose components out of the way while you work. Longer ties are more expensive but more versatile, and you can snip off any extra length.

ANTI-STATIC BAG Use a large anti-static bag as a safe surface for working on any sensitive components. Smaller bags are ideal for storing or transporting components. Most PC parts arrive in anti-static packaging, so don't throw them away.

MEDIUM CROSSHEAD SCREWDRIVER This can be used for almost every screw inside a PC, allowing you to fit or adjust all the major components. Choose one with a long shaft so that you can reach recessed screws.

TORCH This can be particularly useful when connecting a PC under a desk or making adjustments inside its case. A torch will also help you to read text on those components inside your PC that are labelled with small text or simply stamped with information.

FINE PLIERS You can use these to remove and fit jumpers, hold parts in tight spaces and help extract bits that are reluctant to move. You can also use them to cut wires or cable ties, and twist out metal blanking plates from a drive bay.

ANTI-STATIC WRISTBAND Wearing this reduces the chances that static electricity will damage sensitive components such as your expansion cards, motherboard, memory or processor.

STORAGE DEVICE A simple USB flash memory device lets you transfer any drivers or patches you need from another PC. A larger hard disk device is perfect for taking full backups if you're transferring data and programs from another PC.

THERMAL PASTE You may need this for the trouble-free installation of a new processor or graphics card heatsink, or when transferring a processor to a new motherboard. Make sure that you don't buy thermal adhesive by mistake.

BUILD A BETTER PC

CHAPTER 1
ESSENTIALS

Your workspace

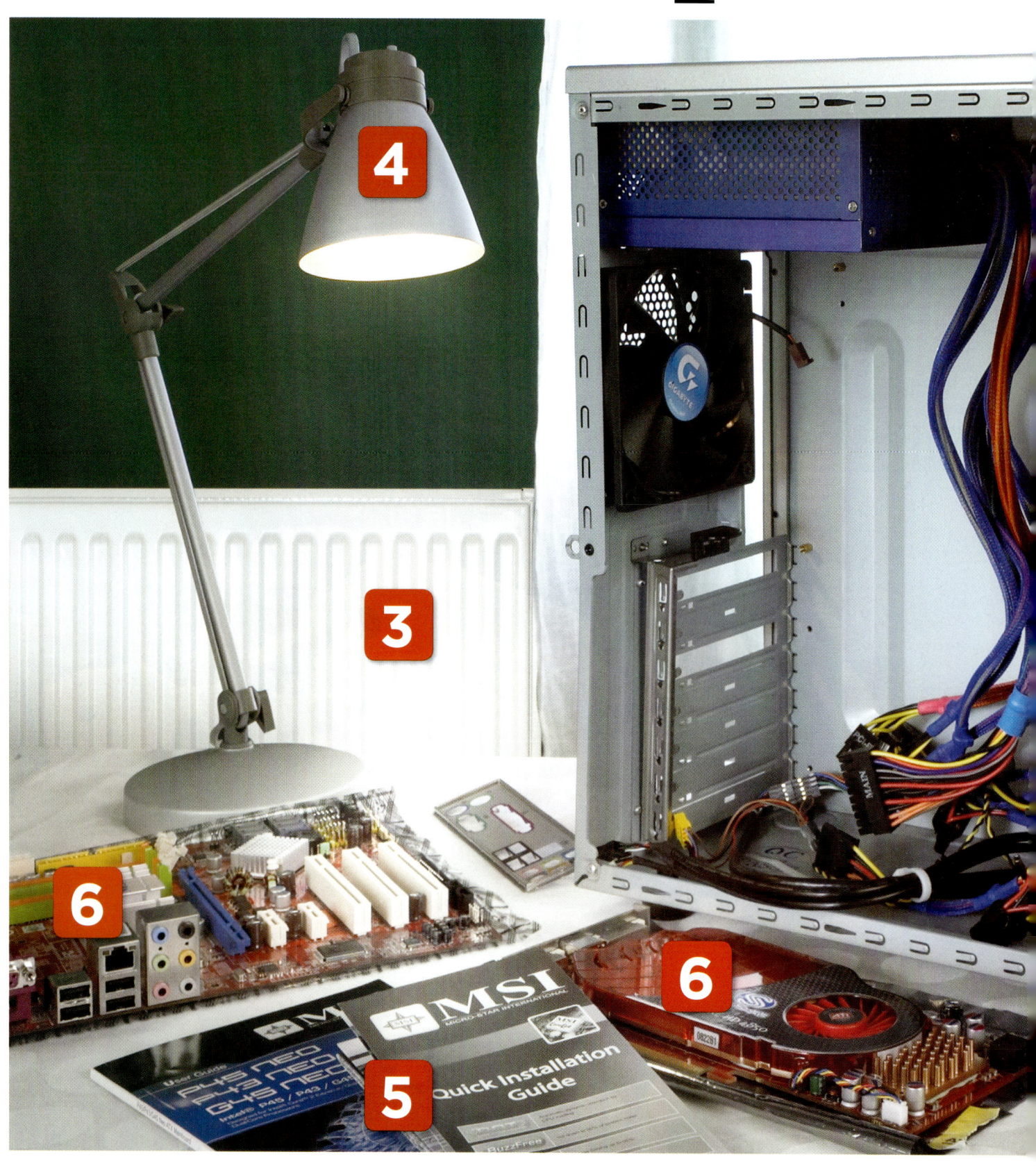

8 · BUILD A BETTER PC

1. DESK
You need a clear desk or table to work on your PC. As cases can have sharp edges, put down a cloth before you start work to prevent scratches. If you haven't got a suitable cloth, lining your desk with paper should do the job.

2. PLASTIC CUP
Screws and clips from inside your case can easily get lost. A plastic cup is a handy way of storing everything so you don't lose them.

3. RADIATOR
It's good to work near a radiator, so you can touch an unpainted part of it to discharge static. Alternatively, wear an anti-static wristband.

4. LAMP
A desk lamp will help make sure that you've got enough light inside your PC.

5. MANUALS
Keep any manuals that came with your kit handy, as they'll help you build your PC correctly.

6. COMPONENTS
Keep your components in or on top of their anti-static bags until you're ready to use them.

CHAPTER 1
ESSENTIALS

Essential skills

BEFORE YOU UNWRAP all the shiny new components you've bought and start shoving them into your case, there are some safety lessons to learn, along with some key skills that will make building your PC much easier. Without these, you run the risk of damaging your computer before you've even turned it on. The worst part is that most of the time, you'll be unable to tell that you've caused any damage until you turn on your PC for the first time. At this point, tracking the problem down can be a real nightmare. We'll take you through the main pitfalls you'll face when building a new computer and, more importantly, how to avoid them.

STATIC
We all know about static electricity: it's the charge that builds up when we walk across a carpet and discharges when we touch someone else. This little flash of electricity may not seem very powerful, but it's potentially fatal for sensitive electronic components. Get a build-up of static and touch your processor, and you may have destroyed one of the most expensive parts of your computer before you've even started.

Fortunately, avoiding problems isn't that hard. If you've got one, wear an anti-static wrist strap. This will prevent static electricity from building up, making it safe to touch any component in your computer. If you haven't got one, don't panic, as there are other ways around the problem. Try and work near a radiator. To discharge any build-up of static, simply touch the unpainted part of a radiator. You're then safe to work. Finally, all computer components come in anti-static bags to protect them. Don't remove any component from its bag until you're ready to fit it.

MAGNETIC SCREWDRIVER
Inside your PC, you'll find that there are lots of parts of your case that are awkward to reach to screw components into place. The easiest way to deal with this problem is to use a magnetic screwdriver. Simply place the screw into the screwdriver and then manoeuvre the screw towards its destination. The opposite is true when removing screws, as a gentle action should mean that a screw comes away attached to the screwdriver, rather than dropping to the floor.

Don't worry about magnetically sensitive devices inside your PC. A magnetic screwdriver isn't powerful enough to cause any damage or wipe any data.

THE RIGHT SCREWS
While the right screwdriver can make your job easier, it's essential to use the right screws to prevent damage. Put a screw that's too long into a hard disk, for example, and you could damage a circuit board and break the whole thing. Where possible, you should use the screws that come with the device, as these are guaranteed to work. Failing that, if your case has special fittings for devices, such as rails for hard disks and optical drives, the correct screws should have been fitted.

Of the different types of screws that are used, the small stubby ones are for hard disks and optical drives, the long screws are for holding expansion cards in place, while the screws with the flat heads are for fitting the motherboard and for some case panels. At all times, make sure that you don't overtighten screws, or you could cause damage. The idea is to tighten screws to the point where your components are held snugly in place.

■ Prevent the build-up of static by wearing an anti-static wrist strap

10 BUILD A BETTER PC

■ Choose the right screw for the right job

■ Check that the cables are all plugged in

THE RIGHT AMOUNT OF FORCE
When you plug components such as expansion cards, memory and a processor into your motherboard, it can be difficult to know how much force you should apply. Our tips should help you get it right. First, make sure that you've lined up your components correctly with the slot or socket – our step-by-step guide to building your PC on pages 48 to 73 will show you how to do this.

Next, make sure that you're applying equal pressure across the device to move it into position. Processors should drop into place with little pressure, memory needs a firm push to click it into place, while expansion cards need a fair push. If you're getting a lot of resistance, stop what you're doing and start over again.

POWER CABLES
When building a PC, it's important to remember you're dealing with an electrical device. Before you plug the power in and turn on your computer, check you've plugged all the power cables in properly, particularly on the motherboard. Loose connections can cause problems.

The fans inside a PC can cause problems, too, particularly if you've got power cables near them. Make sure that all power-carrying cables are clipped out of the way of fans so that you don't cut through them. Power connectors plug in only one way, so if you can't get one in make sure that it's the right way round. Forcing a connector in the wrong way will damage your devices irreparably.

Before you plug in your power cable, make sure that your power supply is set to the correct voltage. Some supplies, although rarely seen today, have a switch that changes the input voltage from 110V (US) to 230V (UK). If you've accidentally got it set to 110V, the supply will be damaged and your motherboard may be affected, too.

TAKE YOUR TIME
The best tip that we can give is to follow each step carefully and take your time. Building a PC isn't a race and, as you're dealing with lots of expensive components, it's best to get it right the first time around. Our step-by-step help will guide you through every step you need to take, while our troubleshooting guides on pages 122 to 141 will help you fix any problems that you may run into.

■ A magnetic screwdriver is a PC builder's best friend

BUILD A BETTER PC 11

CHAPTER 1
ESSENTIALS

Finding and installing drivers

ANY NEW HARDWARE that you buy will come with a driver disc, so that you can install it easily. Some motherboards even have fancy installation wizards that automatically detect which drivers you need and install them automatically. However, while this sounds straightforward, the drivers that you get on the disc are usually out of date.

If you've already got a computer, then your first job is to go on to the internet and download the latest driver files, saving them to a USB key or external hard disk. If you haven't got access to a PC, don't worry. Simply use the drivers that came on the disc until you've got a working computer, and then follow these instructions to download the latest drivers and install them afterwards. Thanks to the internet, getting drivers is incredibly easy and shouldn't take too long.

MOTHERBOARDS

The motherboard is the main part of your PC and it comes with plenty of built-in features, including onboard sound, networking, storage drivers and potentially even graphics. Windows, particularly Vista, will have drivers for many of these things, but if you want the best performance and the best range of features, you'll need the latest drivers.

You can get everything for your motherboard from the manufacturer's website: you'll find the address in your motherboard's manual. If not, then use a search engine to find the URL.

Once you're on the website, there should be a link for Support. Just keep following the links for motherboards and drivers. Eventually, you'll get to a point where you'll need to enter the details of your motherboard to locate the driver download page for your model. It's vital you get exactly the right model in order to get the correct drivers for your computer. If you can't find the details on the box or in the manual, then the motherboard's name is usually written on the board itself.

After you've entered your motherboard's details, you'll be presented with a long list of drivers divided by type, such as graphics or networking. For each heading, download one driver, making sure that you select the latest version. Most driver packages cater for all versions of Windows, but check the details to ensure that you download the correct driver.

GRAPHICS CARDS

If you're using onboard graphics, you'll be able to find the latest drivers on the motherboard

■ ATI gives you a choice of files to download, but the full Catalyst Control Suite is the best choice for new computers

■ You'll need to perform several file downloads to get the latest motherboard drivers

12 BUILD A BETTER PC

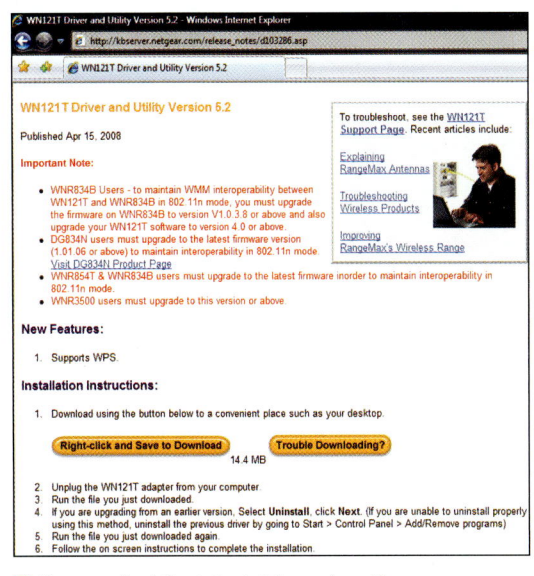

■ You can find the latest drivers for all your devices on the internet

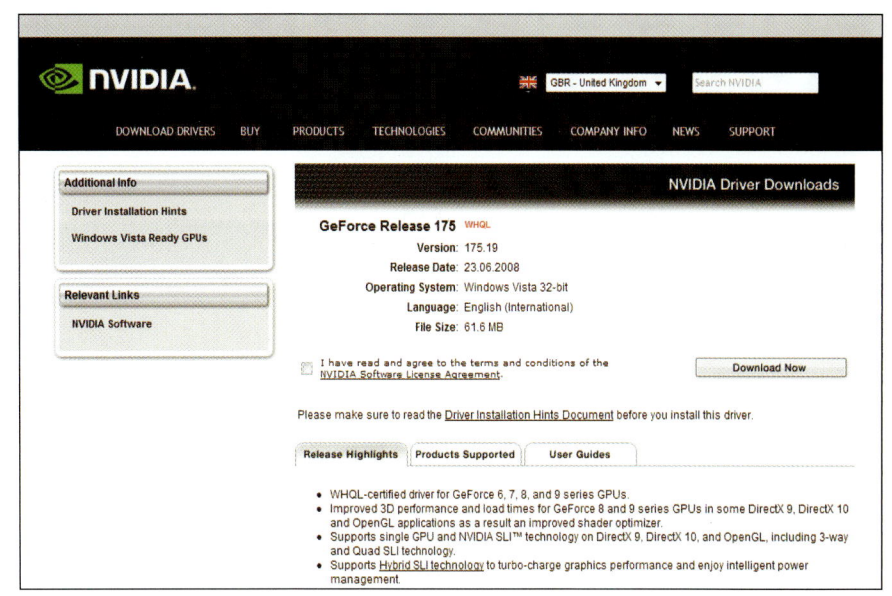

■ Nvidia has a unified driver architecture, so a single download is all you need

manufacturer's website. If you're using a dedicated graphics card, you should download the drivers directly from ATI's or Nvidia's sites. This will ensure that you get the best performance and stability from your graphics card.

NVIDIA

Nvidia uses a unified driver package, so one download will work for most of its graphics cards. This makes installation simple. Visit *www.nvidia.com* and select Download Drivers from the Download Drivers menu in the top-left of the screen. Select the type of card (GeForce for consumer graphics cards) and the series of card that you have, such as 9xxx series for a GeForce 9600 GT. Select your language as English (UK) and click Search. Tick the box to accept the licence agreement and click Download.

It's important to select your graphics card model, as not every driver package has the driver for every graphics card. If you download the wrong package, your card won't install.

ATI

ATI has a similar unified driver architecture to Nvidia. Visit *http://ati.amd.com/gb-uk* and click on Support & Drivers. Click on the Download graphics drivers link. On the next page, select which operating system you'll be installing, select Radeon from the list (consumer graphics cards are all Radeon models), and then select your card. Click Go to be taken to the driver selection page. You should select Catalyst Software Suite, as this includes the driver and the Catalyst Control Panel for configuring settings. Make sure you select your model from the list, or you may get a version of the driver that doesn't support your card.

OTHER DEVICES

If you're installing other hardware, such as a wireless network adaptor, TV tuner, sound card or printer, you'll need to download the latest drivers for these, too. In a similar way to the procedure we've described above, you'll need to visit the manufacturer's website and follow the links until you get to where you can select which device you want to download drivers for. Check a device's manual for full details on the manufacturer's website. If you can't find any information, a Google search for the manufacturer's name should bring up the details you need. Remember to make sure that you get the right driver for your device and for the OS that you require.

REGULAR CHECKS

Once you've got the latest drivers, your job isn't done. You should regularly check manufacturers' websites and see if updates are available. Typically, graphics card drivers are updated monthly, while other devices are updated less regularly.

Driver updates fix known problems and can help your PC become more stable and perform better. It's worth going back to a manufacturer's site to check for updates if you're suffering a problem, as a new driver can often fix this.

Manufacturers' websites are also useful if you want help with a product. You can also find manuals for download, which can be really helpful if you lose your printed version and need to check a detail or plan an upgrade.

TIP
New versions of drivers can sometimes fix problems with your computer. If you're having trouble with a particular device, look for a newer driver before doing anything else.

BUILD A BETTER PC **13**

CHAPTER 2
CHOOSING AN OPERATING SYSTEM

WHILE THE CHOICE of hardware may seem the most important decision when building a PC, it's the operating system that dictates how you'll use your computer. Depending on the type of PC you want, there's a choice between Windows and Linux. Here, we'll take you through the different options so that you get a system you're happy with.

IN THIS CHAPTER

Windows Vista	16
Windows XP	18
Linux	20

CHAPTER 2
CHOOSING AN OPERATING SYSTEM

Windows Vista

IF YOU'RE LOOKING to build a new PC, then it makes a lot of sense to choose Windows Vista. It was released in January 2007 and the recent service pack (SP1) means that a lot of the initial bugs have now been ironed out.

One of the main reasons that people have been reluctant to upgrade to Vista is because of hardware incompatibility. As you're starting from scratch with a new machine, though, this isn't a problem that will affect you. Here we'll examine what it can offer and why you might want to choose it for your new PC.

Vista's main advantage over its rivals is that it's Microsoft's latest operating system and, therefore, the one that most developers will be targeting when writing new applications and drivers for hardware. In fact some software, such as Office 2007, will only work with Vista. It's also the only operating system that supports the gaming technology DirectX 10. There aren't many DirectX 10-only games at the moment, but this is changing. If you want to keep up to date with the latest games and be sure that you'll be able to run all new software, there's no better choice.

Microsoft has also designed Vista to be more secure than XP. For the most part, it's done a good job improving the robustness of the system, boosting the firewall's capabilities and including Windows Defender anti-spyware by default. We'd still recommend dedicated internet security software, but a more secure operating system from the start is a good reason to opt for Vista.

Vista also has User Access Control (UAC) built in, which is supposed to increase the security of your computer by prompting you to allow any action that only an Administrator should do, such as writing to a Windows folder. While it's a good idea in practice and could stop malicious software from infecting your computer, it's a very annoying and intrusive addition that doesn't give you any helpful information on whether you should allow or deny a request. Fortunately, this much criticised addition can be switched off.

LOOKING GOOD
Not all of the new features are hidden under the surface. A lot of work has been put into making Windows easier to use and more pleasing on the eye. The new Sidebar sits down the side of the screen and holds gadgets: little applications for specific jobs, such as showing the weather, the time or displaying post-it notes. There are plenty of gadgets to choose from, too.

The big change with Vista is the built-in search feature, which makes it easier to find your files and programs. After clicking on the Start menu

■ Media Center is the easy way to view photos, videos and pictures, and record TV

■ New gadgets can be added easily

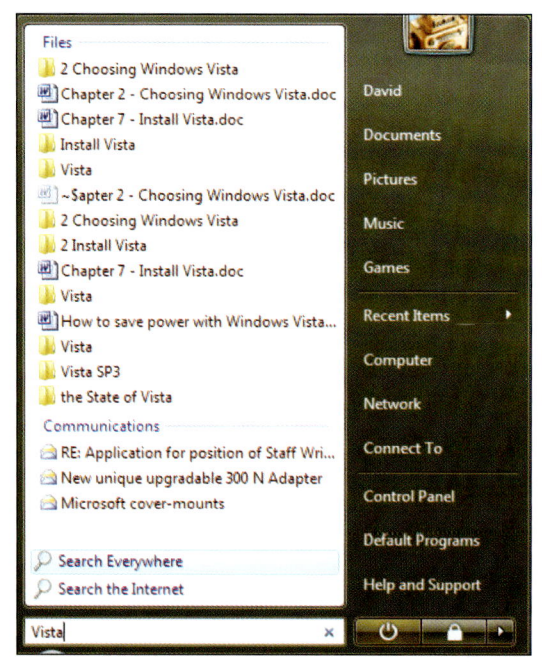

■ Vista's integrated search locates files and apps

DETAILS

Microsoft Windows Vista

DETAILS
www.microsoft.com

PRICE (OEM VERSIONS)
Home Basic	£55
Home Premium	£60
Business	£86
Ultimate	£120

GOOD FOR
Mid-range or faster PC, Media Center computer

MINIMUM REQUIREMENTS
800MHz processor, 512MB RAM, 40GB hard disk space, DirectX 9-compatible graphics card for Aero interface

PRO Easier to use than XP; more stable; Media Center is built in
CON Needs a lot of memory to run smoothly; doesn't support all old hardware and software

VERDICT
Easier to use, more secure and with better support than Windows XP, Vista is the ideal choice for new PCs, particularly high-end computers. If you're building a media centre, it's the only decent choice.

and starting to type, you're presented with a list of items that contain your search terms. This feature integrates with email (Windows Mail in Vista), so all your important information is incredibly quick to find. If you want Vista to search other email clients, such as Mozilla's Thunderbird, or scan new file types, you can download iFilters (*http://ifilter.org*) to add these capabilities.

VERSION AVERSION
While XP came in just two editions (Home and Professional), Vista comes in four versions – Home Basic, Home Premium, Business and Ultimate – so choosing the right one can seem rather daunting. Microsoft has a feature-comparison table on its website (*http://tinyurl.com/mseditions*) to help you make the right decision.

For most people, Vista Home Premium offers the best combination of price and features. Home Basic doesn't give you much for your money, and misses out features such as Media Center and the new Aero interface. Business is designed for the office, which means it includes support for networking at the expense of Media Center. Finally, Vista Ultimate includes all the features of Business and Home Premium, but it comes at a price. It also gives you access to the Ultimate Extras download site, but there's little here that makes it worth £60 more than Home Premium.

Finally, you also get a choice between the 32- and 64-bit versions of Windows. The latter can handle more system memory, while the former is limited to around 3.5GB. However, there are fewer drivers for the 64-bit version and not all software is guaranteed to work with it, so unless you're bent on sticking tons of memory in your new PC and you know that all your hardware will work, stick with the 32-bit version.

MEDIA CENTER
One of the key benefits of Vista Home Premium is that it comes with Media Center. This lets you watch and control your music, videos and photos using a remote control (around £15). If you add a TV tuner (from £15), you can even turn your PC into a hard disk recorder, complete with the free electronic programming guide.

Vista isn't the first version of Windows to include Media Center, but with XP it was an optional version of the operating system and not

■ Vista looks much better than its predecessors

built in as standard. With Vista, as it's part of the operating system, it's easier to configure and more reliable. For this reason alone, if you're looking to build a PC for the lounge, there's no better choice than Windows Vista Home Premium.

PICTURE PERFECT
It's likely that you've got tons of digital photos on your PC, and no simple way to organise them. This is where the new Windows Photo Gallery comes in. This useful utility lets you organise and categorise your photos, assigning simple tags to them. Using it, you can either look through your photos by directory or view them by tags, choosing to see all photos that contain a pet, for example.

POWER PC
The biggest problem with Vista is that it requires a fairly meaty computer to run it smoothly, and we strongly recommend that you have a PC with at least 2GB of memory in order to get the best experience. This means that it's not ideal if you want to build a very low-budget PC. There's also the problem that older hardware, such as printers and scanners a few years old, may not have compatible drivers. If you have a particular bit of kit that you want to keep using and you can't find Vista drivers, then XP could be a better choice. For everyone else, Vista's a big improvement over its predecessor and a great choice for a new PC.

TIP
The Original Equipment Manufacturer (OEM) version of Vista can be bought with any new bit of hardware and is designed for people building a computer. You don't get any telephone support included, but the OEM versions are much cheaper than the full boxed products, and cheaper than the upgrade version.

BUILD A BETTER PC **17**

CHAPTER 2
CHOOSING AN OPERATING SYSTEM

Windows XP

ALTHOUGH WINDOWS VISTA was launched with much fanfare in January 2007, it hasn't quite made the impact that Microsoft had hoped for. In part, this is because XP will run on much lower-specification systems than Vista. In fact, for this reason, XP has had something of a resurgence in the past few months. All Asus's Eee PC mini laptops come with XP installed, for example.

Unlike Vista, with its many versions, XP's choices are simple: Home and Professional. XP Professional is in effect the full XP edition, with Home essentially a stripped-down – and less expensive – version. For example, because Home is targeted towards non-work use, options necessary in a corporate environment, such as Terminal Services (Microsoft's client that allows access to central server data and applications), are disabled in Home. Similarly, because Pro users benefit from more configurable user groups and administration options, such features are thinned out in Home. Finally, remote desktop, which lets you control your computer over a network, is missing altogether from Home.

The only other advantage that Professional has is that it's available in 64- and 32-bit versions, whereas Home is only available as 32-bit. The main difference is that the 64-bit edition can handle memory capacities over 4GB, while the 32-bit version can only accept 4GB of RAM, although only around 3.5GB is usable in practice. The downside of the 64-bit version is that it suffers from poor driver support and not all software will run on it. For that reason, we recommend sticking to the 32-bit version. We'd also recommend XP Home, as you're unlikely to need the more advanced features of XP Professional.

LOWER COST
As well as the more clearly targeted editions of XP's Home and Professional, its pricing is lower than that of Vista, making the older operating system even more tempting in terms of the cost of putting a system together on a tight budget; saving money here means you'll have more to spend on components. So while the two ends of Vista's scale, Ultimate and Home Premium, cost around £120 and £60 respectively, XP Professional and Home Edition can be had for £85 and £50 respectively.

SPEED RUNNER
Pricing isn't the only area in which XP beats Vista. Based purely on the speed of one system running each operating system, XP leaves Vista behind on startup, shutdown and in the opening of applications and programs, which ultimately translates into a faster computing experience.

The reason XP is faster than Vista is to do with the required specifications of the systems on which they were designed to run. When XP was launched in 2001, both Home and Professional editions were designed to run on a PC with a 233MHz processor, 64MB of RAM and just 1.5GB of hard disk space. Compared to Vista, and even the entry Home Basic edition, the difference is gargantuan. Home Basic requires an 800MHz processor, 512MB of RAM

■ XP may be getting old, but it's quick to run and requires lower hardware specifications than Vista

■ XP's familiar interface, stability and reliability still make it a good choice for a new computer

---

DETAILS

Microsoft Windows XP

DETAILS
www.microsoft.com

PRICE (OEM VERSIONS)
Home Edition £50
Professional £85

GOOD FOR
Budget PC, mid-range, high-end, extreme, mini PC

MINIMUM REQUIREMENTS
233MHz processor, 64MB RAM, 1.5GB hard disk space, VGA (800x600), CD-ROM or DVD drive

PRO Excellent software and hardware compatibility; support until 2014; fast on low-specification PCs
CON Being phased out; looks a little dated

VERDICT
Considering its price, performance, hardware and software compatibility, and reliability, XP is still a fine choice for a new PC.

and 15GB of disk space, and things get worse when you move up the scale of available versions: Home Premium, Business and Ultimate each require 1GB of RAM and a sizeable 40GB of free hard disk space. Frankly, Vista is highly resource-intensive and sluggish compared to XP.

SUPPORT GROUP

Although the cost and speed may be tempting you to consider using XP, you might be concerned about the support now offered to XP by Microsoft. As with any new product release, Microsoft has to prioritise resources – and developers – towards the newest arrival. Support for XP cannot be indefinite, and Microsoft's support cycle always suggested that XP would eventually be dropped.

Microsoft starting phasing out Windows XP in June 2008. However, this doesn't mean that it's no longer available, as some resellers and retailers still have copies of the operating system. The current view is that while major retailers won't stock boxed copies of Windows XP, smaller resellers will be able to sell the OEM versions (see Tip, below) until the end of January 2009. Extended support for XP, including free security updates, will continue until April 2014, by which time even the most ardent XP user may be considering upgrading.

YOU CAN RELY ON IT

The final reason that Windows XP is still a good choice for a new system is its stability and reliability. Hailed as one of the most stable operating systems Microsoft has built to date, XP benefits from three service packs, as well as extensive driver support for hardware across the board. Vista is still relatively young compared to its predecessor, and will undoubtedly become more stable and reliable as its life cycle progresses, but XP has had seven years' worth of work and support put into making it the number one operating system worldwide. In the future, given the amount of user support XP has globally, hardware and software developers will continue to support XP as they have previous operating systems, probably until 2014 as well.

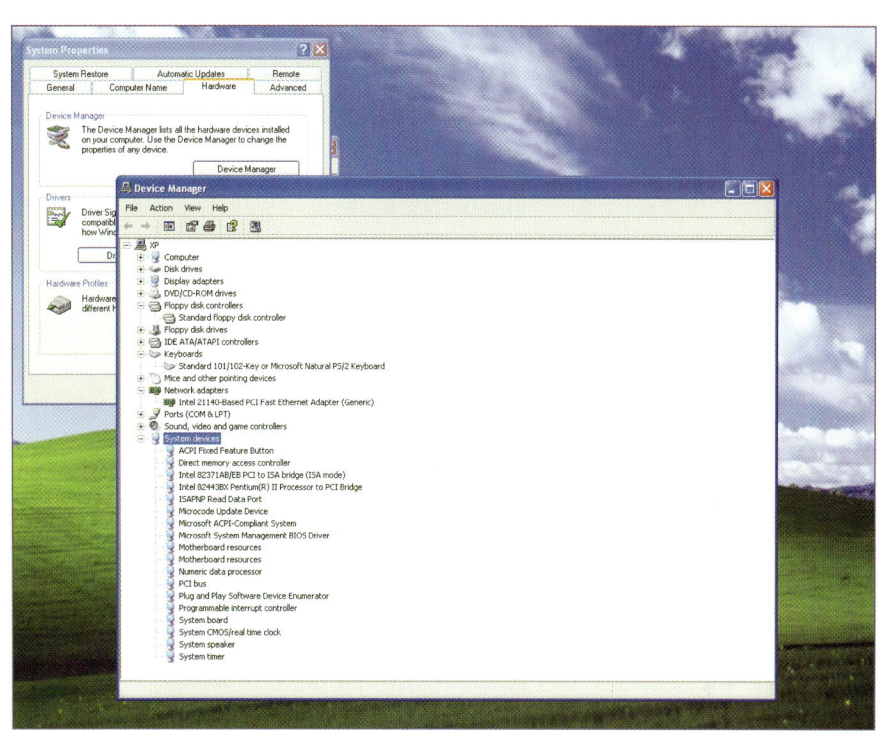

■ You'll have no problems getting hardware or software to work with XP

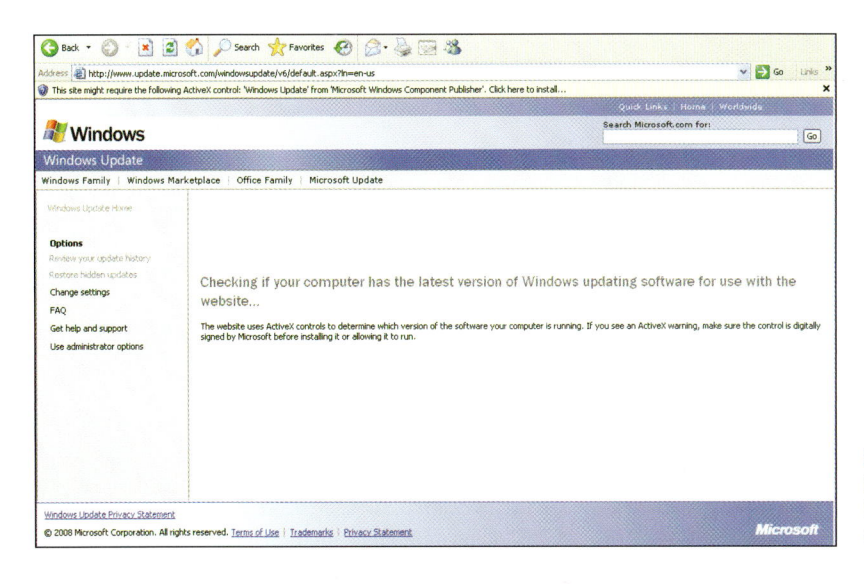

■ Support is a key concern for older applications, but Microsoft has announced it will support XP until 2014

TIP
The Original Equipment Manufacturer (OEM) version of Windows XP can be bought with any new bit of hardware and is designed for people building a new computer. You don't get any telephone support included, but the OEM versions are much cheaper than the full boxed products, and less expensive than the upgrade version.

BUILD A BETTER PC   **19**

CHAPTER 2
CHOOSING AN OPERATING SYSTEM

Linux

LINUX HAS A reputation for being tricky to use and something that only those who like to mess around with command lines should even bother with. While to a certain degree this reputation is justified, Linux has come on in leaps and bounds in the past few years, and is now arguably just as easy to install as Windows. It's also being used by many companies in mainstream laptops. The current bunch of mini laptops, including Asus's Eee PC and Acer's Aspire One, all run a version of Linux with a simplified menu.

Linux, then, can be just as good a choice as Windows. Here we'll examine why you might want to install Linux on your PC.

OPEN BORDERS
The main benefit of Linux is that it's totally free. As an open source product, it costs nothing no matter what you want to use it for. The result has been that different companies have taken Linux and modified it to create their own version, or distributions (distros), of the operating system.

The downside to this is that there's a large number of different versions to choose from, each with its own slightly different installation routine and slightly different way of working. While this can be confusing, we recommend Ubuntu. This manages to get a good balance between ease of use and power, and is a popular choice within the Linux community. There are full download and installation instructions on page 102.

A FAMILIAR DESKTOP
If you decide to install Linux, you'll find that you end up with a desktop that doesn't look a million miles away from Windows. In fact, from the desktop, you can select Computer from the Places menu and browse through files in a Windows Explorer-style file manager. All the usual drag-and-drop functions are available, and you can even create files and folders in the same way as you can in Windows. From this point of view, using Linux is just as easy as using Windows.

More than just sharing a similar way of managing files, you'll find that Linux shares a lot of applications with Windows, such as the OpenOffice free office suite and the Firefox web browser. What you may find surprising, though, is that if you use Ubuntu, you'll find it easier to install these applications than if you run Windows. Using the Add/Remove Programs application you can browse additional software to install from an easy-to-use menu. Ubuntu downloads any applications you want to install automatically. Try and do that with Windows.

That said, there's no getting away from the fact that your Windows applications won't install on Linux. While you'll be able to find free open source equivalents for most of your Windows applications, not every type of application will be listed. You may be lucky enough to find an application for download from the web, but there's no standard installation routine for Linux, so getting a new application installed can be difficult.

UPDATED
Just as with Windows, Ubuntu is at risk from malicious hackers looking to exploit security vulnerabilities in the operating system. Fortunately, Ubuntu also has its own free updates. A message

■ The Linux desktop is similar to Windows

■ Adding new applications is incredibly simple

DETAILS

Ubuntu Desktop Edition

DETAILS
www.ubuntu.com

PRICE
Free

GOOD FOR
Budget, mid-range PCs

MINIMUM REQUIREMENTS
700MHz processor, 384MB RAM, 8GB hard disk space

PRO Free; simple application installation
CON Hardware support not as good as in Windows; poor games support

VERDICT
As it's completely free, Ubuntu is an attractive choice where cost is a primary concern. Even where this isn't the case, if you want a PC for the internet and office work, Ubuntu's great.

pops up when new updates are ready to be installed. Clicking on it lets you select the updates you want to install, which are then downloaded automatically from the internet and installed on your computer. In this way, Ubuntu is just as easy to use and keep updated as Windows.

HARDWARE

While you'll find that Ubuntu will install flawlessly on most computers, there are times when you'll have hardware that doesn't work properly as there aren't drivers for it. Wireless network adaptors are one good example of hardware that you can have problems with. However, a fair number of hardware manufacturers make Linux drivers available on their websites. What you don't get, though, is a simple installation file to run. Instead, installing drivers can be a real pain. Fortunately, if you search the internet for help, you'll find lots of forums that can talk your through installation.

Before choosing to install Linux, you may be best off running Ubuntu from CD (see our instructions on page 102) to see if you like the look and feel of the OS. If you do, check that drivers are available for the hardware and peripherals that you'll want to use.

TRICKY TIMES

Finally, while Linux has improved enormously, there are the odd times where it proves itself to be a bit tricky to deal with. Installing drivers is one such area, but there are other things that are difficult. Trying to troubleshoot problems in Linux can be very difficult, and sometimes there's no choice but to revert to a command line to get something done. This shouldn't put you off, and if you're interested in tinkering with your new computer and want to learn some new skills, Linux is a good way to go.

CONCLUSION

It's hard not to be taken in by Linux's charms, especially as it's free. With Firefox and OpenOffice easy to install from inside Ubuntu, Linux is a great choice for a budget or mid-range PC whose primary job is going to be browsing the internet, sending email and using office documents.

If you want a wider choice of applications, have lots of peripherals and other hardware, then Windows is the better choice. If you'll be building a higher-end PC, particularly if gaming is a consideration, you should also use Windows.

■ Familiar applications, such as Firefox, are the same in Linux as in Windows

■ Linux's file browser is similar to Windows Explorer

■ Linux is free, so it's great for a budget PC

TIP
There are tons of help forums and lots of friendly Linux users out there. If you're having a problem, search the internet and you're bound to find an answer or at least a site where you can ask for assistance.

BUILD A BETTER PC 21

CHAPTER 3
CHOOSING YOUR HARDWARE

CHOOSING THE RIGHT components for your PC can be daunting. Here we'll explain the ins and outs of the latest peripherals, and we've also put together recommended specifications and upgrade advice for different budgets and PC use.

BUILD A BETTER PC

IN THIS CHAPTER

Components explained	24
Budget PC	30
Mid-range PC	32
High-end PC	34
Extreme PC	36
Media Center PC	38
Mini PC	40
Essential peripherals	42

CHAPTER 3
CHOOSING YOUR HARDWARE

Components explained

WE'VE INCLUDED SOME example specifications for PCs later on in this chapter, but it's good to get an understanding of the different components before you go out and buy the parts for your PC. That way, you'll have a better understanding of why we've made our recommendations, and you'll know when to choose faster components.

CASES

The first place to start is with the type of case that you'll use. This will dictate the look of your PC, and how many hard disks and optical drives you can add to it. The quality of the case can also dictate just how loud your finished computer will be, so it's worth getting something decent.

SIZE

Cases come in two sizes: ATX and microATX. ATX cases are the regular size and take all modern motherboards, while microATX cases are smaller and only take microATX motherboards.

For most general-purpose desktop PCs, you're best off with a standard ATX case. You don't have to pay the earth to get something decent, though. Generally, around £25 to £30 will get you a well-made case, such as Gigabyte's GZ-X1. If you're looking to build a more powerful PC, then spend a bit more. As well as ending up with a more attractive computer to suit your expensive components, you'll get a higher-quality model, too. This will be easier to build and it will be more stable, so you'll end up with a quieter PC that doesn't vibrate as much.

If you're planning to build a PC for the living room, you should choose a home theatre case. These are designed to look like hi-fi components, to fit in with your other entertainment gear. Silverstone's Grandia GD01 (around £125) is a great choice, with room for a full-size motherboard and plenty of storage. It also comes with a built-in Media Center remote control receiver and LCD screen, though it's quite large. Smaller media centre cases that take microATX motherboards are available, but be careful, as most of these will require you to install a laptop-sized optical drive. These are generally a lot more expensive than standard desktop components, and there's also a trade-off between size and performance.

BAREBONES

If you've got your mind set on a tiny PC, then you're best off buying a barebones kit. These come with a motherboard and power supply pre-installed in a tiny case, so you have to choose whether you're going to install an AMD or Intel processor before you buy. Be warned, though: choosing a small PC means there'll be less room inside for hard disks, and not all of them will take a dedicated graphics card. That said, Asus's T3-M2NC1PV (AMD) and T3-P5945GC X (Intel) both cost around £90, and accept dedicated graphics cards. Shuttle (*www.shuttle.eu*) is another popular manufacturer of barebones cases.

PROCESSOR

The processor is the brains of the computer and plays a massive part in dictating how quickly your

■ Make sure the case you choose is suitable for the type of PC you want to build

PC will run. You've got a choice between AMD and Intel processors, and you need to make sure that you match your processor to your motherboard. In both cases, you should buy at least a dual-core processor. These in effect have two processors inside one chip, which makes multitasking (running more than one application at once) more effective. Old single-core processors are no cheaper, so are best avoided.

INTEL

Intel has the best range of processors at the moment, from budget all the way up to high-end. There are, however, a few things you need to understand about them in order to ensure you get the right motherboard.

All Intel's processors fit into a motherboard with a LGA775 socket. The choice isn't that easy, though, as you also have to consider the processor's speed to find a compatible motherboard. An Intel processor's speed (quoted in GHz, such as 2.66GHz) is really two things: an external bus multiplied by a multiplier. For example, the 3GHz Core 2 Duo E8400 has a 333MHz external bus and a x9 multiplier.

To run a specific processor in a motherboard, you need one that supports the processor's external bus speed. However, the external bus speed is often quoted as the front side bus (FSB) speed, which is the external bus speed multiplied by four (quad-pumped). So, the E8400 can also be said to have a 1,333MHz FSB. Typically speaking, the newer the motherboard, the greater the range of processors it supports. We'll cover motherboard support on the following page.

For the budget buyer, Intel's Celeron dual-core processors are the best choice. Despite the old-sounding name, these processors are essentially the same as the Core 2 Duo products. Prices start from around £36 for the E1200, they have an 800MHz FSB and will work with all modern Intel motherboards.

The Core 2 range has products with 800MHz, 1,066MHz, 1,333MHz and 1,600MHz FSBs. You'll need a modern motherboard to support the 1,333MHz and 1,600MHz models. The 2.2GHz E4500 (around £80), which has an 800MHz FSB, is a good mid-range choice. Those looking for a fast processor should choose the 3GHz E8400 (around £110), which has a 1,333MHz FSB.

Intel also has a range of quad-core processors, which are like having two Core 2 Duo products in one chip. These Core 2 Quads can be quite expensive, though. The 2.4GHz Q6600 (around £150) has a 1,066MHz FSB and is good value, but the 2.66GHz Q9450 (around £200) has a 1,333MHz FSB and offers amazing power for the money. If cash is no object, the 3.2GHz Core 2 Extreme QX9770 (around £1,000) has a 1,600MHz FSB and is incredibly fast, plus it can be easily overclocked.

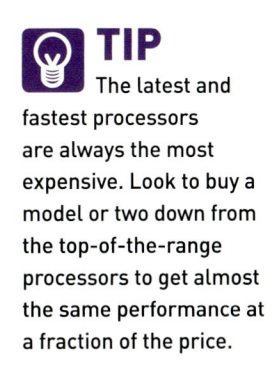

■ You need to get a motherboard that supports your chosen processor

■ A barebones case is a quick way to build a new PC

TIP
The latest and fastest processors are always the most expensive. Look to buy a model or two down from the top-of-the-range processors to get almost the same performance at a fraction of the price.

FREE TOOLKIT

when you claim 3 issues of Computer Shopper DVD version for just £1

Your FREE Toolkit

This incredibly useful general purpose set is perfect for PC repairs and any handy work. The toolkit contains 26 durable pieces in a neat compact case.

- **9 assorted bits** (Philips: No.1, 2 & 3, Slotted: 4.0mm, 6.0mm & 7.0mm, Torx: T10, T15 & T20)
- Adaptor
- Magnetic tip handle
- Mini long nose pliers
- Mini slide cutter
- Stainless steel tweezers
- Sockets 1/4" Drive (7mm, 8mm, 9mm & 10mm)
- Extension Bar
- 6 precision screwdrivers (2 Philips and 4 slotted)

WORTH £9.99

SAVE 26%

YOUR GREAT DEAL
- 3 issues for £1
- Save 26% on the shop price
- FREE Toolkit
- FREE delivery to your door
- Get every issue before it hits the shops

CALL NOW ON 0844 844 0031

Order securely online at **www.dennismags.co.uk/computershopper** entering offer code **G0811BBP** or return the invitation below

---

COMPUTER SHOPPER — FREE TOOLKIT INVITATION [UK ONLY]

☑ **YES!** Please start my subscription to Computer Shopper with **3 issues for £1 and send me my FREE Toolkit**. I understand that after 3 issues for £1, my subscription will automatically continue at the great low rate of just £21.99 every 6 issues **(saving 26% on the shop price)**. If I am not completely satisfied, I can write to cancel my subscription during my introductory period and no further money will be taken from my account.

YOUR DETAILS – Please complete in BLOCK CAPITALS

MR/MRS/MS   FORENAME
SURNAME
ADDRESS
POSTCODE
DAYTIME PHONE   MOBILE NO.
E-MAIL   YEAR OF BIRTH

Your details will be processed by Dennis Publishing Ltd (publishers of Computer Shopper magazine) and our suppliers in full accordance with UK data protection legislation. Dennis Publishing Ltd may contact you with information about our other products and services. Please tick if you prefer NOT to receive such information by post ☐ email ☐ phone ☐ mobile phone messaging ☐. Dennis Publishing Ltd occasionally shares data, on a secure basis, with other reputable companies that wish to contact you with information about their products and services. Please tick if you prefer NOT to receive such information by post ☐ phone ☐. Please tick if you DO wish to receive such information by email ☐ mobile phone messaging ☐. If the recipient of this subscription is under 18 please tick here ☐.

Gift subject to availability. Offer limited to 1 per household. Dennis Publishing reserves the right to replace the gift shown with one of equal or greater value. Please allow 28 days for delivery.

☐ **Direct Debit Payment**
Please start my subscription with 3 issues for £1. After 3 issues, I understand that my subscription will continue at the low rate of just £21.99 (Saving 26%) every 6 issues – unless I write to tell you otherwise

Instruction to your Bank or Building Society to pay by Direct Debit

Please complete and send to: Freepost RLZS-ETGT-BCZR, Dennis Publishing Ltd, 800 Guillat Ave, Kent Science Park, Sittingbourne ME9 8GU
Name and full postal address of your Bank or Building Society

To the manager: Bank name
Address
Postcode
Account in the name(s) of
Branch sort code
Bank/Building Society account number
Signature(s)
Date

Originator's Identification Number: 7 2 4 6 8 0

Ref no. to be completed by Dennis Publishing

Instructions to your Bank or Building Society
Please pay Dennis Publishing Ltd. Direct Debits from the account detailed in this instruction subject to the safeguards assured by the Direct Debit Guarantee. I understand that this instruction may remain with Dennis Publishing Ltd and, if so, details will be passed electronically to my Bank/Building Society.

Banks and building societies may not accept Direct Debit instructions for some types of account

Please return to:
Freepost RLZS-ETGT-BCZR, Computer Shopper Subscriptions, 800 Guillat Avenue, Kent Science Park, Sittingbourne, ME9 8GU

You will be able to view and amend your subscription details online at www.subsinfo.co.uk

Offer Code: G0811BBP

CHAPTER 3
CHOOSING YOUR HARDWARE

Intel has Extreme Editions of its processors. These let you increase the processor's multiplier for easy overclocking. The downside is that they're very expensive. The £1,000 Core 2 Extreme QX9770, mentioned on the previous page, is supported only by the latest motherboards. The QX6850 is slightly better value at £600, and has a 1,333MHz FSB. Unless you're serious about overclocking, though, the normal Core 2 Duo and Core 2 Quad processors are better value.

Finally, Intel has recently announced its new range of processors: the quad-core Core i7 series. These are completely different to the previous range of processors and have integrated memory controllers, like AMD's processors. To use one of these processors, you'll need a brand new motherboard (Intel's X58 chipset is currently the only one) and you'll have to use DDR3 memory.

AMD
AMD's processors have suffered in comparison to those offered by Intel in recent years, but the new Phenom range of processors is getting better, and the older Athlon series is great value, although they are being phased out. While AMD processors' speed is worked out in the same way to Intel processors (external bus multiplied by multiplier), all AMD processors have a 200MHz external bus speed, so they work with most motherboards. All AMD processors fit into motherboards with AM2 sockets. However, Phenom processors won't work in all AM2 motherboards and get the best performance when installed in an AM2+ motherboard, so check for compatibility before you buy. Fortunately, AM2+ is backwards-compatible, so you can buy a newer motherboard and install an Athlon X2 instead if you prefer.

The 2.2GHz Athlon 64 X2 4200+ (around £43) is great value for a budget computer, while the 2.6GHz Athlon 64 X2 6000+ (around £70) is great for mid-range computers. If you want something faster, then a Phenom's the best choice. Currently the quad-core 2.5GHz Phenom X4 9850 Black Edition (around £150) is the best choice.

In both cases (Athlon 64 X2 and Phenom) the Black Edition means that the processor's multiplier can be changed for easy overclocking. Unlike Intel, AMD doesn't charge a premium for these processors.

MOTHERBOARDS
Once you've chosen your case and processor, the next step is to work out what kind of motherboard you're going to install. The starting point will depend on whether you want to go for an Intel or AMD processor. In both cases, it's

■ Make sure that your motherboard has enough expansion slots

usually worth spending a little bit more to get a motherboard that will support the widest range of processors, so that you can upgrade your PC at a later date. Also, make sure that you get the right size motherboard to fit your case (ATX or microATX), remembering that microATX boards can also fit inside ATX cases.

INTEL
Choosing an Intel motherboard can be tricky, as you need to make sure that you buy one that supports the front side bus speed of your chosen processor. Typically speaking, for budget computers a motherboard that uses Nvidia's GeForce 7100 or Intel's G31 Express chipsets are a good bet. These support processors with FSBs up to 1,333MHz and have onboard graphics. Intel's P43 chipset is the next stage up in terms of performance, although most boards that use it still only support 1,333MHz FSB processors.

If you want greater performance, look for a motherboard with Intel's P45 chipset. These support 1,600MHz FSB processors and, usually, ATI's CrossFire technology. For the same processor support but with Nvidia's SLI technology, you'll need a motherboard with an nForce 790i chipset.

AMD
Choosing an AMD board is comparatively easy, as any AM2+ motherboard will take one of AMD's current processors and future processors for some time to come. That said, what you want to achieve will dictate the chipset that you buy. If you're

> **TIP**
> 32-bit Windows only supports a maximum of 4GB of RAM and then only uses around 3.5GB of it, so it's not worth buying more memory than this. The 64-bit versions don't have this limitation.

BUILD A BETTER PC **27**

CHAPTER 3
CHOOSING YOUR HARDWARE

looking to build a budget computer or Media Center PC, motherboards that use AMD's 780G chipset are a good bet. These are well priced and, depending on the manufacturer, often have HDMI outputs for high-definition video.

Moving up, if you want better performance and ATI's CrossFire technology, look for a board that uses AMD's 790X chipset. For Nvidia's SLI technology and high-end performance, the nForce 650a SLI chipset is a good choice.

MEMORY

The type of memory that you buy will depend on your processor and motherboard. For Intel-based systems, the motherboard dictates the type of memory you can install and there's a choice of DDR2 and DDR3 motherboards. DDR3 memory is more expensive and not worth buying, unless you've bought a new Core i7 system, in which case you have to use it.

SPEED

Just as with processors, DDR2 memory comes at different speeds. The two main options are 800MHz (also known as PC2-6400) and 1,066MHz (also known as PC2-8500). AMD processors have the memory controller integrated into the chip. This dictates what speed memory they can access. All AMD Athlon 64 X2 processors can run PC-6400 RAM; Phenoms can run PC-8500 RAM.

Intel Core 2 systems have the memory controller on the motherboard, and memory speed is limited by this. The speed should not exceed the processor's FSB speed. As a general rule, then, processors with a 1,066MHz FSB or faster can run PC-8500 memory; processors with an 800MHz FSB can run PC-6400. Memory is backwards-compatible, so you can run faster memory at a slower speed.

For budget and mid-range systems, we recommend a minimum of 1GB of PC-6400, which should cost around £15. Upgrading to 2GB will make your PC smoother to run and will cost around £30. Fitting faster PC-8500 RAM, where supported, will improve your computer's performance and should cost from around £50. In both cases buy your memory in matched pairs, consisting of two memory sticks. Motherboards have two memory channels, so fitting memory to each channel improves performance.

GRAPHICS CARDS

If you don't intend to play the latest games and aren't interested in watching HD movies, you don't need to bother with a dedicated graphics card and should get a motherboard with onboard graphics. Otherwise, you'll need a motherboard with a PCI Express (PCI-E) x16 slot.

For watching HD movies smoothly, Sapphire's Radeon HD 3450 (£39) is a good choice. This card will decode Blu-ray and HD DVD movies, taking the strain off your processor, and add an HDMI output to your computer. For games, Sapphire's HD 4850 (£110) is the best card to buy. It's incredibly quick in games and great value, although it struggles to run some of the latest games, such as Crysis, at maximum detail settings. For the ultimate performance, Leadtek's Winfast GTX 260 (£194) provides stunning performance.

Both Nvidia and ATI have technology – SLI and CrossFire, respectively – to let you run two graphics cards together for more performance. However, the gains are small compared to the cost.

STORAGE

Whatever PC you're building, we recommend that you buy a DVD writer. These can be bought for as little as £11. Our current favourite drive is Pioneer's DVR-215 (£17). This will write all types of DVD. If you want to write Blu-ray discs, LG's GGW-H20L (£147) is the best choice, and it will also let you play Blu-ray and HD DVD films, the latter of which can be bought very cheaply.

Finally, you'll need to get a hard disk that's big enough for all your files. While you can get an 80GB hard disk for £21, we don't recommend it, as it's poor value. Instead, spend around £28 to get a 250GB hard disk. If your budget will stretch, look to spend £40 for a 500GB disk or more for disks up to 1TB in size.

■ You need a PCI-E x16 slot and a powerful graphics card to play the latest games

Built your own desktop?
Fancy building your own laptop too?

LogiQ Barebone Laptop Chassis — £349
Intel Centrino 2 Ready, 15.4" Screen, Built in DVD-RW, 1.3m px Webcam
Product Code: 3310-3210

Intel Core 2 Duo T9400 Processor — £259
2.53GHz Speed, 1066MHz FSB, 6MB Cache, 3 Year Warranty
Product Code: 1122-3458

2GB Buffalo Laptop Memory — £17
DDR2 800Mhz, 200 Pin, 1 Year Warranty
Product Code: 3790-1050

320GB Fujitsu Laptop Hard Drive — £54
2.5" Drive, 8MB Cache, Shock Protection, 3 Years Warranty
Product Code: 1012-1486

Azurewave Wireless N Lan Card — £17
Mini PCI Express, 802.11 a/b/g/n compatible
Product Code: 3810-6250

Windows Vista Home Premium — £69
64bit edition, OEM copy, Media Included
Product Code: 3010-1441

So you've built your own desktop and you're pretty pleased with yourself. But what happens when you need computing mobility? Well you could get yourself an off-the shelf laptop, but as soon as you modify it you will violate the warranty. So how about putting those new computer build skills you've developed to more good use and build your own laptop instead?

At PC Nextday we have a massive selection of laptop barebone chassis and laptop components so you can build your own laptop with the exact specification that's right for you. Visit our on-line store at www.pcnextday.co.uk for more information.

ORDER NOW AT
www.pcnextday.co.uk

Download our hands on guide to building your own laptop at:

pcnextday.co.uk/laptopbuild

pcnextday
www.pcnextday.co.uk

CHAPTER 3
CHOOSING YOUR HARDWARE

Budget PC

THIS PC IS about as cheap as it's possible to get. It costs around £183, yet can still perform most everyday tasks, such as surfing the web and sending emails, typing documents and creating spreadsheets. It even has a dual-core processor, so can encode video at a reasonable speed, and the 250GB hard disk leaves a fair amount of room for images and music.

It won't do anything particularly quickly, though. You'll certainly struggle with video editing, and the relatively small amount of RAM may cause you problems when editing large images, such as digital photos taken in RAW mode. Playback of high-definition films is also out, as is playing games. The PC is upgradable, though, and will make a good base for future upgrades so long as you don't get too ambitious with the components you want to fit.

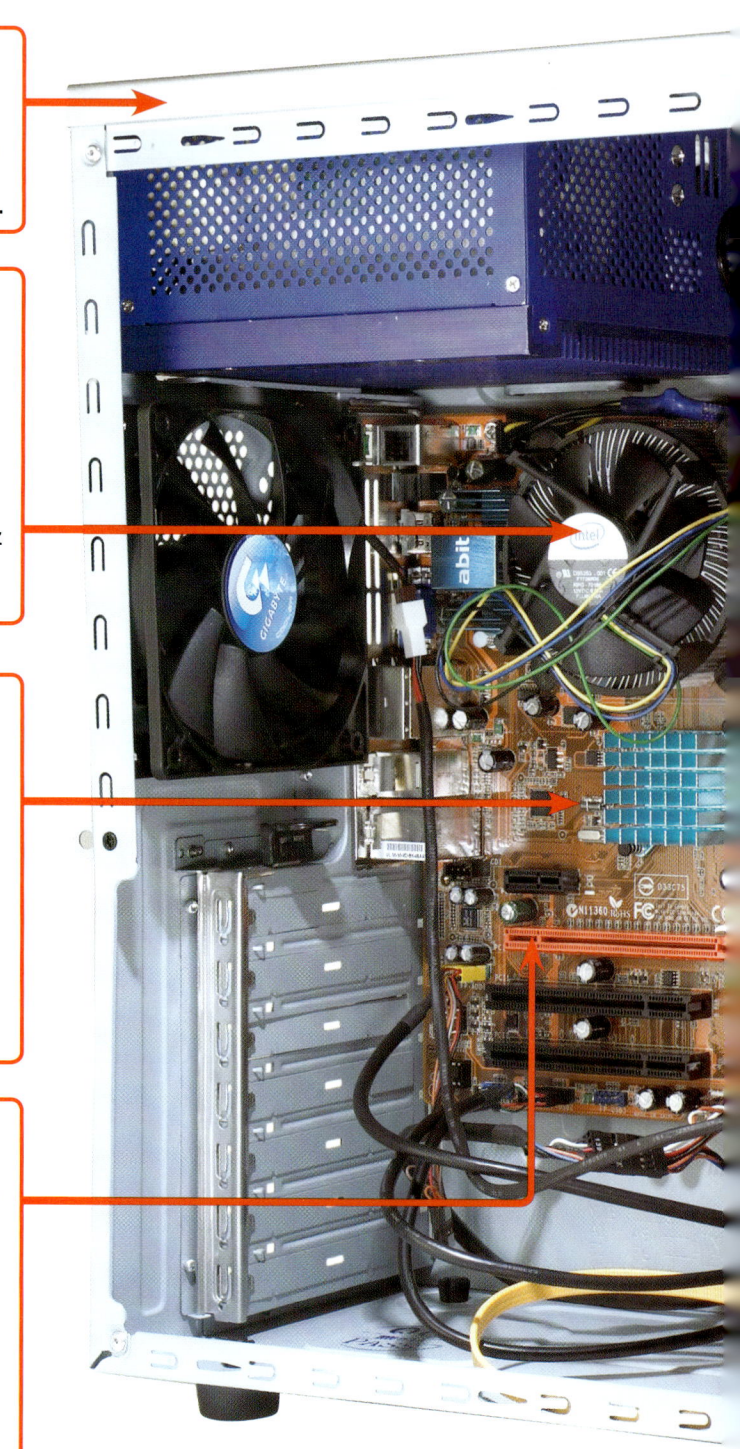

CASE This case is fairly good value and doesn't look bad either. With its screwless design, it's pretty easy to build, too. Consider upgrading to an Antec P182 (£87) if you want a bit more room and a more attractive PC.

PROCESSOR The 1.6GHz Celeron E1200 is the cheapest dual-core processor you can buy. It will perform reasonably well in multithreaded applications, such as video encoding, but it will struggle with programs that only use one core. You could get a significant speed boost by upgrading to a 2GHz Pentium Dual Core E2180, which costs around £42.

MOTHERBOARD The PC's motherboard is a MicroATX model. It has all the usual features, such as integrated networking and sound, but it doesn't have as many slots for expansion cards as a full-size motherboard. If you need more room for expansion cards, you should spend £52 on MSI's P43 Neo-F, but you'll need to buy a dedicated graphics card to use with this board.

GRAPHICS CARD The motherboard has integrated graphics, which are fine for Linux but no good for games or high-definition video playback. A cheap card, such as Sapphire's £29 Radeon HD 3450, will give you high-definition video playback when coupled with the processor upgrade mentioned above, but for games you should spend £110 on Sapphire's Radeon HD 4850 and upgrade to Windows.

SHOPPING LIST
Recommended minimum specifications

PROCESSOR	
Intel Celeron Dual Core E1200	£29
(AMD Athlon 64 X2 4200+	£29)
MOTHERBOARD	
Intel: Abit I-N73HD	£41
(AMD: Gigabyte GA-MA78GM-S2H	£54)
CASE	
Gigabyte GZ-X1	£28
HARD DISK	
Maxtor STM3250310AS 250GB	£28
OPTICAL DRIVE	
Pioneer DVR-215	£17
OPERATING SYSTEM	
Ubuntu Linux	Free
MEMORY	
1GB Corsair Value Select DDR2 PC2-5300	£15
POWER SUPPLY	
Antec Basiq Power 350W ATX 12V PSU	£25
TOTAL	**£183**

OPTICAL DRIVE The PC's DVD writer is fine for writing all kinds of discs, with the exception of Blu-ray. It's not worth upgrading to a Blu-ray drive, though, as your processor and graphics won't be able to handle high definition video, so the only upgrade you should consider is a second DVD drive to make copying discs easier.

MEMORY 1GB of memory is more than enough to run Linux, although you may notice some slowdown when running multiple applications or dealing with large images. Fitting 2GB of Corsair Value Select RAM will cost you £29 and make your PC run much faster.

HARD DISK Hard disks are now such good value that even a PC this cheap still has a fair-sized 250GB disk. This will leave plenty of room for your operating system, applications and even plenty of images, music and video. It's possible to fit an even cheaper disk, such as Maxtor's 80GB STM380215AS for £21, but the £7 saving isn't worth it for the amount of storage you'll sacrifice.

BUILD A BETTER PC   31

CHAPTER 3
CHOOSING YOUR HARDWARE

Mid-range PC

CASE The CM690 is clean and sturdy, and looks great. There's plenty of room inside, but it's not the quietest of cases. For something slightly more attractive and quieter, upgrade to Antec's P182 (£79).

PROCESSOR This provides plenty of power for gaming and multi-application use. If you're tempted to indulge in a quad-core processor for a jump in overall performance, the Q6600 costs around £116.

A MID-RANGE PC should be capable of performing a variety of day-to-day tasks well, without specialising in one particular area. Such systems need to be solid across the board, but will inevitably lack a bit of edge due to constraints on price. For example, a good mid-range PC will be able to play the latest games at reasonable system settings or allow you to open applications such as iTunes or Windows Media Player while browsing the internet and opening your email client.

For a mid-range PC, such multitasking as this should be possible as long as you avoid resource-intensive tasks, such as image editing or video encoding. A system like this should be able to perform these tasks fairly well, but not at the speeds to be expected from a high-end PC.

GRAPHICS CARD The HD 4850 is well worth the cost, but will struggle to run the latest games such as Crysis at high detail settings. Look for Leadtek's Winfast GTX 260 graphics card (£194) for the ultimate gaming performance.

MOTHERBOARD Incredibly fast and capable of supporting all Intel's latest processors except the brand new Core i7, this board is a great choice for most computers. The lack of RAID means those that want more storage options should upgrade to a different board, such as Biostar's TPower I45.

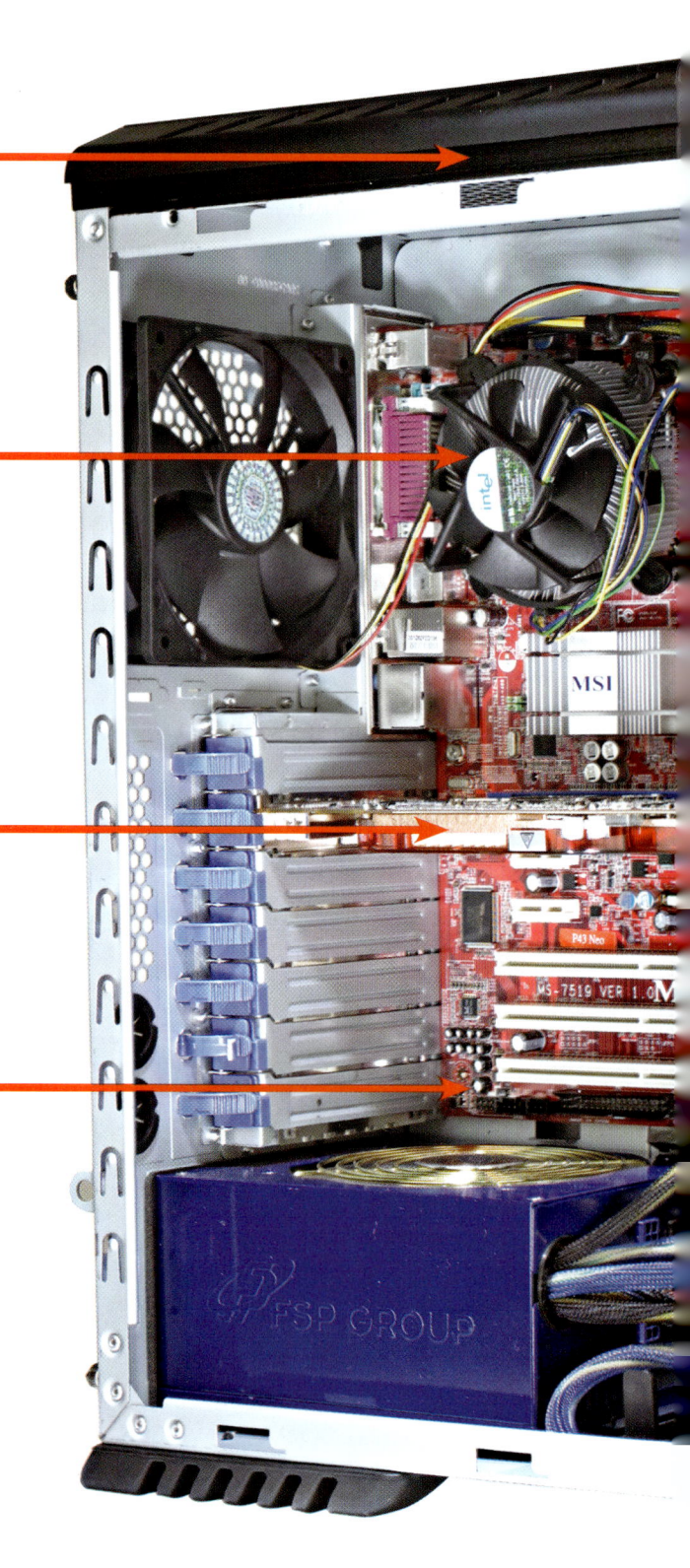

32 BUILD A BETTER PC

SHOPPING LIST
Recommended minimum specifications

PROCESSOR	
Intel Core 2 Duo E8400	£110
(AMD Athlon 64 X2 6000+	£70)
MOTHERBOARD	
Intel: MSI P43 NEO-F	£52
(AMD: ASUS M3A-H/HDMI	£50)
CASE	
Cooler Master CM690	£60
HARD DISK	
500GB Samsung HD502IJ Spinpoint F1	£40
OPTICAL DRIVE	
Pioneer DVR-215	£17
OPERATING SYSTEM	
Windows Vista Home Premium	£60
MEMORY	
2GB Corsair PC2-6400 C4 XMS2 DHX	£40
GRAPHICS CARD	
Sapphire HD 4850	£112
POWER SUPPLY	
Corsair 550W VX Series	£55
TOTAL	**£546**

OPTICAL DRIVE Pioneer's DVR-215 can write quickly to all DVD formats. If you want to watch HD movies and record to Blu-ray discs, LG's GGW-H20L (£147) is a great upgrade.

MEMORY 2GB is enough to push applications and games at a fair pace, but with memory prices at a low, a 4GB kit of Corsair PC2-6400 DDR2 RAM (TWIN2X4096-6400C5) can be found for just £16 more.

HARD DISK More than enough space to store music, photos, games and applications, though Samsung's HD753LJ 750GB offers 250GB more space for £57.

BUILD A BETTER PC **33**

CHAPTER 3
CHOOSING YOUR HARDWARE

High-end PC

PROCESSOR The Core 2 Duo processor has two cores running at 3GHz, so will be quick in applications that take advantage of one or both cores. If you want to edit high-definition video, you should consider upgrading to a quad-core processor, such as the Core 2 Quad Q9450 for around £200.

THIS IS A powerful PC. Its fast dual-core processor will handle the vast majority of tasks with few problems, while its 4GB of RAM means you're unlikely to run out of memory. You'll also have trouble filling the 1TB hard disk, which is one of the fastest available. Its motherboard has several expansion slots, as well as support for DDR3 memory, so you can upgrade when it becomes more affordable. The power supply can also handle plenty of extra hardware. The Radeon HD 4850 graphics card is brand new and remarkably powerful for its price.

However, while the processor is certainly quick, it won't be as speedy as a quad-core processor in multithreaded applications, such as video encoding. In addition, the graphics card won't be able to handle the most demanding games, such as Crysis, at the highest resolutions and detail settings, and the PC lacks a Blu-ray drive for high-definition video playback.

GRAPHICS CARD The Radeon 4850 is an excellent card for the money, but it can only just manage a playable frame rate in Crysis at 1,680x1,050 with 4x anti-aliasing. If you want to make sure the most graphically intensive games play smoothly at high resolutions, you should consider an upgrade to an Nvidia GeForce 260 GTX, which costs around £220.

MOTHERBOARD This motherboard supports all Intel's processors except the brand new Core i7. It also supports RAID, so you shouldn't need anything faster. However, it only supports CrossFire, so you'll need an SLI board if you want to use Nvidia's dual-graphics technology.

CASE Antec's P182 has tons of room for extra hard disks, optical drives and cooling. It should be good enough for all but the most extreme of PCs.

34 BUILD A BETTER PC

SHOPPING LIST
Recommended minimum specifications

PROCESSOR	
Intel Core 2 Duo E8600	£173
(AMD Phenom X4 9850 Black Edition	£130)
MOTHERBOARD	
Intel: Asus P5Q-E	£97
(AMD: Asus M3A-H/HDMI	£50)
CASE	
Antec P182	£87
HARD DISK	
Samsung Spinpoint F1 HD103UJ 1TB	£92
OPTICAL DRIVE	
Pioneer DVR-215	£17
OPERATING SYSTEM	
Windows Vista Home Premium	£60
MEMORY	
4GB Corsair DDR2 PC2-8500 TWIN2X4096-8500C5DF	£90
GRAPHICS CARD	
Sapphire Radeon HD 4850	£112
POWER SUPPLY	
Corsair TX 750W	£84
TOTAL	**£812**

OPTICAL DRIVE The DVD writer can read and write every kind of DVD available. It can't read or write Blu-ray discs, though, so to back up huge amounts of data and play high definition films, you'll need to upgrade to a Blu-ray writer such as the LG GGW-H20L, which is £147.

MEMORY The DDR2-8500 memory runs at 1,066MHz and should prove to be fast enough for all Windows applications.

HARD DISK You can never have too much hard disk space, and 1TB is as large as you can get in a single disk. If you're worried about losing data, you should fit a second identical drive for RAID or backups.

BUILD A BETTER PC

CHAPTER 3
CHOOSING YOUR HARDWARE

Extreme PC

AN EXTREME PC is one on which no expense has been spared. Such a system is built without compromise using only the best and most powerful components, and will be incredibly fast in all Windows applications and games. Our system has two hard disks for the operating system and program files arranged in a RAID 0 configuration, which gives a speed boost as both disks work together. There's a second disk with a huge 1TB of storage for your documents.

The PC also has an optical drive that can read and write Blu-ray discs, as well as play HD DVDs, so you'll have plenty of space to back up your files and be able to play high-definition films. It's all wrapped up in a stylish case, with four fans to keep everything cool. Its only disadvantages are that all the powerful components will use a lot of power, and the computer may be quite noisy.

PROCESSOR It doesn't get any faster than the Core 2 Extreme QX9770, which is also easily overclockable. The Q9550 isn't much slower and is £540 cheaper, though.

MEMORY The Corsair RAM runs at a huge 1,066MHz, and its heat spreaders make it look the business. There's also 4GB, which is more than enough even for memory-hungry Vista. If you want the ultimate in performance, consider upgrading to the even faster PC2-9600 (1,200MHz) RAM for around £170.

GRAPHICS CARD This is the fastest graphics card currently available, and the only one able to play Crysis at very high resolutions with all the graphical effects turned on.

MOTHERBOARD With support for all the latest Intel processors (except the new Core i7) and ATI's CrossFire, you shouldn't need another motherboard. Those looking for SLI graphics should buy a motherboard with a 780i or 790i chipset, which will cost around £150.

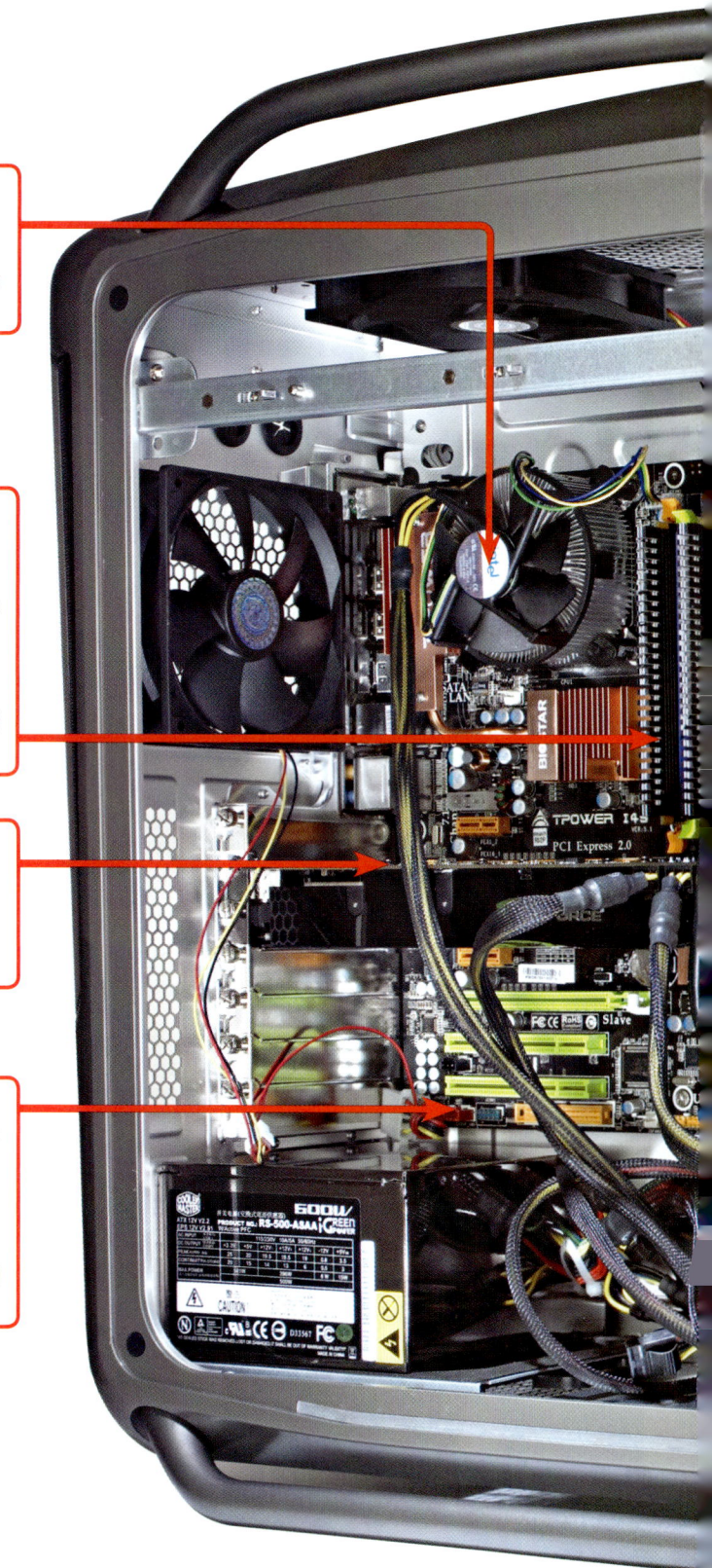

36   BUILD A BETTER PC

SHOPPING LIST
Recommended minimum specifications

PROCESSOR	
Intel Core 2 Extreme QX9770	£955
(AMD Phenom 9950 Black Edition	£120)
MOTHERBOARD	
Intel: Biostar TPower I45	£121
(AMD: Asus M3N78 Pro	£63)
CASE	
Cooler Master Cosmos S	£175
HARD DISK 1 (system)	
2x Western Digital Caviar Blue 640GB WD6400AAKS (RAID 0)	£114
HARD DISK 2 (storage)	
Samsung Spinpoint F1 HD103UJ 1TB	£92
OPTICAL DRIVE	
LG GGW-H20L Blu-ray writer/HD-DVD	£147
OPERATING SYSTEM	
Windows Vista Home Premium	£60
MEMORY	
4GB (2x 2GB) Corsair TwinX DDR2 PC2-8500	£101
GRAPHICS CARD	
MSI N280GTX-T2D1G	£351
POWER SUPPLY	
Tagan 1100W BZ PipeRock Modular PSU	£153
TOTAL	**£2,269**

OPTICAL DRIVE There's no kind of disc this drive can't handle. It can play both Blu-ray and HD DVD discs, and write to Blu-ray discs for up to 25GB of data. Cheaper 8.5GB writable DVDs are covered, too. If you want to copy discs or leave a DVD in one drive while using the other, you should add a DVD writer, which will cost you around £15.

CASE The Cosmos S looks great and is fairly easy to build, with loads of room for expansion. It'll also keep your internal components cool with its four fans, but this has the potential to make it quite noisy. Alternatively, you could add a water cooling kit to keep the noise down.

HARD DISK Two 640GB hard disks in RAID 0 mode provide fast disk access. A separate 1TB disk provides plenty of storage space for your files. Look to add another 1TB hard disk in RAID 1 mode to protect your data.

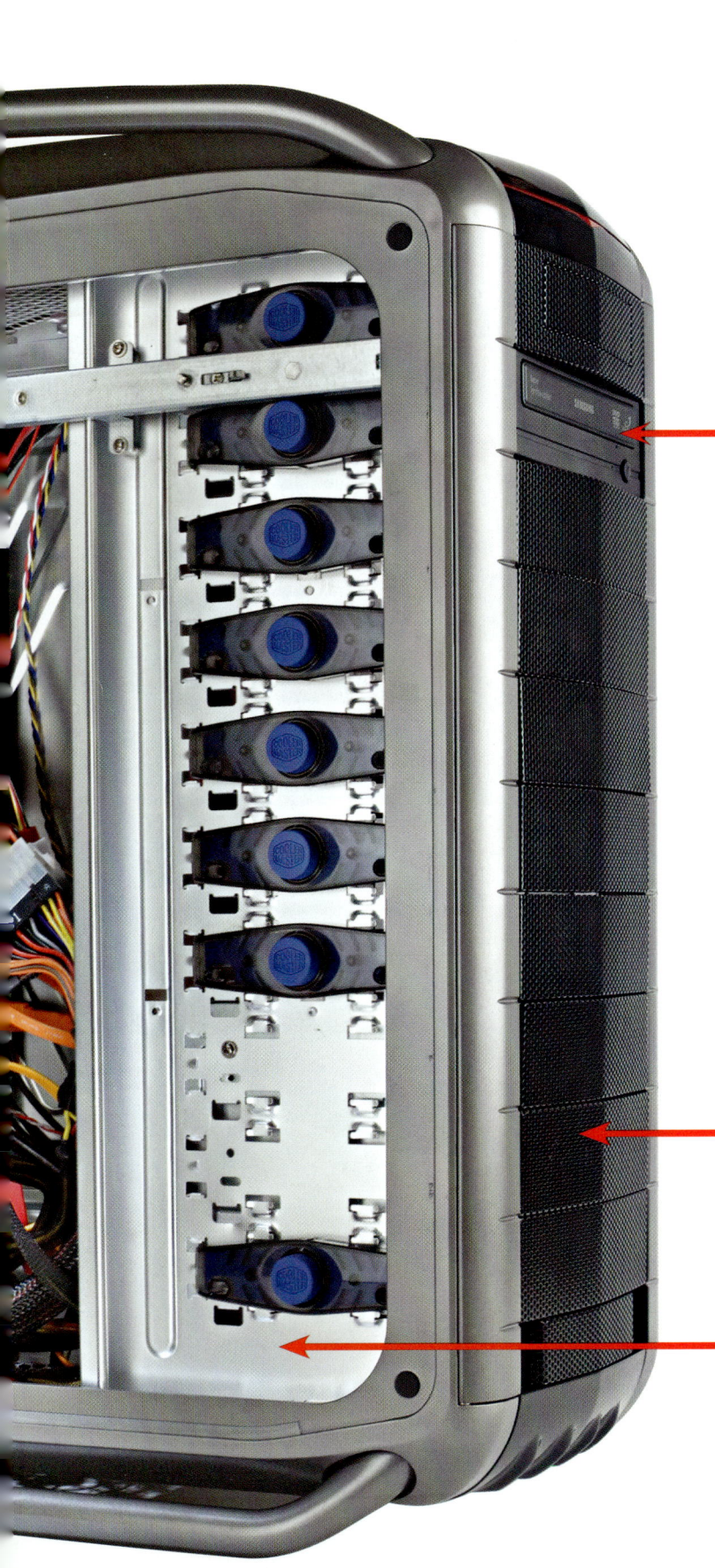

BUILD A BETTER PC

CHAPTER 3
CHOOSING YOUR HARDWARE

Media Center PC

A MEDIA CENTER PC is designed to sit in your living room and connect to your TV, making all your videos, pictures and music available via a remote control. With a TV tuner, you can record your favourite programmes, while an HD optical drive means you can watch movies in high definition.

As this PC will be on display more than a regular desktop system, it's important to choose a case that fits in and looks like a hi-fi component rather than a computer. Unless you want to play games, you can get by with a lower-spec processor and entry-level graphics card.

To make life easy for yourself, Windows Vista Home Premium is the only operating system worth installing, as its integrated Media Center is the best you can buy.

PROCESSOR The 1.6GHz Pentium Dual Core E2180 should provide more than enough power. If you're planning on using your Media Center as a regular PC, a Core 2 Duo E8400 (£105) will add more power.

GRAPHICS CARD The Radeon HD 3450 is a cheap way to add HDMI to your computer and provides an easy way to decode HD movies. Make sure you buy the retail version, so that you get the ATI DVI-to-HDMI adaptor that can carry sound. If you want to play games, upgrade to Sapphire's HD 4850 (£110).

MOTHERBOARD A decent microATX motherboard with support for 1,333MHz FSB processors should suit most Media Center computers.

CASE The Grandia GD01 looks stunning and has plenty of room inside, plus it's got a built-in Media Center remote receiver and comes with a remote control. However, it's very large. Smaller cases can be bought, but be careful as you may need to buy expensive laptop-sized components to fit in it.

38 BUILD A BETTER PC

SHOPPING LIST
Recommended minimum specifications

PROCESSOR	
Intel Pentium Dual Core E2180	£42
(AMD Athlon 64 x2 4200x	£29)
MOTHERBOARD	
Intel: Abit I-N7340	£41
(AMD: Gigabyte GA-MA78Gm-S2H	£54)
CASE	
Silverstone Grandia GD01	£123
HARD DISK	
500GB Samsung HD502IJ Spinpoint F1	£40
OPTICAL DRIVE	
LG GGC-H20L	£70
OPERATING SYSTEM	
Windows Vista Home Premium	£60
MEMORY	
2GB Corsair PC2-6400 C4 XMS2 DHX	£40
GRAPHICS CARD	
Sapphire Radeon HD 3450	£29
POWER SUPPLY	
Corsair 550W VX Series	£55
TV TUNER	
Terratec Cinergy DT USB XS Diversity	£62
TOTAL	**£562**

OPTICAL DRIVE The GGC-H20L can burn DVDs and play HD DVD and Blu-ray discs, so it's great for watching movies. If you want to record Blu-ray discs, LG's GGW-H20L (£147) is a great upgrade.

MEMORY 2GB is more than enough for Media Center, but with memory prices so low and for extra performance across the board, a 4GB kit of Corsair PC2-6400 DDR2 RAM (TWIN2X4096-6400C5) can be bought for £56.

HARD DISK There's more than enough space to store music, photos, games and applications here, though Samsung's HD753LJ 750GB offers more space for £57. This is a good upgrade if you've got tons of media files and want to record a lot of TV.

BUILD A BETTER PC

CHAPTER 3
CHOOSING YOUR HARDWARE

Mini PC

GRAPHICS CARD The onboard graphics are fine for regular applications and Windows. The PCI-E x16 slot can't take a full-length card, so this PC isn't ideal for games.

IF YOU WANT a small PC that won't take up much desk space, you should invest in a barebones mini PC. These tiny computers usually come with a built-in motherboard and power supply, so you only need to add an optical drive, processor, memory and hard disk to complete your PC. You need to make sure that you buy the right model for the processor you're intending to install, as you can't replace the motherboard. These kinds of computer are typically a lot more attractive than regular computers and are a good choice for people that don't have a lot of space.

Mini PCs are typically less powerful than full desktop systems, as there's less room inside for lots of hard disks and large, powerful graphics cards. That said, a lot of mini PCs have PCI Express x16 graphics slots, so you can add games capability quite easily.

CASE There's not much room inside this case. If you want to fit a powerful graphics card or add more hard disks, look for a larger barebones kit.

40   BUILD A BETTER PC

SHOPPING LIST
Recommended minimum specifications

PROCESSOR
Intel Core 2 Duo E8400 — £110
(AMD: Athlon 64 X2 6000+ — £70)

CASE
Intel: Asus T3-P5945GCX (includes motherboard and 300W power supply) — £87
(AMD: Asus T3-M2NC51PV (includes motherboard and 300W power supply) — £100)

HARD DISK
500GB Samsung HD502IJ Spinpoint F1 — £40

OPTICAL DRIVE
Pioneer DVR-215 — £17

OPERATING SYSTEM
Windows Vista Home Premium — £60

MEMORY
2GB Corsair PC2-6400 C4 XMS2 DHX — £40

TOTAL — **£354**

OPTICAL DRIVE Pioneer's DVR-215 will burn all DVDs and CDs. If you also want to record to Blu-ray discs, LG's GGW-H20L (£147) is a fantastic upgrade.

MEMORY 2GB is enough for most tasks, but for extra performance across the board, a 4GB kit of Corsair PC2-6400 DDR2 RAM (TWIN2X4096-6400C5) costs £56.

PROCESSOR The 3GHz Core 2 Duo E8400 is a very quick processor than can cope with any job. If you want even more performance, upgrading to the Core 2 Quad Q9450 for around £200 is a good choice.

HARD DISK More than enough space to store music, photos, games and applications, though Samsung's 750GB HD753LJ offers more space for £57. This is a reasonable upgrade if you've got tons of media files and want to record a lot of TV.

BUILD A BETTER PC

CHAPTER 3
CHOOSING YOUR HARDWARE

Essential peripherals

ALTHOUGH GETTING THE base specifications for your PC and choosing the right operating system is incredibly important, you should also start thinking about the other peripherals you want to use. If you're sitting in front of your computer all day, buying a decent monitor and a comfortable keyboard and mouse is incredibly important. Don't scrimp and save on the extra peripherals, as you'll end up not enjoying using your new PC. Here, we'll talk you through the options that are available to you.

MONITORS

The monitor is your window into your computer. When you use your PC, it's this display that you'll be staring at all the time. Getting one that produces a decent image and fits your needs is, therefore, incredibly important.

If you haven't looked at computer monitors in a while, you'll be surprised at the increased choice available. For starters, regular 'square' monitors are pretty much a thing of the past, replaced by widescreen monitors. These make watching films more pleasant and make working with things such as large spreadsheets much easier. With wider resolutions than standard monitors, things such as Windows Vista's Sidebar fit more comfortably on the screen and still leave plenty of rooms for documents.

Widescreen monitors, like standard displays before them, come in a range of different sizes and resolutions. At the bottom of the pile are budget 17in and 19in models, which have a 1,440x900 resolution. These typically start at around £110. However, in our eyes they're not worth it. Instead, 20in monitors, such as LG's Flatron L204WS, are slightly larger and easier on the eye than 19in models and cost only a little more from around £130. The main benefit, however, is that they have a resolution of 1,680x1,050, so you get a lot more information onscreen. If you'd like something a little bigger, 22in models, such as LG's Flatron L227WT, have the same resolution and cost around £200.

If you want to take the next step up, you'll need a 24in monitor, such as ViewSonic's VX2435wm. These have a resolution of 1,920x1,200, so are capable of displaying full 1080p HD video. For standard Windows use, this large desktop is a pleasure to use. If money's no object, opt for an even bigger screen with an even larger resolution. Dell's 3008WFP is a massive 30in monitor with an incredible 2,560x1,600 resolution, although at £1,033 it's incredibly expensive.

When choosing a suitable monitor, it's worth being able to decipher the specifications to make sure you get one suitable for your needs. The viewing angles (horizontal and vertical) describe how far from straight on you can get before the picture deteriorates. Higher viewing angles are better, particularly if you want to use your monitor to show films to more than one person.

The brightness of a monitor is measured in candela per square metre (cd/m^2). The higher the number, the brighter the picture, so the easier your monitor will be to see. Brightness levels from 300cd/m^2 should be chosen.

The contrast ratio of a monitor tells you the difference between the darkest shade (black) and the lightest shade (white) that the monitor can produce. Many modern monitors use dynamic contrast ratios, where the backlight is dimmed to increase the range of shades that can be produced. Typically, a monitor with a contrast ratio of 1,000:1 or higher should be able to produce dark blacks and bright whites.

TIP
If your PC has two graphics outputs – most graphics cards do – you can run two monitors together and split the Windows desktop over both.

■ A 20in widescreen monitor is a great choice

42 BUILD A BETTER PC

■ A 24in monitor has a high resolution, which is perfect for Windows applications and movies

The final specification that you'll come across is the response time. This measures how long it takes the monitor to change a pixel from black to white and back to black, although some manufacturers 'cheat' and quote a grey-to-grey time. High response times imply that the picture will take a long time to change, so fast-moving action, as in games, could end up with ghosting and smearing. In our extensive tests we've noticed that as long as a monitor has a response time of 25ms or lower, you won't get any problems. So don't get drawn into paying more money for a monitor just because it has an incredibly quick advertised response time.

The only other option to consider is the type of inputs you want on your monitor. If the PC you're building has a digital DVI output, look for a monitor with a matching input. This will give you the best-quality picture. If you want to watch HD movies, then look for a monitor with an HDMI connection or HDCP support on its DVI input. If your PC only has an analogue D-sub output, you'll need a monitor with one of these. Most monitors that support DVI also have an D-sub input, too. If you want to connect a games console or regular DVD player, you'll need a monitor with SCART, S-video, composite or S-video inputs. These are a lot rarer, though.

KEYBOARDS AND MICE

The keyboard and mouse remain the main way that we interact with our computers. Buying the right set is crucial if you want to make your computer easy to use. The most cost-effective way to buy a new keyboard and mouse is to get a set that includes both.

Most sets will include wireless peripherals. These are reliable and generally have long battery lives. With no cables to clutter up your desk, we highly recommend these products. The main choice you'll have to make is whether you want a regular keyboard or an ergonomic model.

Regular keyboards, such as Logitech's Cordless Desktop LX710 Laser (£27), are easiest for most people to use, as they place the keys in a straight line. For touch-typists, ergonomic keyboards can be better, as the keys are placed more naturally for the typing position. However, we've never got on very well with the full-on ergonomic models with the 'split' in the middle of the board. We've found that Logitech's Cordless

■ The Desktop Wave's curved keyboard fits perfectly under your hands and makes typing easier

BUILD A BETTER PC 43

ADVANCE Technologies

http://www.advancetec.co.uk Tel:. 0870 777 3786

ATFX Systems come with a 3 Year Limited Warranty
Extended Warranty Options Available Online
ATFX PCs use Genuine Microsoft Windows www.microsoft.com/piracy/howtotell

ATFX GT-TI

Features:
Gigabyte Motherboard
Intel Core 2 Duo E8400 3.0GHz
OCZ 2GB DR2 PC2-6400 800MHz Memory
BFG GeForce 256MB 8600 GT ThermoIntelligence
CoolerMaster Dominator 690 Black Nvidia Case
600W Power Supply
20 x Dual Layer DVD-Writer
320GB 7200RPM HardDisk Drive
Microsoft Windows Vista Home Premium 32-Bit
& Office 90days Trial

£499 inc vat

Free Keyboard & Mouse
* TFT Monitor not included

CyberSnipa Stinger Gaming Mouse
£29.32 inc vat

Cyber Snipa Spotter Webcam USB
£22.31 inc vat

AT Elite
Business Machine

Intel Pentium® E2180 Dual Core 2.0GHz
Asus Motherboard
Gb LAN - 256MB Integrated Graphics
SoundMAX 6-channel Sound Card
1GB DDR2 667MHz Memory
250GB 7200rpm 8MB SATAII Hard Drive
20x Dual Layer DVD±RW Drive
Coolermaster Mini ATX Case
Software
- Windows XP Home - AntiVirus Software
Office Trial Edition (90 Day)

£271 inc vat

* TFT Monitor not included

AT Matrix
Gaming System

AMD Phenom Quad 9950 Black Edition 2.6GHz
Asus Motherboard with HDMI
Gb LAN - NVIDIA GeForce 8200 Graphics
8-channel Sound Card
2GB DDR2 667MHz Memory
320GB 7200rpm 8MB SATAII Hard Drive
20x Dual Layer DVD±RW Drive
NZXT Midi ATX Case
Software
- Windows XP Home - AntiVirus Software
Office Trial Edition (90 Day)

£449 inc vat

Free Keyboard & Mouse
* TFT Monitor not included

CHAPTER 3
CHOOSING YOUR HARDWARE

■ These surround-sound speakers can connect to your DVD player as well as your PC, making them ideal for use in a home-entertainment setup

Desktop Wave (£42) provides a decent balance between comfort and ergonomic design. It has a slight 'smile' to it and each key is at a slightly different height to match the differences in finger length. It's a great keyboard if you're going to be doing a lot of typing.

Although wireless mice are fine for using Windows, if you play a lot of games a wired mouse is a much better option. This is because they don't have as much lag in them, so each mouse movement is replicated instantly in your game – essential if you want to get that accurate head shot. In this case, we'd recommend buying a dedicated gaming mouse, such as Razer's Death Adder (£40).

If you love playing the latest games, you should think about buying a mouse mat, rather than using the surface of your desk. With the right mat, such as the ICEmat 2nd Edition (around £30), you'll get a low-friction surface, so your mouse will glide around effortlessly.

SPEAKERS
To get the best out of your computer, you need to invest in a decent set of speakers. Don't rely on any built into your monitor, as they'll never be able to produce the clean balanced sounds of a dedicated set. Fortunately, buying speakers doesn't have to be expensive.

First, work out what kinds of speaker you want. Standard 2.1 sets have two stereo speakers and a sub-woofer, which produces rich thumping bass. If you primarily use your computer for music or games, then these kinds of speakers will suit your computer. The best set we've reviewed, Logitech's X-230, costs only £30. For this, you'll get incredibly rich and detailed sound.

Next, you've got the choice of surround-sound speakers. These are ideal if you want immersive sound around you when you're watching films and want to enjoy the full soundtrack, for example. Surround-sound speakers typically come in 5.1 or 7.1 speaker configurations, where the .1 is the bass subwoofer and the 5 and 7 refer to the number of satellite speakers. To be honest, 7.1 sets aren't worth it unless you'll be using your computer in a massive room. Besides, the extra two speakers and cables mean that you're just adding clutter to your home. A 5.1 set will suit most people.

Again, there's a choice of sets to consider. Standard 5.1 PC speakers, such as Logitech's X-540 (£52), use analogue mini-jack plugs that connect to the sound card's outputs at the rear of

■ A decent set of 2.1 speakers will produce rich sounds in games and music

BUILD A BETTER PC **45**

CHAPTER 3
CHOOSING YOUR HARDWARE

your PC. To enjoy surround sound on your DVDs and HD movies, you'll need software capable of decoding the sound to analogue outputs. Windows Media Center will decode Dolby Digital soundtracks, but not DTS; CyberLink's PowerDVD will do all formats, but you'll need to upgrade to the full version from any version that came bundled with your optical drive.

Alternatively, buying 5.1 speakers with a built-in decoder, such as Logitech's Z-5500 Digital (£200), means that you can connect your computer digitally to the speakers and let them do the hard work of decoding. For this to work, you'll need to have an S/PDIF output from your PC. The Z-5500 speakers have optical and coaxial S/PDIF inputs and can decode Dolby Digital and DTS soundtracks. They also have 5.1 channel analogue inputs, so you could still let your PC do the audio decoding. The benefit of this system is that you can also connect your regular DVD player to the speakers, so you can use them for your home cinema setup, too.

TV TUNERS
With Media Center now built into Windows Vista Home Premium, turning your computer into a fully fledged hard disk recorder simply requires you to add a TV tuner. With Media Center's excellent free programme guide, you'll find a PC the easiest hard disk recorder to use. When you make your choice there are a few things to consider.

First, it's not worth buying an analogue-only tuner. The analogue TV service is being turned off over the next few years, leaving only digital TV. That said, if you can't get very good reception for digital TV, look to get a hybrid tuner with both digital and analogue capabilities; this way you can use the best signal but still switch over to digital when the time comes.

The best choice for most people is a digital tuner. As Media Center can handle two tuners at once, allowing you to record one channel while watching another, it makes sense to buy a TV card with dual tuners. This doesn't have to be expensive, as Terratec's Cinergy FT USB XS Diversity (£60) shows. This USB tuner plugs into a spare USB port, but you can also get internal tuners that plug into a spare PCI or PCI Express slot for similar money. The Diversity tag means that the card can use both tuners to improve the quality of your TV reception. However, using it in Diversity mode means that you can only watch a single channel, as with a single-receiver TV tuner.

Finally, Freesat now means that you can get HD TV for free, and some cards give you this ability on your PC. To use the service, you'll need to have a satellite dish, such as those provided by Sky. The downside to Freesat at the moment is that Media Center doesn't currently have support for the service, so you'll have to use the software bundled with the card. It's rumoured that an update to Media Center will add Freesat support soon.

■ A dual tuner allows you to watch one TV channel while recording another

BUILD A BETTER PC

Step into
the Game with the SAPPHIRE HD4000 series

ATI RADEON NO.1 MANUFACTURER

SAPPHIRE HD4600 Series
HDMI - DX10.1 - CrossFireX - HDDVD/BluRay

SAPPHIRE HD4850 TOXIC
HDMI - OverClocked - QUIET Cooling - CrossFire

SAPPHIRE HD4870 TOXIC
HDMI - OverClocked - Vapor-X Cooling - CrossFire

SAPPHIRE HD4870 X2
Dual 4870 VPU's - HDMI - DX10.1 - CrossFire

ATI CROSSFIRE X TECHNOLOGY

ATI RADEON PREMIUM GRAPHICS

HDMI HIGH DEFINITION MULTIMEDIA INTERFACE

3DMARK vantage

Windows Vista

SAPPHIRE

CHAPTER 4
BUILDING YOUR PC

THE MAIN TASK you have when building a PC is making sure that you put all the components together correctly so that your new computer works first time. Our detailed step-by-step advice will help you put any PC together from start to finish.

IN THIS CHAPTER

Taking the case apart	50
Installing the power supply	52
Installing the motherboard	54
Installing an Intel processor	58
Installing an AMD processor	59
Installing memory	60
Fitting the internal cables	62
Installing a hard disk	64
Installing an optical drive	66
Installing a graphics card	68
Installing expansion cards	70
Putting the case back together	72

CHAPTER 4
BUILDING YOUR PC

Taking the case apart

TIP
If you're having trouble taking your case apart, look out for hidden screws that may be holding it together.

REMOVE THE FRONT Many cases require you to remove the front panel. Some simply lift off, but check for screws and clips inside.

SCREWS Most cases are held together by screws that need to be removed. Thumbscrews such as these can be undone without a screwdriver.

50   BUILD A BETTER PC

HOW TO...
Take the case apart

1 REMOVE THE SIDES
Start by taking off the side panels to get inside the case. As noted on the diagram opposite, you might need to take the front panel off first to get at the screws to remove the side panels. Some cases, like the one pictured, have thumbscrews, so you don't even need a screwdriver. If your case has a second panel, make sure that you remove this, too, so that you can work on both sides of the case when you're inside it.

2 TAKE OUT INNARDS
Once you're inside your case, you need to check it for accessories. It's common for manufacturers to put spare screws, proprietary drive rails and instruction manuals inside. Take out everything that isn't screwed into place. Look for silica gel taped to the side as well. Remove any packaging so that you're left with a bare interior.

3 REMOVE OPTICAL DRIVE BLANKING PLATES
In order to fit your optical drive later, you may need to remove some plastic and metal blanking plates. At this point, if you haven't had to already, it's probably helpful to get the front of the case off. Your case's manual will tell you how to do this, but most cases simply unclip from the inside.

Look for the 5¼in drive bay into which you'll fit your optical drive. Match this up to the front panel. On some cases this will be the top one, which will have a flap to hide the optical drive from view, so that you don't have to get one the same colour as your case. On other cases, you'll have a plastic blanking plate on the front panel that should unclip.

Inside the case, you'll find a metal blanking plate that you will need to remove. By gently rocking it backwards and forwards, you should be able to break the connection. Be careful not to cut yourself doing this.

4 REMOVE FLOPPY DRIVE BLANKING PLATES
If you're planning to fit a memory card reader or floppy disk drive, you'll need to follow the same steps you did for the optical drive. Find the 3½in drive bay you want to use and break off the metal blanking plate. Next, pop out the corresponding plastic blanking plate on the front panel.

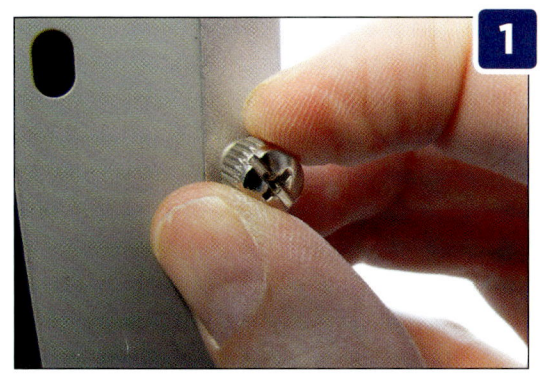

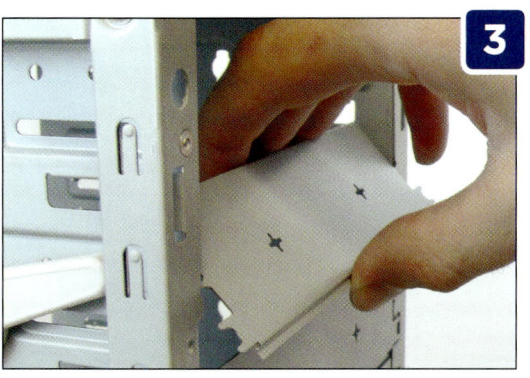

TIP
The inside of the case can have sharp edges, so be careful when you remove any blanking plates.

BUILD A BETTER PC   **51**

CHAPTER 4
BUILDING YOUR PC

Installing the power supply

The ATX connector provides power to your motherboard

The SATA connector is for hard disks and optical drives

A standard PCI Express graphics card connector

The newer 8-pin PCI-E power connector

The secondary motherboard power connector

A connector for floppy disks and memory card readers

The Molex connector is for hard disks

> **TIP**
> Tuck any unwanted cables out of the way inside the case to improve airflow and keep your PC tidy.

52 BUILD A BETTER PC

HOW TO...
Install the power supply

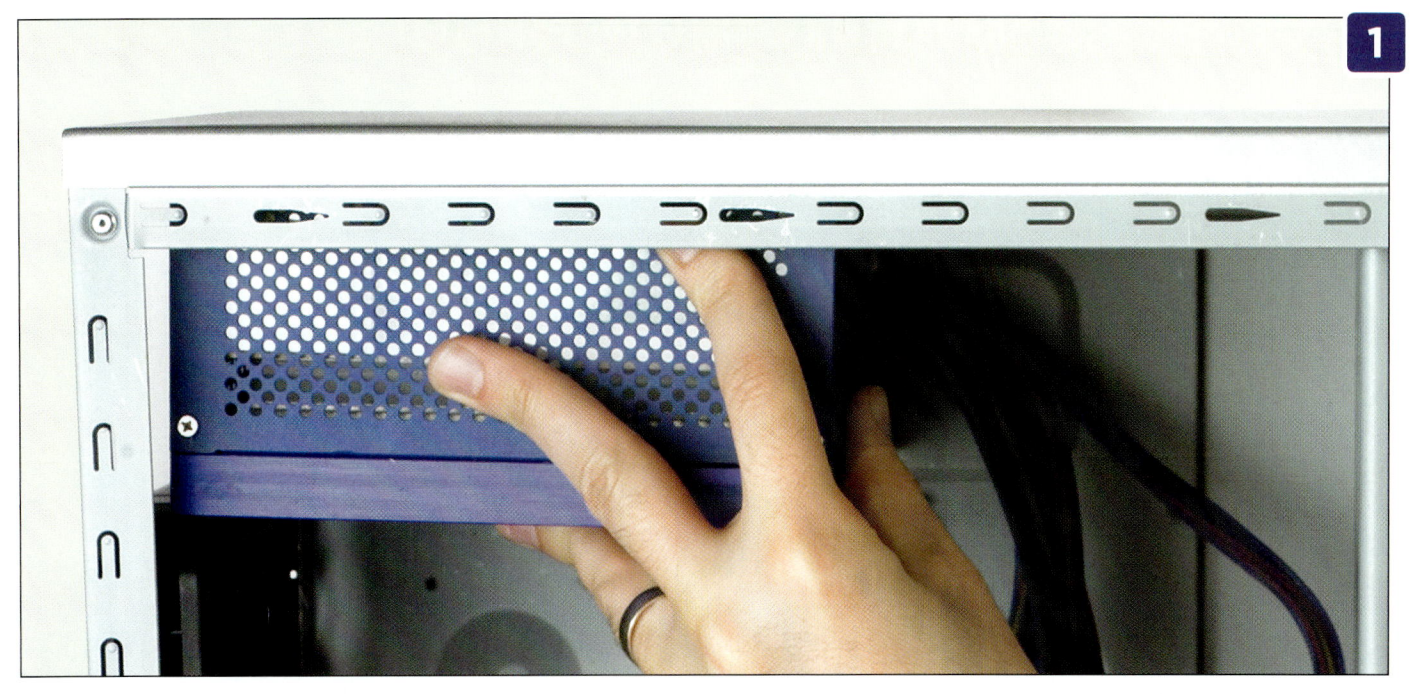

1. FIT SUPPLY ON TO SHELF
If your power supply fits at the top of your case (some cases have space at the bottom), you'll see a small shelf for it to rest on. Slide the power supply on to this shelf and push it backwards until it makes contact with the back of the case.

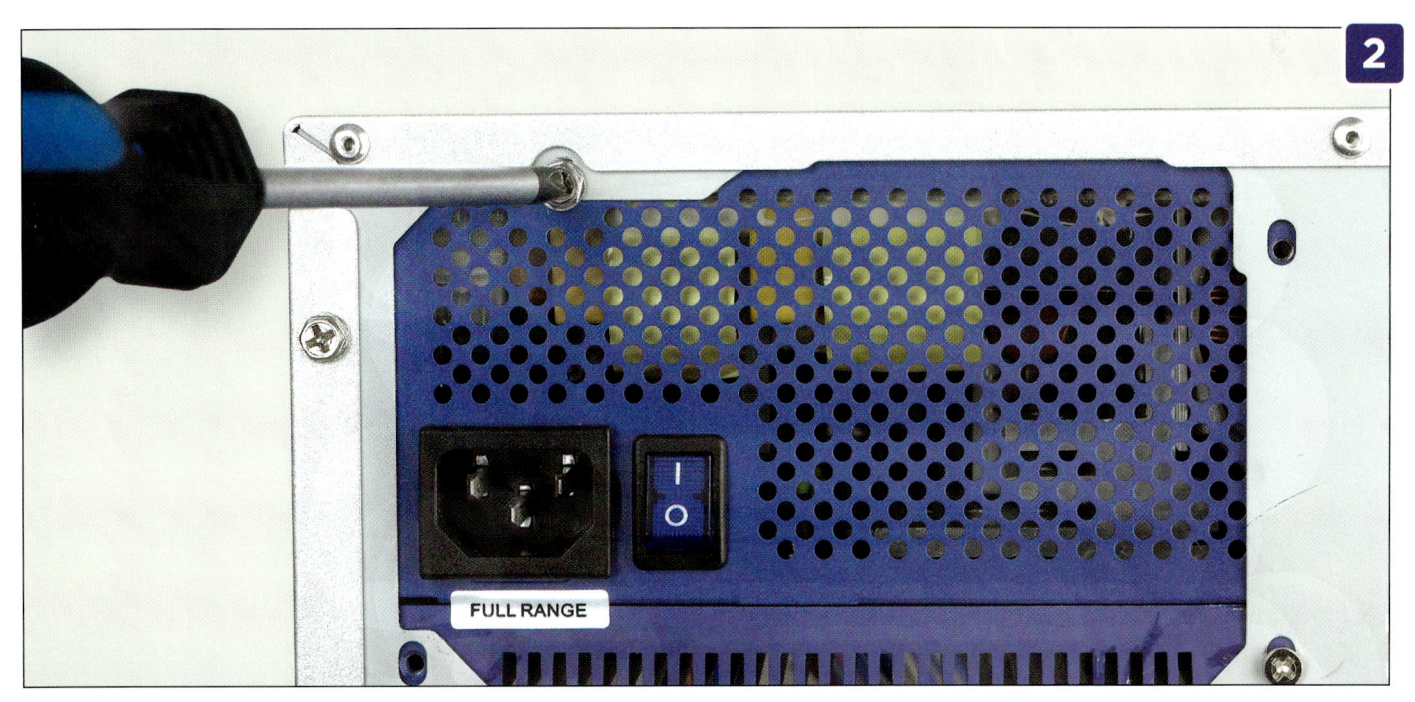

2. SCREW IN SUPPLY
If your power supply is the correct way round, its screw holes will match up with those in the back of the case. If they don't, remove the supply and rotate it 180°. Use four screws to attach the power supply securely to the case.

CHAPTER 4
BUILDING YOUR PC

Installing the motherboard

SATA PORTS These are for hard disks, newer DVD writers and Blu-ray drives.

EXPANSION SLOTS These are used for internal peripherals such as TV tuners and graphics cards.

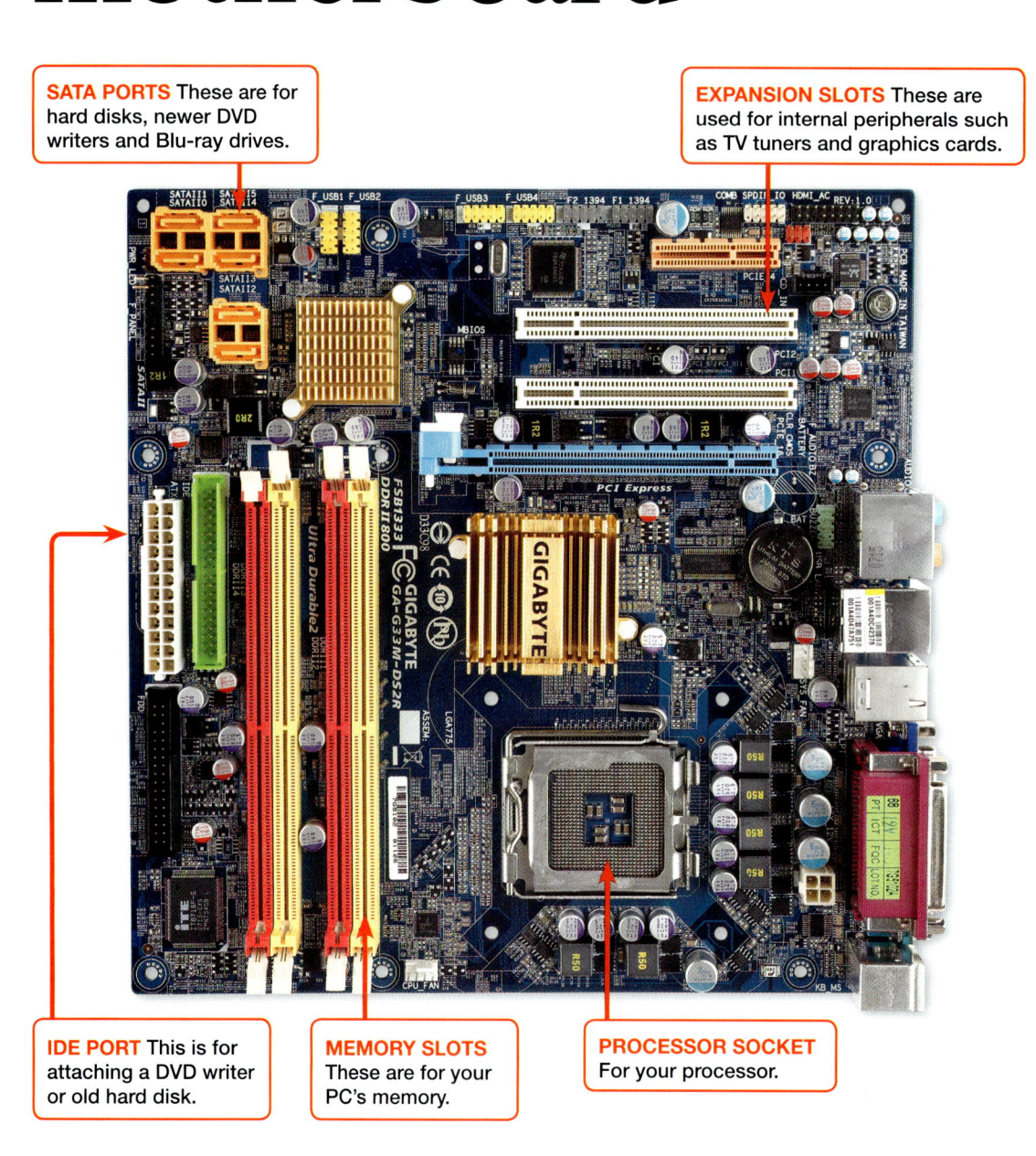

IDE PORT This is for attaching a DVD writer or old hard disk.

MEMORY SLOTS These are for your PC's memory.

PROCESSOR SOCKET For your processor.

REAR PANEL CONNECTORS These ports are fixed on your motherboard.

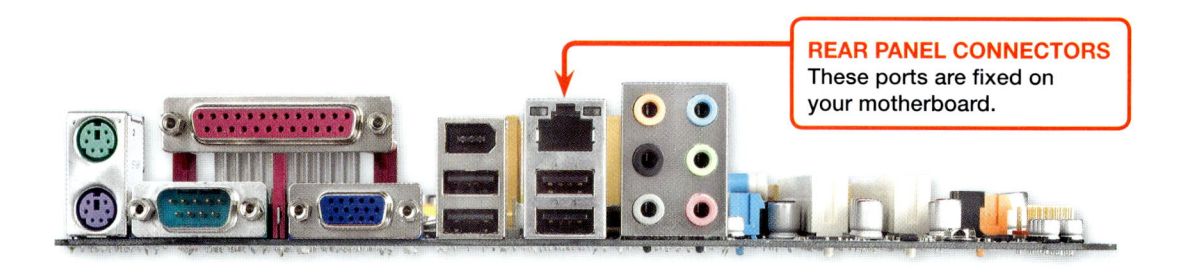

TIP
Blanking plates can be difficult to fit. Push them in until they click, but don't worry if they're not entirely level around the sides.

54 BUILD A BETTER PC

HOW TO...
Install the motherboard

1 UNPACK THE BOARD
Open your motherboard's box. You'll see lots of cables, a driver CD, a metal blanking plate with holes cut out and a manual. Take these components out and put them to one side, as you'll need them later on.

The motherboard will be inside an anti-static bag and resting on top of anti-static foam. Slide the motherboard out of the bag, but leave it attached to the foam for now. Place the motherboard and foam on top of the anti-static bag, and take out the metal blanking plate.

2 MEASURE BLANKING PLATE
The blanking plate fits into the case, and gives you access only to the ports that your motherboard has. However, some motherboard manufacturers use generic blanking plates that fit their entire range of boards. With these, you may need to remove some metal covers to give access to your motherboard's ports.

The easiest way to see is to hold the blanking plate up to the motherboard until the cutouts match the ports on your board. The blanking plate should be pushed against the motherboard with the ridge pointing out, so any text is readable. It will only fit one way, so manoeuvre it until it's the right way. Make a note of any ports that are covered.

3 REMOVE UNNECESSARY BITS
If you need to remove any parts of the blanking plate, you should do that now. You'll have two options for doing this. First, you may have to remove a bit of metal, in a similar way to the metal blanking plates on your case. These should be rocked gently out until the metal snaps.

Second, some ports may be covered by a flap. In this case, the flap should be bent inwards (towards where the motherboard will be). Make sure that you bend it far enough for the motherboard's port to be given enough clearance to pass underneath.

4 INSTALL THE BLANKING PLATE
From the inside of the case, you need to take the blanking plate and push it into the gap at

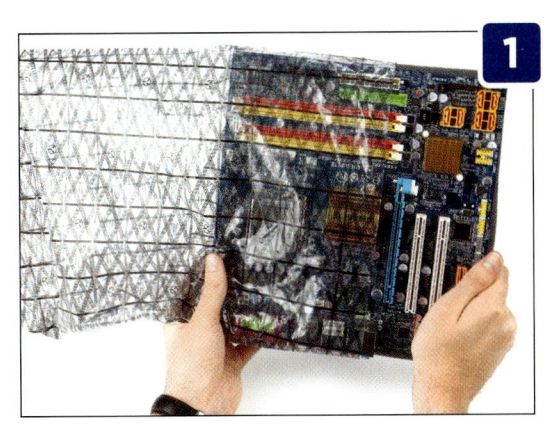

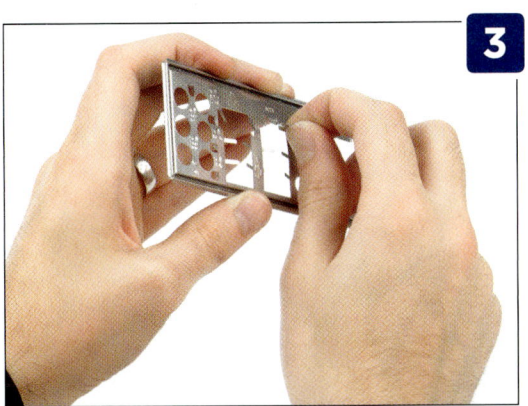

TIP
Motherboards can require a bit of force to be inserted. Push from the sides of the board; don't force any components, as this could cause damage.

BUILD A BETTER PC **55**

CHAPTER 4
BUILDING YOUR PC

the rear of the case. Remember to align it so that it's the same way up as when you measured it against your motherboard.

The ridge round the outside of the plate should clip into the hole. Be warned that this can be really fiddly and the blanking plates don't always fit perfectly. It should, however, clip into place and remain stable without any support.

5 MEASURE WHERE THE MOTHERBOARD GOES
Next, you need to see where the screw holes for the motherboard will go. Lie the case flat on the desk and make sure that all the internal cables are out of the way. When you've got a clear case, take the motherboard off its foam backing and slide it gently into the case. Make sure that its rear ports are pushed up against the blanking plate correctly. Take a note of where the screw holes in the motherboard go, and remove the board. Place it back on its foam.

6 FIT THE RISERS
You need to fit risers where you noted the screw holes. These will be included with the case and look like tall copper screws. Their job is to hold the motherboard off the bottom of the case, so it isn't shorted out when its contacts touch the metal. The risers simply screw into the pre-drilled holes in the case. Use as many risers as there are screw holes in the motherboard, making sure that you screw them tightly into position with your fingers.

7 SLIDE THE MOTHERBOARD INTO PLACE
Put the motherboard back in the case, making sure that all its screw holes have risers underneath. If some are missing, check to make sure that you haven't screwed the risers into the wrong place. You'll probably notice that the motherboard has a tendency to be slightly off from the risers. This is normal, and is caused by pressure from the backplate pushing against the motherboard. Simply line up the motherboard's ports with the backplate and push the motherboard towards it until the screw holes line up. This will take a bit of gentle force.

8 SCREW THE MOTHERBOARD DOWN
With the motherboard in place, you can start to screw it in. Start with the corners, holding the motherboard firmly, so that its screw holes line up with the risers that you put in.

When screwing the screws in, don't use too much pressure as you don't want to break the motherboard. Ideally, you want the screws tight enough for the board to be secure, but not so tight that it feels as though the board is going to start cracking.

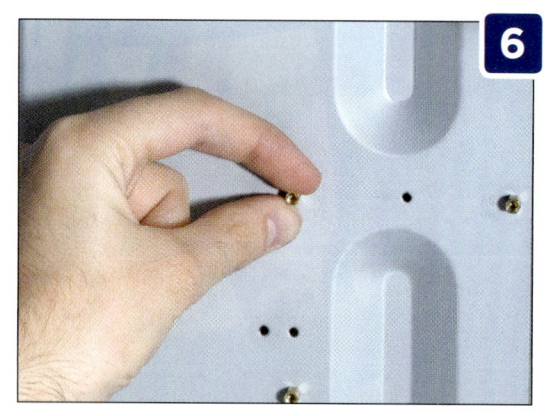

Once you've done the corners, you can put screws in the other holes. How many you put in is up to you, but you shouldn't need to do all of them to make the motherboard secure. Keep going until the motherboard is firmly in place.

9 IDENTIFY ATX CONNECTORS

With the motherboard in place, you're ready to connect it to the power supply. There are two connectors that you'll need to plug in. The first is the ATX connector. On modern motherboards, you need a 24-pin connector. There's only one of these on the power supply. However, as older motherboards only required a 20-pin connector, there's usually a four-pin connector that can be detached. Make sure that this is connected and that you have an unbroken 24-pin connector.

10 PLUG IN ATX CONNECTOR

You need to plug this 24-pin connector into the matching connector on the motherboard. This should be easy to find, but it's usually located by the IDE ports on the right-hand side of the motherboard.

The ATX connector will only plug in one way, so you can't get it wrong. Once it's lined up the connector should plug in smoothly. There's a clip on it to hold it in place. This will require gentle pressure to get it to clip in, but no more. If you're having to force the cable, then the chances are that you've got the connector the wrong way round. Once the cable is in place, give it a gentle tug to make sure that it's secure.

11 IDENTIFY SECONDARY CONNECTOR

Modern motherboards also have a secondary power connector. On most boards this is a single four-pin connector, but some require eight-pin connectors. Check to see what your power supply has, as you may need to buy an adaptor.

In a similar way to the 24-pin connector, the eight-pin connector on power supplies can be split into two. If your motherboard only has a four-pin connector, you'll have to split it into two halves. Only one of these will plug into the motherboard.

12 CONNECT SECONDARY CONNECTOR

Locate the secondary motherboard power connector. Your board's manual will tell you exactly where it's located, but on most motherboards it's near the processor socket. Next, plug the power supply's secondary connector into it. This plug will only go in one way, so there's no chance of getting it wrong. The connector should slide gently into the plug. You'll need to apply a bit of force in order to get the clip to lock into place, and you should hear it click when it's in properly.

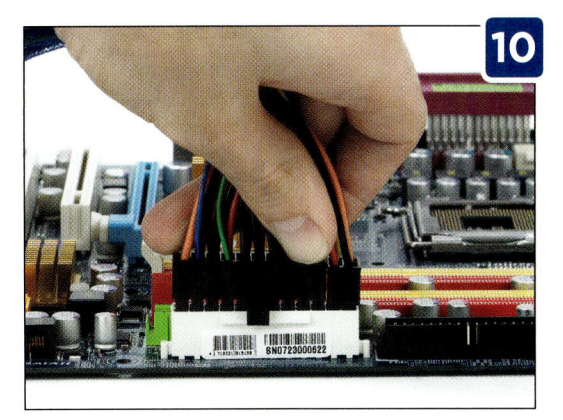

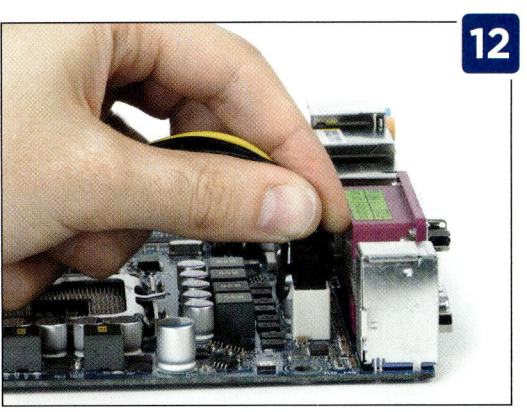

TIP
Make sure that the power connectors are in properly by giving them a gentle tug.

BUILD A BETTER PC **57**

CHAPTER 4
BUILDING YOUR PC

HOW TO...
Install an Intel processor

1 LIFT THE PROCESSOR CAGE
Intel's LGA-775 sockets are covered by a cage. A new motherboard will also have a plastic cover on top. First, remove this cover. It should easily unclip. To access the socket, unclip the handle that runs down the side of the socket and lift it up. This releases the retaining clip for the main cage.

Lift the main cage up and out of the way to expose the socket. Be careful not to touch any of the pins inside the socket, as bending them will stop the processor from working correctly.

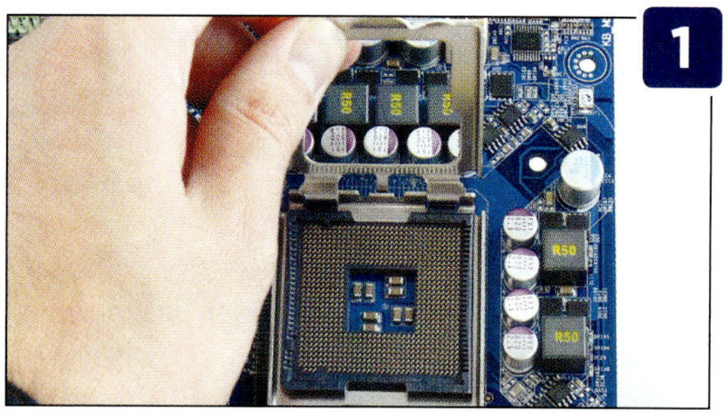

2 INSTALL THE PROCESSOR
The processor has two cut-out notches in its sides, which line up with the ridges in the socket. This prevents the processor from being put in the wrong way round. You'll also notice an arrow on the processor. This should line up with the corner of the socket that has its pins arranged diagonally.

Line the processor up and sit it gently in the place. If it doesn't sit properly, then you've got it the wrong way round. Once you're happy with the processor's position, close the drive cage and pull the retaining handle down. This should take a bit of force, but if it feels like there's too much resistance, check that the processor is seated properly.

3 THERMAL PASTE
Thermal paste fills in micro-cracks in the surface of the processor and the surface of the cooler, ensuring that there's efficient heat transfer between the two. Some fans come pre-coated with thermal paste, in which case you can skip this step.

If it doesn't, you'll need to apply your own. This is easy to do. First, squeeze a tiny blob of thermal paste into the middle of the processor. Take a thin bit of card and use this to spread it, so that the surface of the processor is coated. Don't spread it over the side of the cage, and add more thermal paste if you don't have enough.

4 ATTACH THE FAN
Most Intel coolers clip into the four round holes on the outside of the processor socket. If you're not using an Intel reference cooler bundled with your processor, check the cooler's instructions; some need a backplate screwed to the motherboard.

For all other coolers, you'll see four feet. Make sure that all the feet are rotated away from the direction of the arrow. Line up the cooler so that the four feet touch the holes in the motherboard. It's best to try and get the power cable pointing towards the header on the motherboard marked CPU (we'll cover this later).

Starting at diagonally opposite sides, push the four feet into the place. You'll need some force, and the feet should click into position. When done, check the cooler is seated properly and that it isn't wobbly. If it is, make sure the feet are properly in position.

> **TIP**
> The plastic clips on Intel coolers can be annoying to fit. Make sure the black plastic clips are raised before fitting the cooler, and push diaganolly opposite clips in together.

BUILD A BETTER PC

HOW TO...
Install an AMD processor

1 OPEN THE SOCKET LEVER
AMD's processors fit into AM2 or AM2+ sockets. The sockets are compatible with each other, so the installation instructions are the same.

To fit the processor in the socket, first lift the lever. This unclips to one side and rises vertically above the board. This will move the socket very slightly, aligning the holes in the plastic socket with the connectors beneath. The processor should drop into place with no force, hence the socket's type: zero insertion force (ZIF).

2 FIT THE PROCESSOR
The processor can only fit one way into the socket. Make sure the arrow on top of the processor is aligned with the arrow on the processor socket. Gently push the processor into place. You should feel it click into position when it's all the way in. If it feels like you have to use too much force, stop and check that the processor is correctly aligned.

Once the processor is all the way in, check round it to make sure that it's sitting flush against the plastic socket. If it's not, push gently down on the sections that aren't flush. Push the lever down and clip it back into place to secure the processor.

3 THERMAL PASTE
Thermal paste fills in micro-cracks in the surface of the processor and the surface of the cooler, ensuring that there's efficient heat transfer between the two. You may find that your fan comes pre-coated with thermal paste, in which case you can skip this step.

If it doesn't, you'll need to apply your own. This is simple to do. First, squeeze a tiny blob of thermal paste into the middle of the processor. Take a thin bit of card and use this to spread it, so that the surface of the processor is coated. Don't spread it over the side of the processor, and add more thermal paste if necessary.

4 FIT THE COOLER
If you're using a third-party cooler, check its instructions for how to fit it. If you're using an AMD cooler that came with your processor, fitting it is simple. Around the processor socket is a plastic cooler mount, with two nodules sticking out. These are designed to hold your cooler's clips.

Take your cooler and open its handle. Fit the metal clip without the handle on it over one nodule and push it snugly against the mount. Place the cooler flat across the top of the processor. Push the cooler's remaining metal clip over the second nodule and close the handle. This will require a bit of force to get the handle all the way down. We'll cover connecting the fan's power connector later.

TIP
If you bend the pins on your AMD processor, a credit card slid into the row of bent pins can be used to straighten them.

BUILD A BETTER PC **59**

CHAPTER 4
BUILDING YOUR PC

Installing memory

DUAL MEMORY Motherboards have dual memory channels. Installing two memory modules – one in each channel – can increase performance. The slots to use are usually the same colour, but check your motherboard's manual first.

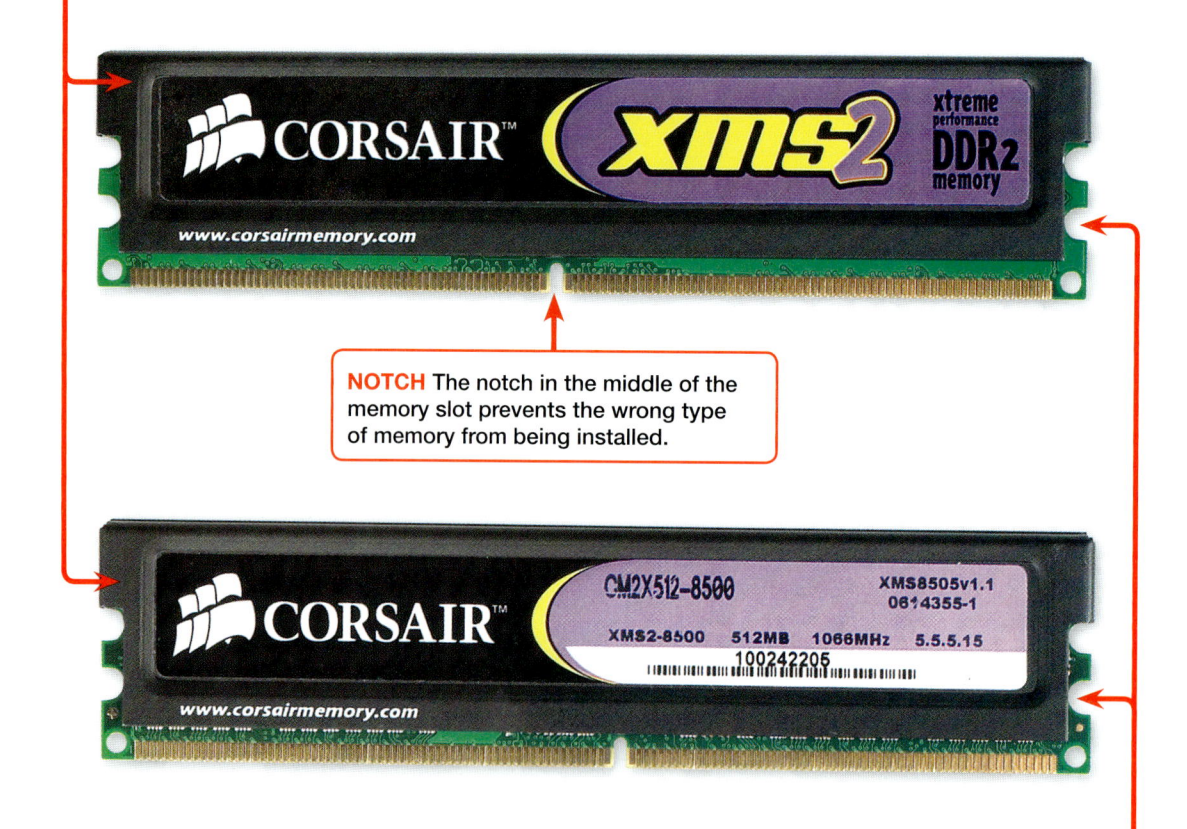

NOTCH The notch in the middle of the memory slot prevents the wrong type of memory from being installed.

CLIPS The clips at the side of the memory slot hold the RAM in place. You open them to install memory, and they close automatically when the RAM is installed.

TIP Make sure your memory is lined up properly before you insert it to prevent damage.

60 BUILD A BETTER PC

HOW TO...
Install memory

1. IDENTIFY WHICH SLOTS TO USE
Presuming that you've bought memory in a kit with two sticks of RAM, you should now identify which slots you're going to install the memory in. As noted opposite, the slots to use are usually the same colour, but you should check your motherboard's manual carefully to make sure that you're using the right ones.

To be doubly safe, the slots will also be numbered to make it easier to follow the motherboard manual's instructions.

2. OPEN THE RETAINING CLIPS
To install your memory, you need to open the clips on either end of the slot into which you're going to insert your memory stick. Pick the first slot and push open these clips; they should open gently without any force, clicking as they open.

The clips should open to around 45°, but don't force them further open when you feel resistance.

3. LINE THE MEMORY UP
To fit the memory, you need to slide it into the slot. Make sure that the notch in the memory lines up with the ridge in the socket. If it doesn't, then you've got the memory the wrong way round. If the memory still doesn't fit, then you're using the wrong type of memory. Check the memory's instructions and motherboard's manual to see what type you need.

4. CLIP THE MEMORY INTO PLACE
Once the memory module is lined up, press firmly on both sides to push it into place. The clips should spring back and click into position. Check the clips are in place and nestled against the notches in the side of the memory module. If they're not, try pushing the memory down a bit further. You can also push the clips up to help them lock into place.

Once your first module is in place, repeat these steps for any remaining modules.

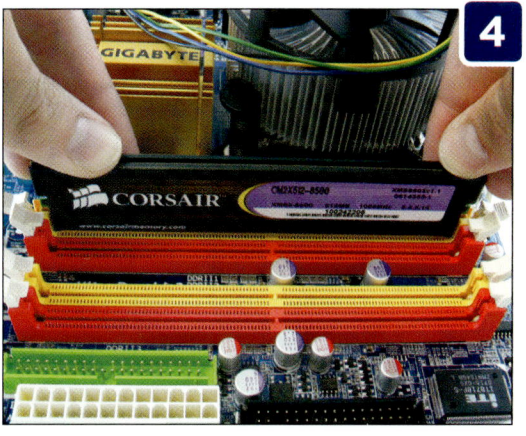

TIP
Push down evenly on both sides of the module, or you'll find it hard to get the retaining clips to lock into place.

BUILD A BETTER PC

CHAPTER 4
BUILDING YOUR PC

HOW TO...
Fit the internal cables

1 POWER
To get your PC to turn on when you push the power button, you need to connect the power switch to the motherboard. Among the loose cables in your case, you'll find a two-pin connector. This will usually be marked PWR SW, but check the case's manual if you're not sure.

This needs to be connected to the power jumpers on the motherboard. Typically, these will be located on the bottom-right of the motherboard and will be marked, although you should double-check your motherboard's manual to make sure. The connector will just plug over the two pins and should connect easily.

2 RESET
If your case has a reset switch – not all do – then there will be a similar connector to the power switch, with RESET SW written on it. Connecting this to your motherboard lets you restart your PC after a major crash, as it resets the hardware and forces your computer to reboot.

To connect it, you need to find the reset jumpers on the motherboard. These will be near the power switch, but you should read your motherboard's manual for an exact location. Simply push the connector over the two pins to connect the switch. It doesn't matter which way round this connector goes.

3 POWER AND HDD LEDS
The HDD connector connects to an LED on the front of the case and lights up when the hard disk is in operation. This is useful, as you can see whether your PC's working or if it's crashed.

As this connects to an LED, it must be connected correctly. The cable should be marked as positive and negative (usually written on the plug). The motherboard HDD jumper will also have a positive and negative port. Check your motherboard's manual carefully to make sure that you get this right, and then connect the cable.

Do the same thing for the power LED, which will have a similar connector. This must be connected the right way round, so make sure that you get the positive and negative connectors aligned.

4 USB
If your case has front-mounted USB ports or a card reader, you'll need to connect these to spare headers on your motherboard. In all likelihood, the cable in the case will be marked USB.

Your motherboard will probably have spare connectors marked USB, but the manual can tell

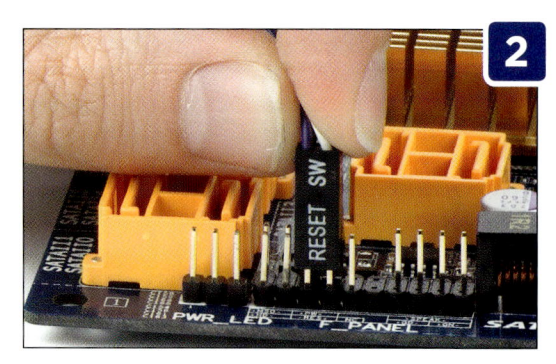

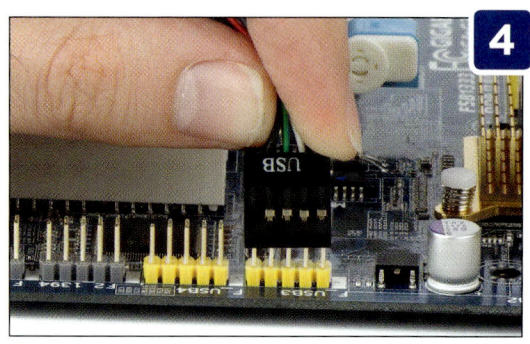

62 BUILD A BETTER PC

you exactly where these are. USB connectors take power, so you need to plug the cable in the right way round. Fortunately, the USB ports on most cases have a single plug that can only be connected to the motherboard in one way. If it doesn't, you'll need to check the case's and motherboard's manuals carefully to make sure that you install the connectors correctly.

Assuming you're using a block connector, plug it into a spare USB header on the motherboard. We'd recommend using the closest header to the cable to avoid draping cables everywhere.

5 FIREWIRE
Front-mounted FireWire cables plug in much the same way as USB cables. Again, look for a spare FireWire header on the motherboard (the manual will explain where these are), and then connect the FireWire cable to it. The cable might be marked as 1394, as FireWire is also known as i1394.

6 AUDIO
Front-mounted audio ports also need to be connected to the motherboard if you want to be able to plug in your headphones and a microphone. Fortunately, most motherboards and cases have a single block connector that plugs into the front audio connector on the motherboard.

Your motherboard's manual will have full details of where this is connected, but it's usually located by its back panel. Again, there's only one way to connect this cable, so just slide it gently into place. If your case has a Speaker header, plug this into the appropriate connector on the motherboard. This is used to give warning beeps.

7 FANS
It's common for modern cases to have extra fans pre-fitted. These help increase airflow through the case and keep your PC cool. While fans can be connected directly to the power supply, it's better to connect them to spare fan headers on the motherboard. This way, the motherboard can automatically control the fan speed and keep your PC running as quietly as possible.

If your fans end in three- or four-pin connectors, you can plug them into your motherboard. Look at the manual to find a spare fan connector and then plug in the fan's power connector. Three-pin connectors can plug into four-pin ports and vice versa. The cables can also only plug in one way, so it's easy to get it right.

8 CPU FAN
The processor fan, which we installed earlier, can now be connected to the motherboard. In the same way as system fans, the processor's fan speed is controlled by the motherboard based on the processor's temperature. This keeps your computer as quiet as possible.

There's a special connector for the processor fan on the motherboard, which is often called CPU FAN. Check your motherboard's manual for its location. This is likely to be a four-pin connector, but three-pin processor fans can also plug in. The connector can only go in one way, so just plug it in.

TIP
LED connectors need to be connected the right way round, or you'll break the light.

BUILD A BETTER PC **63**

CHAPTER 4
BUILDING YOUR PC

Installing a hard disk

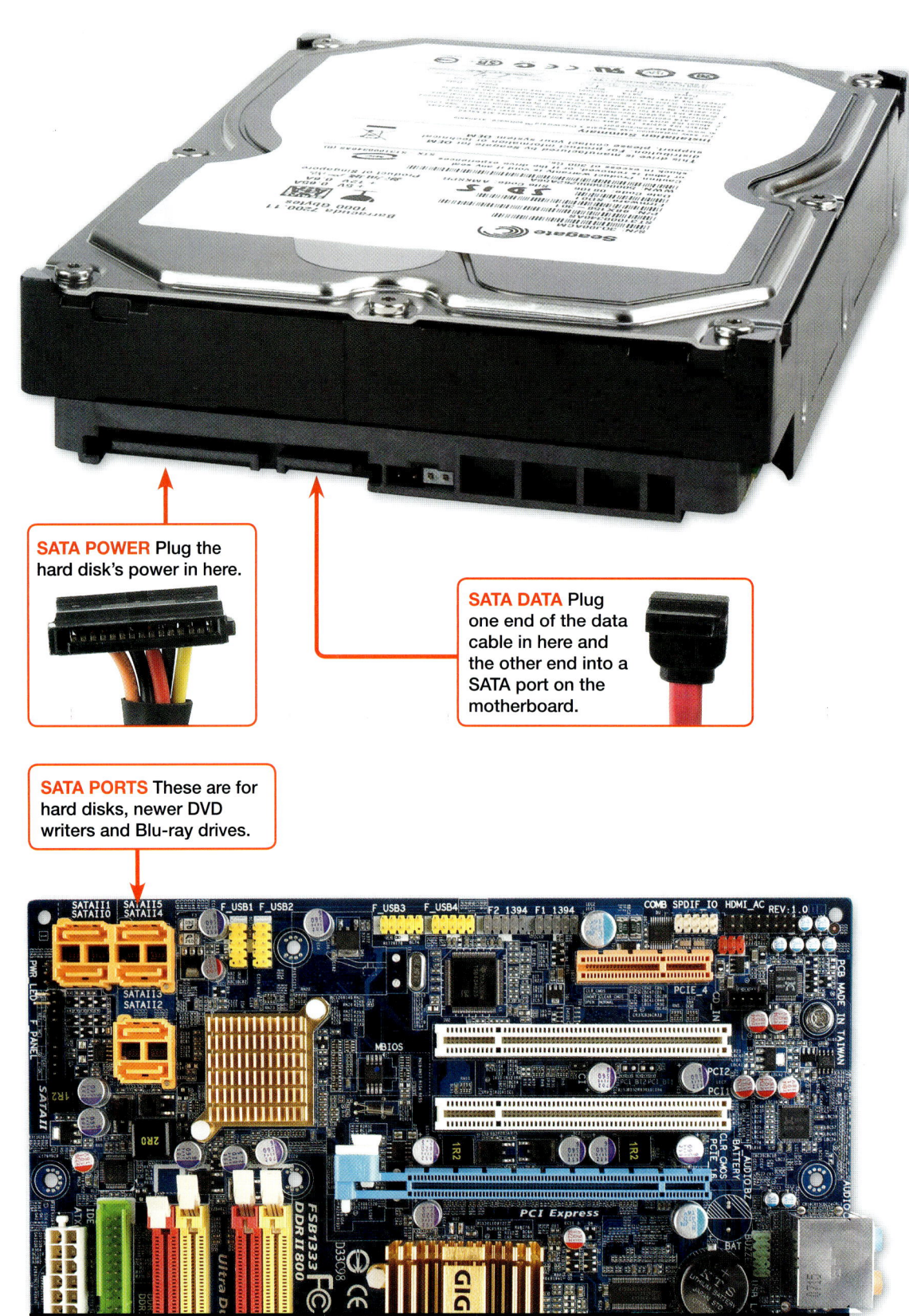

SATA POWER Plug the hard disk's power in here.

SATA DATA Plug one end of the data cable in here and the other end into a SATA port on the motherboard.

SATA PORTS These are for hard disks, newer DVD writers and Blu-ray drives.

TIP
If you're installing more than one hard disk, plug the one you want to boot from in the lowest-numbered SATA port. The BIOS will pick this hard disk as the boot drive by default.

64   BUILD A BETTER PC

HOW TO...
Install a hard disk

1 FIT HARD DISK INTO A BAY
To fit a hard disk, you need to find a 3½in drive bay. Be careful not to use one of the external bays, which have a cutout on the front of the case, as these are designed for memory card readers and floppy disk drives.

If your case has drive rails or screwless fittings, you'll need to read the case's manual for instructions on how to fit these drives. For other cases, slide the hard disk into a spare drive bay, until the screw holes in the side of the drive line up with the holes in the drive bay. The disk should then be secured with four screws: two either side of the case. Suitable screws should have been provided with the hard disk or case. Screw these up tightly, so that the drive doesn't wobble.

2 PLUG IN SATA POWER
In the main picture opposite, you can see the SATA power connector on the hard disk and on the power supply. Locate the correct connector from your power supply and plug it into the back of your hard disk. It only goes in one way and clicks when it's connected. Be extremely careful when plugging it in, as downwards pressure can break the clip surrounding the power connector. If you do this, the power plug won't stay in place.

3 PLUG IN SATA DATA CABLE
Unlike IDE, SATA uses a simple and thin connector to carry data. Your motherboard will ship with several SATA cables, so take one of these from the box. Plug it gently into the rear of the hard disk. It will only plug in one way and will click when it's properly connected.

Be careful when you plug it in, as downwards pressure can break the connector and prevent the SATA cable plugging in.

4 PLUG SATA DATA CABLE INTO MOTHERBOARD
Next, you need to find a spare SATA port on your motherboard. These are usually located at the bottom-right of the board and are numbered. The lower the number, the higher up the boot chain your hard disk is. So, if you're installing more than one hard disk, make sure the drive from which you're going to boot is plugged into the lowest-numbered port. Check the motherboard's manual to ensure that all the ports do the same thing; some boards have ports reserved for RAID.

Connecting the SATA cable is easy, as it will only plug in one way. It will click when the cable is connected properly.

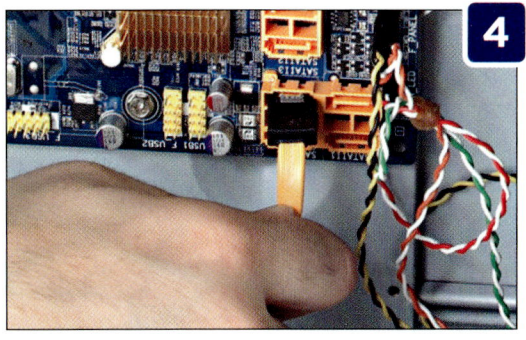

> **TIP**
> SATA connectors on hard disks can be broken easily, so be careful when inserting and moving cables.

BUILD A BETTER PC **65**

CHAPTER 4
BUILDING YOUR PC

Installing an optical drive

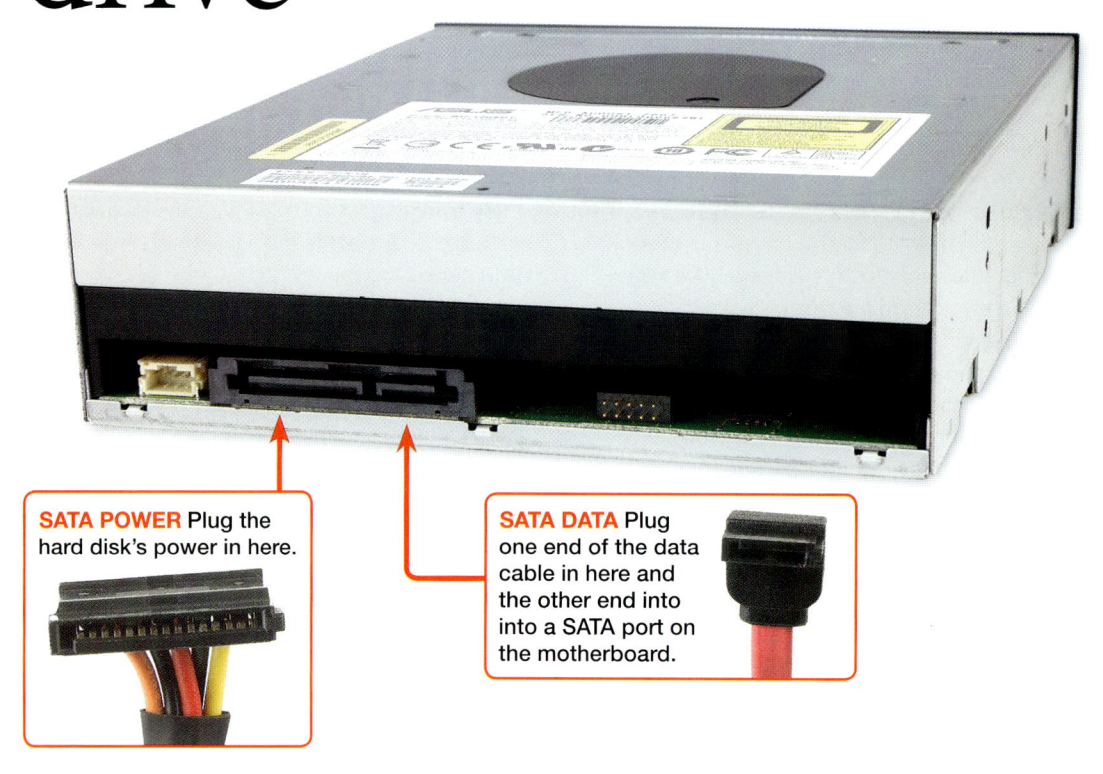

SATA POWER Plug the hard disk's power in here.

SATA DATA Plug one end of the data cable in here and the other end into into a SATA port on the motherboard.

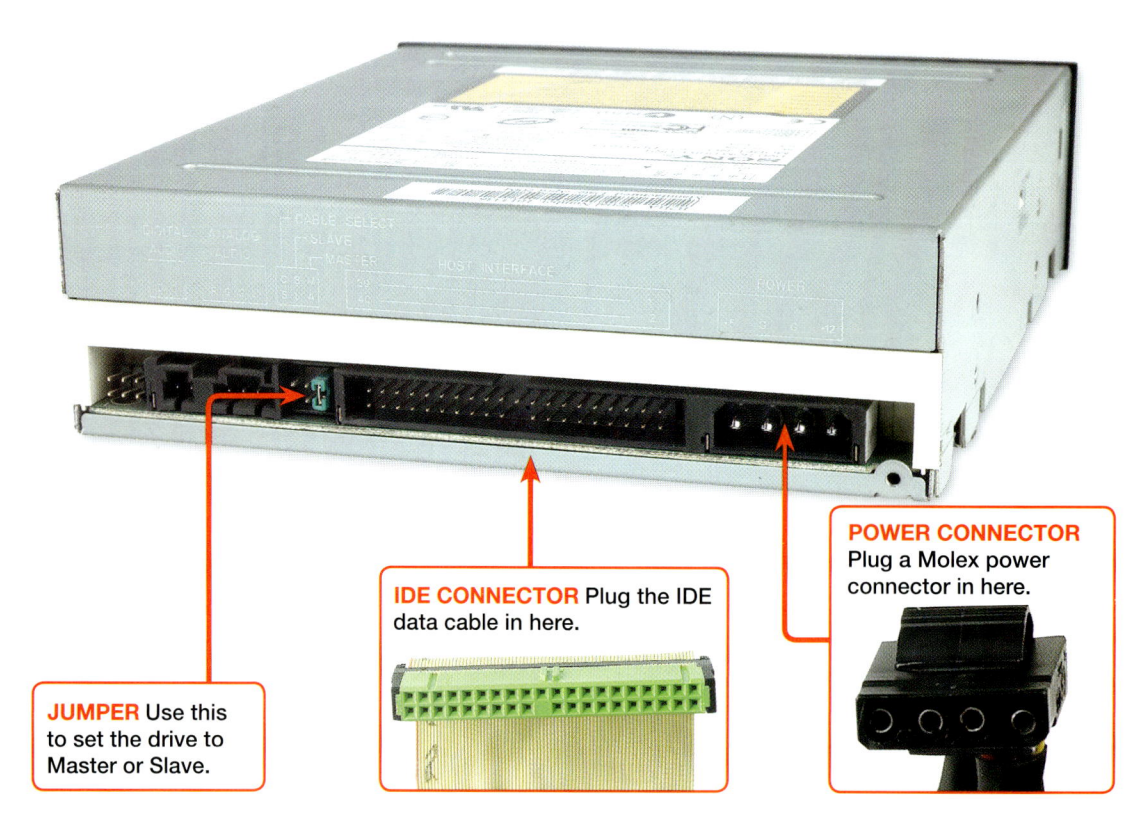

POWER CONNECTOR Plug a Molex power connector in here.

IDE CONNECTOR Plug the IDE data cable in here.

JUMPER Use this to set the drive to Master or Slave.

TIP If you're installing more than one IDE drive, you'll need to set the jumpers on the rear so that one drive is the master and the other the slave.

66 BUILD A BETTER PC

HOW TO...
Connect an optical drive

1 FIT THE DRIVE
First, fit the optical drive into a spare 5¼in drive bay in the case. Some cases have flaps at the front to hide the optical drive from view. If you have a screwless case or your drives need to be fitted on runners, consult your case's manual for full instructions.

Other cases require you to screw the drive into place. The optical drive needs to be slid into the case from the front. This often means that you need to have the front of the case removed, if you haven't done that yet. Slide the drive into the bay. The front of it needs to be flush with the case where there's no flap, and slightly further back if you've got a drive flap.

To tell where the drive should be, push it in until the screw holes in its side match up with the round screw holes inside the case. Now use the four screws (provided with the optical drive or case) – two either side – to hold the drive in place.

2 FIT THE IDE CABLE
Most optical drives use the older IDE data connector. If yours uses SATA, follow the instructions for fitting a hard disk (page 64). An IDE cable is a wide ribbon cable. It's harder to plug in than SATA, but shouldn't cause any problems if you know what to look out for. First, the cable can only plug in one way due to a blocked-off connector in the cable. Second, the coloured cable (red or white depending on the cable provided with your motherboard) goes to the right of the connector closest to the power connector. Simply plug the cable in gently. Try and do it as straight as possible in order not to bend any pins on the drive.

3 FIT THE POWER CABLE
Optical drives tend to use a Molex power connector. This is the large four-pin connector on your power supply. Locate a free one and push it into the drive's power connector. Use a bit of force to get it to connect properly. Once you think it's in, give it a gentle tug to make sure it's secure.

4 FIT THE IDE CABLE INTO THE MOTHERBOARD
Now you're ready to plug the cable into the motherboard. Don't get the connector confused with the floppy disk connector; check your motherboard's manual for its location. The IDE connector can only plug in one way, thanks to a notch in the motherboard's connector. Plug the cable gently in as straight as possible to avoid bending any pins.

TIP
If your IDE cable doesn't have a notch in it, face the red cable towards the power connector on the drive.

BUILD A BETTER PC **67**

CHAPTER 4
BUILDING YOUR PC

Installing a graphics card

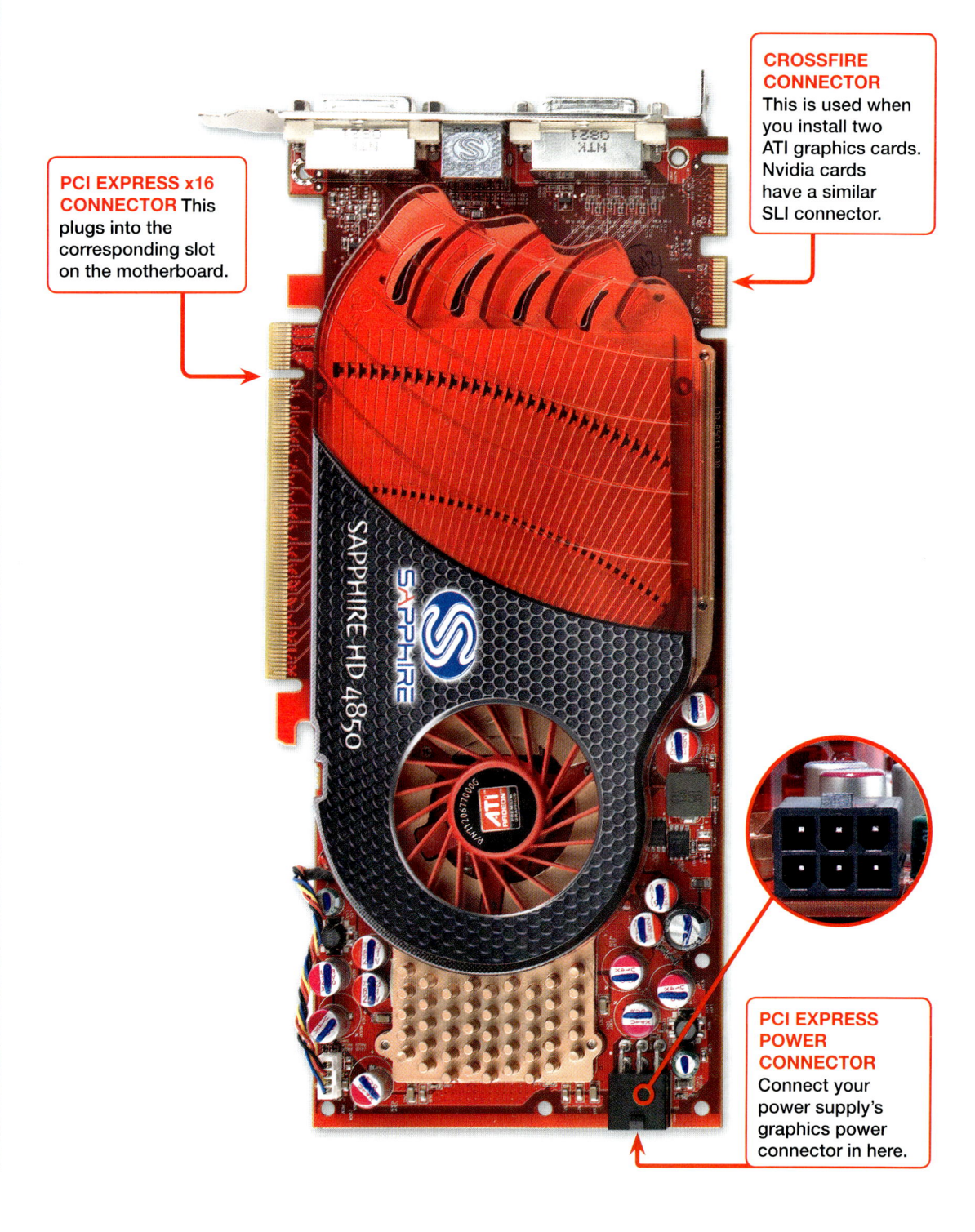

PCI EXPRESS x16 CONNECTOR This plugs into the corresponding slot on the motherboard.

CROSSFIRE CONNECTOR This is used when you install two ATI graphics cards. Nvidia cards have a similar SLI connector.

PCI EXPRESS POWER CONNECTOR Connect your power supply's graphics power connector in here.

TIP
PCI Express x16 slots typically have retaining clips. You'll need to use this clip if you need to remove a graphics card later.

68 BUILD A BETTER PC

HOW TO...
Install a graphics card

1 REMOVE BLANKING PLATE
To fit a graphics card, you'll need to locate the PCI Express x16 slot and remove the associated blanking plate. If you're going to fit a double-height card, then you'll need to remove the blanking plate for the next expansion slot as well.

The steps will differ according to your case, so check its manual for full details. Typically, blanking plates are either individually screwed in place, or a single retaining bar holds them all in place. Remove whatever's holding the blanking plates in place. Some blanking plates just lift out, while others are attached to the case and need to be rocked backwards and forwards to snap them out.

2 PLUG CARD INTO SLOT
With the blanking plates free, you can put your card into the case. This is easy to do: simply line up the graphics card's connector with the slot in the case. The card should look like it's upside down, with the fan pointing towards the bottom of the case.

Pressure on both sides of the card should be enough to make sure that it ends up seated in the expansion card slot properly. You should check the card when you think it's in place to ensure that you've made proper contact. If you can still see some of the card's slot sticking out, then push the offending side in a bit further.

3 SCREW CARD IN PLACE
How you remove the blanking plate will depend on how you attach your card securely, so check the case's manual for full details. In most instances, you'll need to screw the card into place. Line up the top of its connector with the screw hole in the case and screw it into place so that the card can't move in its slot.

4 CONNECT POWER ADAPTOR
Most modern graphics cards require a secondary power source to run. These will need a dedicated PCI Express six-pin power connector. This is on most modern power supplies, but if yours doesn't have one, a Molex-to-PCI Express adaptor is often bundled with graphics cards. The PCI Express power connector can only plug in one way and can be pushed easily into place.

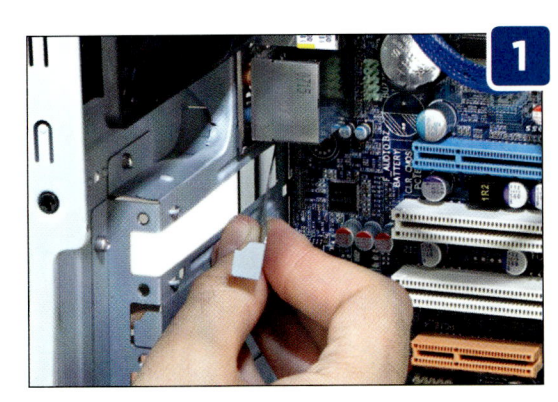

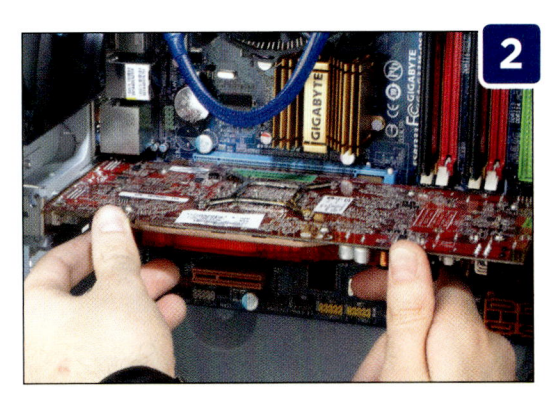

TIP
Don't forget to plug in the PCI Express power connector (if required), or your PC may not turn on.

BUILD A BETTER PC **69**

CHAPTER 4
BUILDING YOUR PC

Installing expansion cards

PCI SLOTS An older type of expansion slot, but there are plenty of cards that will fit them.

PCI EXPRESS x1 SLOT The newest type of expansion slot. Also look out for x4 slots, which look similar but are longer.

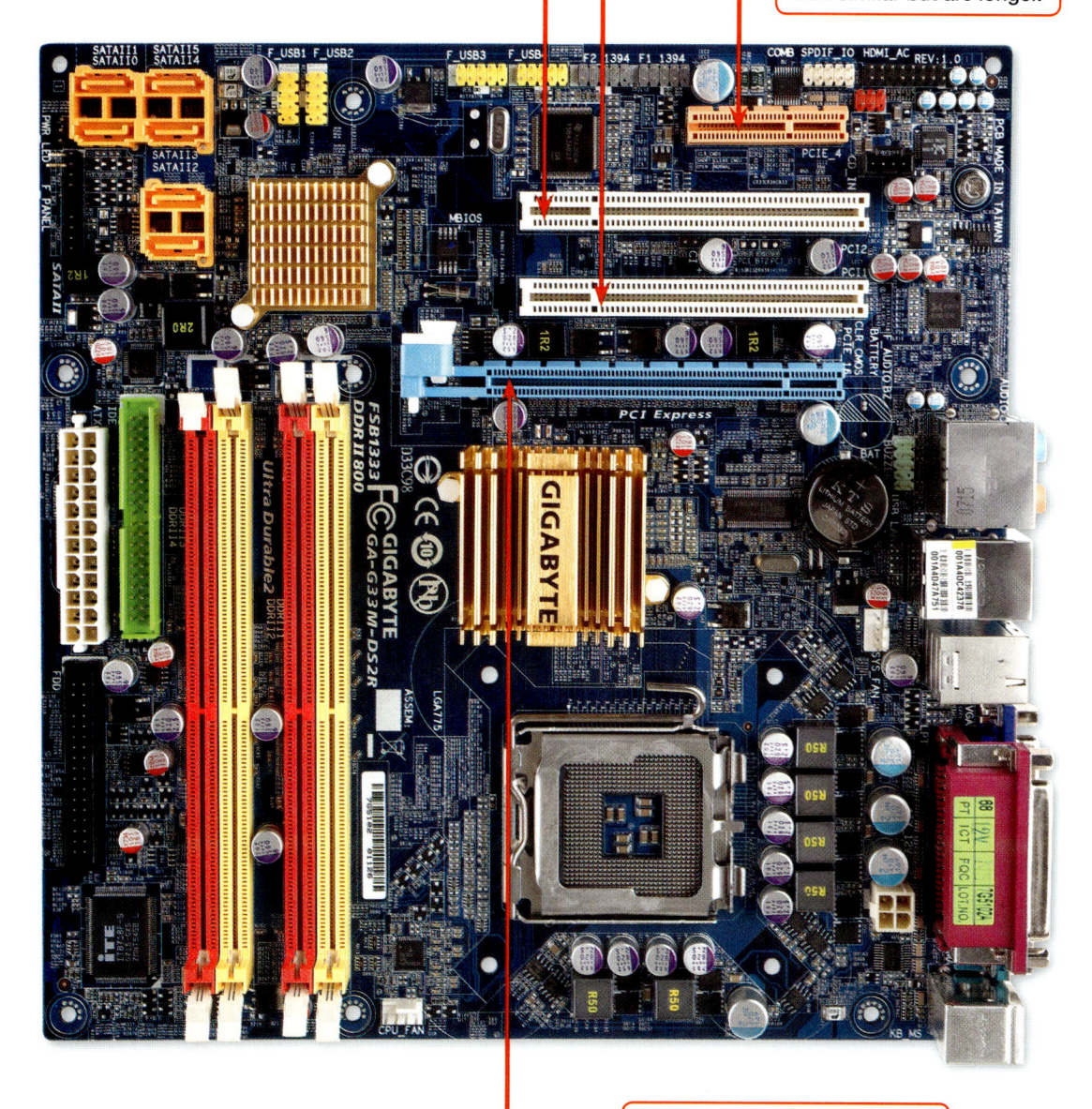

PCI EXPRESS X16 SLOT If you don't install a dedicated graphics card, this slot can be used for expansion cards.

TIP
PCI Express cards can fit in a higher socket type, so an x1 card can fit in an x4 slot and so on.

70 BUILD A BETTER PC

HOW TO...
Plug in expansion cards

1. LOCATE SPARE SLOT
Before you start, carefully read the instructions that come with your expansion card as some require you to install software first. If yours does, you'll need to finish building the PC and install the operating system and necessary software before fitting the expansion card.

When you're ready, find a spare slot (PCI or PCI Express) on your motherboard. Ideally, leave a gap between other expansion cards, such as your graphics card, to increase airflow and keep your PC running cool.

2. REMOVE BLANKING PLATE
To fit an expansion card, you'll need to remove the expansion slot's blanking plate. The steps will differ according to your case, so carefully check its manual for full details. Typically, blanking plates are either individually screwed in place or held in place by a single retaining bar. Remove whatever's holding the blanking plates in place. Some plates just lift out, while others are attached to the case and need to be rocked backwards and forwards to snap them out.

3. FIT THE CARD
PCI and PCI Express cards are fitted in the same way. Line up the connector on the bottom of the card with the slot you want to put it in. Slots have notches part of the way along, which you need to line up with the gap in the card's connector. When you've done this, push the card into place. It will take a bit of force to get the card to slide home properly. If the card doesn't feel like it's going to go into the slot, remove it and make sure it's lined up and that you're trying to install it into the correct slot. When the card is in place, check round it to make sure the connector is firmly in the slot. If the card doesn't look level, apply pressure to the part of the card sticking up until it clicks into place.

4. SCREW IT IN
When your card is firmly in place, you need to secure it in its slot. As some cases use proprietary fixing methods, check your case's manual for instructions on how to do this. If you need to use a screw, line up the screw hole in the card's blanking plate with the screw hole in the case. Tighten the screw up to the point where the card feels firm and doesn't wobble in the slot.

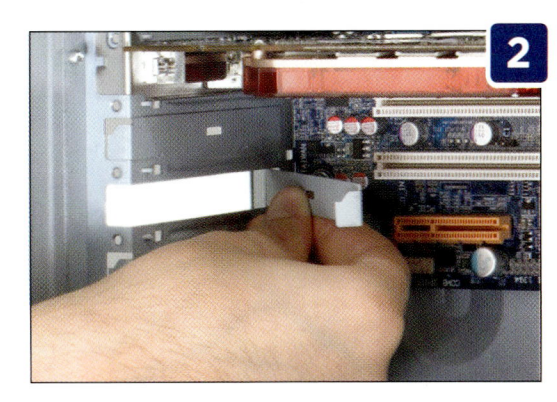

TIP Try and use alternate slots to improve airflow and stop adjacent cards from heating each other up.

BUILD A BETTER PC

CHAPTER 4
BUILDING YOUR PC

HOW TO...
Put the case back together

1 CABLE TIDY
If the inside of your computer is neat and tidy, you'll get better airflow and keep it cooler. A neat PC is also easier to work on should you need to install an upgrade.

One way to keep your case tidy is to fit cable ties. Simply locate loose cables that are running in the same direction and loop a cable tie around the bunch. Slide the strap through the buckle and pull it tight. The ratchet should click into place and stop the cable becoming undone. If it doesn't, you've inserted the strap the wrong way into the buckle. You can clip the long strap off when you're done. For extra neatness, loop the strap through drive bays in the case. This will anchor your cables out of the way.

2 KEEP CABLES OUT OF FANS
It's worth double-checking that none of your power cables is in the way of the fans inside your PC. If they are, you run the risk of severing your cables when you power your PC on for the first time. Pull any loose cables out of the way of fans and secure them with cable ties if necessary. The processor fan (particularly on Intel's designs) is often the worse culprit for snagging cables, so check this one carefully.

3 ATTACH FRONT
Check your case's manual for the exact fitting instructions. If you removed its front, now is the time to fit it again. Line its clips up with the holes in the case and push firmly to reattach it. If you find that your optical drive sticks out too far, you've probably fitted it incorrectly. Undo its screws (or fixings if your case is screwless) and slide it further into the case. Screw it back in and fit the front of the case.

4 ATTACH SIDES
Check your case's manual carefully for full fitting instructions. For most cases, fitting the side panels is a matter of lining up their clips with the grooves on the inside of the case. Take each panel in turn, slide it into place and attach it firmly with a screw.

5 CONNECT NETWORK CABLE

If you want to connect your PC to a broadband router via an Ethernet cable, now's the time to plug it in. Vista's installation can use a network connection to search for updated drivers, so having a network connection can make your installation smoother. Even if you're not using Vista, being able to connect straight to the internet after installing an operating system is really useful.

6 CONNECT KEYBOARD AND MOUSE

To install an operating system, you'll need to connect a mouse and keyboard. Most motherboards support older PS2 keyboards and mice, and newer USB peripherals, too. PS2 keyboards plug into the purple port and mice into the green one. Simply line up the notch in the plug with the one in the port in the back of your computer and push.

For USB keyboards and mice, plug the connector into a free USB port– it will only go one way. For other USB devices, check their manuals before plugging them in. Many devices require you to install drivers first, so you'll have to install an operating system before you can plug them in.

7 CONNECT SPEAKERS

You can connect your speakers to your PC now. This is useful, as after installing an operating system you'll be able to check instantly whether the sound is working properly. How you connect your speakers will depend on the number you're plugging in. Generally speaking, surround-sound speakers have colour-coded cables, so you just need to match the cable with the same-coloured port on the back of your PC. For stereo speakers, plug a 3½mm jack into the green port on the back of the PC. Headphones generally connect to the green port on the front of the case.

8 PLUG IN MONITOR

Finally, you need to connect your computer to a monitor. This is simple. If your screen has a DVI input and your graphics card has a DVI output (pictured), you need a DVI-to-DVI cable. These are D-shaped, so they will only plug in one way. Line up the cable with the graphics card's connector and push the cable straight in. Screw it in place using the thumbscrews on either side of the connector. Repeat this on job on the monitor.

If your monitor has a blue analogue D-sub connector, you've got two options. For graphics cards with DVI outputs, you'll have to plug in a DVI-to-D-sub connector first. You can then plug the D-sub cable into this and the monitor. If you're using onboard graphics with a D-sub output, plug the cable directly into this and the monitor. Just like DVI connectors, D-sub connectors are D-shaped, so they'll only plug in one way.

TIP DVI-to-VGA adaptors will let you plug in an analogue monitor if you've only got DVI outputs.

CHAPTER 5
BUILDING AN ATOM PC

EVEN THE LOWEST-SPECIFICATION desktop will draw a lot of power when in use. If you're looking to build a power-efficient system, there's another way: Intel's Atom processor. Designed to save power, it can form the basis of an incredibly cheap, low-powered and fully fledged Windows system. Here, we'll show you how to build one.

IN THIS CHAPTER

Building a power-efficient
  computer   76

BUILD A BETTER PC   **75**

CHAPTER 5
BUILDING AN ATOM PC

Building a power-efficient computer

INTEL'S NEW ATOM processors may not have the full power of regular desktop processors, but they're incredibly power-efficient and great value. For this reason, they're used in a lot of mini laptops, such as Asus' Eee PC 901. The same company also uses an Atom inside its new desktop computer, the Eee Box. This tiny PC is perfect for light use, such as office applications, email and web browsing, but it doesn't have an optical drive and can't be upgraded.

Over the next four pages, we'll show you how to build a small, upgradable Intel Atom-based PC using the Silverstone Mini-ITX case for just £225. This system's performance will be similar to Asus's Eee Box, but it will have a DVD writer, a larger hard disk and more memory. While it uses more power than the Eee Box – 30W rather than the Eee Box's 16W – it's still extremely power-efficient compared to the 100W or more that an average desktop PC uses. This system could save you more than a third on the electricity costs of running a computer.

Our shopping list on page 79 shows you which parts we recommend for building an Intel Atom Mini-ITX PC. The only parts specific to this guide are the motherboard, case and Molex-to-4-pin-processor power adaptor. You can use any 2½in or 3½in SATA hard disk and any slim, laptop-sized optical drive, so a bigger hard disk or different optical drive will still work in your Atom PC. The computer is perfectly capable of running Windows Vista and XP, and comes with the appropriate drivers on CD for either operating system.

The only tools you'll need are two Phillips screwdrivers: one medium-sized and a small jeweller's version. You'll also need a reasonably large table to work on and a good reading light so you can see what you're doing.

1 TAKE THE CASE APART

Remove the three screws at the back of the case, slide it backwards and lift it off. You'll now need to remove the drive tray. There are two screws at the back and two lower down at the front, so remove them all. The front and the rear screws are different, so make a note of which is which. Take out the external power supply and the bag containing the optical back plate and screws, and set them aside.

Next, you need to fit the motherboard. First, find its backplate in the box that it came in. With the rear of the case facing towards you, position the backplate so that the round keyboard and mouse holes are on the left and the shiny side is facing towards you. Push the backplate into the hole at the back of the case from the inside, and it will pop into place.

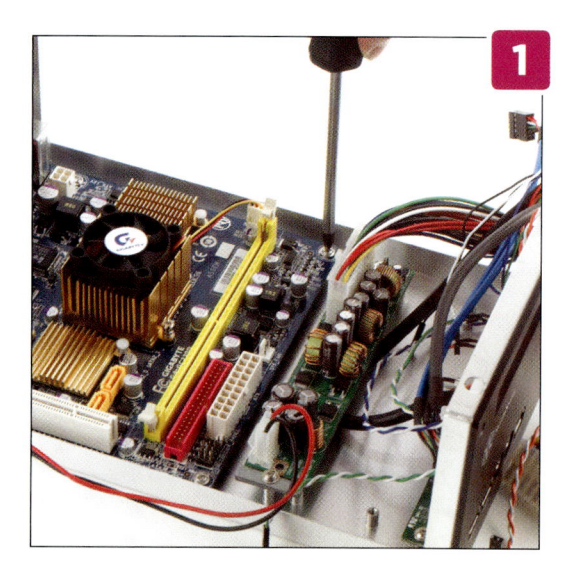

Now remove the board from its anti-static bag and lower it into the case on to the four screw mounts, with the ports for the keyboard, mouse, USB, audio, and so on, towards the rear. You'll have to line up the ports with the holes in the backplate and push them through. Now find the four remaining round-headed screws and use them to secure the motherboard. You'll need to push the motherboard gently against the springy backplate to make the screw holes line up. It's easiest to put each screw in a couple of turns before tightening them up one by one.

2 INSTALL THE MEMORY

Take your memory module and look at the connector on the bottom. You'll notice it has a notch about half-way along its length. This matches up to a ridge on the yellow memory card slot on the motherboard. Make sure the levers at either end of the memory card slot are open, line up the notch with the ridge and slide the module into the slot. Push it down at both ends simultaneously so the levers click into place.

Take the IDE ribbon cable out of the motherboard box and find the long red socket marked IDE. Line up the ridge on the plug with the notch on the socket and plug it in. Now take the thin yellow SATA cable out of the motherboard box and plug it into one of the two yellow SATA 2 ports on the motherboard. The cable plug and the socket are both L-shaped, so the plug will only fit in the socket one way.

Take the large rectangular 20-pin power connector and plug it into the rectangular power socket marked ATX on the motherboard. Again, the connector will only fit one way. Line up the lever clip on the plug with the notch on the socket and push it gently until it clicks into place. Plug your Molex-to-processor power adaptor into one of the power supply's Molex connectors, and plug the small square processor power plug into the small square socket marked ATX_12V at the back of the motherboard. Again, it will only fit one way, so line up the lever clip with the notch on the socket and push the plug in.

3 CONNECT USB PORTS

A cable marked HD Audio and AC 97 is connected to the front of the case with two plugs. The Gigabyte motherboard has high-definition audio, so you'll need the HD Audio plug. It has a blanked-off hole in the bottom that corresponds to a missing pin on the green motherboard audio header, which is marked F-Audio and is at the back of the motherboard next to the audio outputs. Position the plug so that the blanked-off connector matches up to the missing pin and plug it in.

Now find the blue cable with a plug marked USB. This also has a blanked-off hole, which corresponds to a missing pin on the yellow motherboard header marked F_USB1. Line up the plug with the socket and plug it in.

The front panel also has a FireWire cable, but the Gigabyte motherboard doesn't have FireWire, so tuck the cable out of the way.

4 CONNECT INTERNAL CABLES

You now need to plug the cables that connect to the power and hard disk lights and power button into the headers on the motherboard. The headers are labelled F_PANEL and are next to the large ATX power connector. The function of each pin is written next to it, but for a clearer view you can look at the diagram in the motherboard's manual. Each connector has a coloured and a white wire; the coloured wire is positive and the

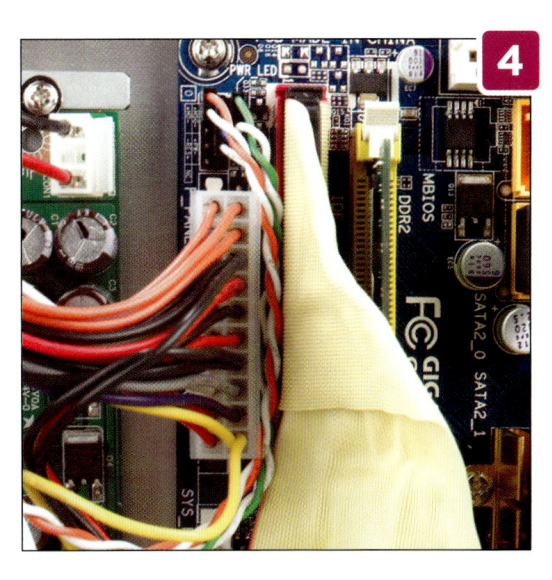

TIP

You can save even more electricity by following our power-saving guide on page 112.

BUILD A BETTER PC 77

CHAPTER 5
BUILDING AN ATOM PC

white is negative. Plug the connector marked HDD LED into the header marked +HD-, matching the coloured wire to the + pin. Do the same for the connector marked POWER SW. The POWER LED connector has three pins; connect it so that the connector's coloured positive cable is nearest the edge of the motherboard.

5 INSTALL THE HARD DISK
The next step is to fit the hard disk. The procedure is the same whether you're fitting a 2½in or 3½in disk, as they both have screw holes in the same place. Put the hard disk on your desk with the circuit board side facing up, and the data and power connectors on the rear facing towards you. Pick up the drive tray and position it that so the long flanges on the sides are facing upwards and the raised screw holes are on the right. Put the tray on top of the hard disk and line up the four screws in the middle of the metal sheet on the right of the tray with the four screw holes on the bottom of your disk. Screw the disk into place with the four small countersunk screws that came with the case.

6 FIT THE OPTICAL DRIVE BACKPLATE
To fit the slim optical drive, you first need to attach the supplied backplate that converts the optical drive's laptop connector to a standard PC IDE connector. Plug it into the back of the slim optical drive and use your small Phillips screwdriver to secure it with the screws supplied.

Put the drive tray flat on your desk with the hard disk's connectors facing towards you. The optical drive has a cutout that corresponds to a raised shelf in the drive tray. Line up the front of the drive with the front of the tray and the cutout with the raised shelf, making sure the drive's bezel is hanging over the front of the tray. Now gently press down on the top of the drive so it slides into the tray. Don't screw the drive in yet.

Put the drive tray back in the case and screw it back into place using the two countersunk screws at the rear and the rounded screws at the front. Postion the optical drive so that the bezel lines up with the hole in the front of the case and secure it with the four tiny screws.

7 CONNECT THE OPTICAL DRIVE
When plugging in the optical drive and hard disk, route the power cables under the drive tray so they don't foul on the lid when you close the chassis. The optical drive is powered by a floppy drive power connector, which is the small, flat, white plug. The power socket on the back of the optical drive has four pins with a flat plastic shelf underneath. Plug in the power connector with its flat underside next to the flat shelf. The hard disk uses a SATA power connector, which is the wide,

> **TIP**
> There's not much room inside this case, so make sure that you don't get any cables trapped when you're putting it back together.

SHOPPING LIST

Gigabyte GA-GC230D motherboard and processor www.lambda-tek.com/componentshop	£55
Silverstone LC12B mini-ITX case http://linitx.com	£87
Optiarc AD-5590A laptop DVD writer www.lambda-tek.com/componentshop	£25
DiamondMax 21 160GB SATA hard disk www.lambda-tek.com/componentshop	£24
2GB Kingston 533MHz DDR2 RAM www.lambda-tek.com/componentshop	£25
Molex-to-4-pin processor power adaptor http://tinyurl.com/molextoprocessor	£3
Moulded IEC mains lead http://tinyurl.com/mainslead	£6
TOTAL AMOUNT	**£225**

flat, black plug. This has an L-shaped hole that corresponds to the L-shaped ridge on the hard disk's power connector. Match up the hole and the ridge and gently plug in the connector.

The IDE ribbon connector plugs into the long connector on the back of the optical drive. Match the blanked-off hole on the plug to the missing pin on the optical drive's connector and plug it in. The yellow SATA data cable plugs into another L-shaped connector in the back of the hard disk.

8 PUT THE CASE BACK TOGETHER

Finally, put the case lid back on, making sure you don't foul any cables, and screw it back together. Plug in your keyboard, mouse and monitor, plug the mains power cable into the external power supply and the power supply into the PC. Now turn on the PC, and press the Delete key repeatedly. This will take you into the PC's BIOS setup program. Use the arrow keys to go to Advanced BIOS Features and press Return. Now go to First Boot Device, press Return and select CD-ROM. Go to Second Boot Device, press Return and select Hard Disk. Now put your operating system disc in the optical drive. Press F10, then Y and Return to save your changes. The PC will reboot, and when the Press any key to boot from CD or DVD message appears press a key to go into your operating system setup program.

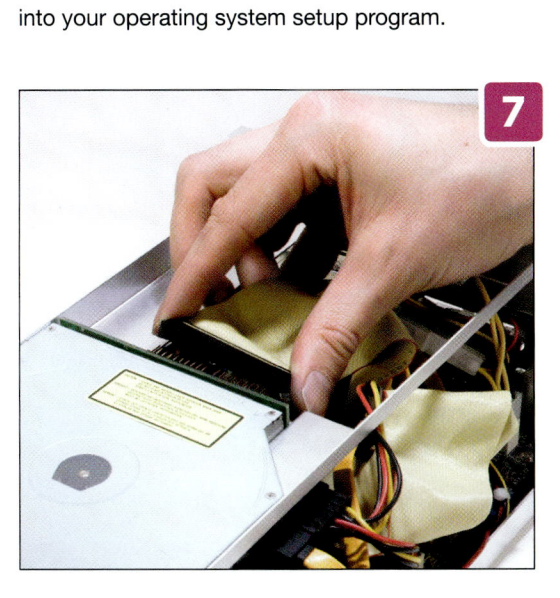

BUILD A BETTER PC 79

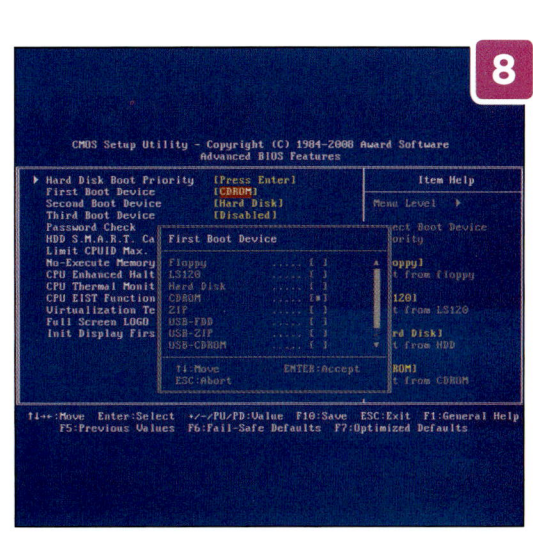

CHAPTER 6
POWER ON

BEFORE YOU CAN install an operating system on your newly assembled PC, you'll need to change a few settings in the BIOS. The BIOS is where you can configure the speed of your processor and memory, make settings such as a system password and choose the time at which the PC boots up every day. In this chapter, we'll show you how to access the BIOS and make the appropriate changes.

IN THIS CHAPTER

Into the BIOS	82
Edit the BIOS	83

CHAPTER 6
POWER ON

Into the BIOS

THE BIOS IS part of the motherboard, and is arguably one of its most important components. If it gets physically damaged or corrupted by a virus, there's a good chance that you won't be able to use your computer at all.

Thankfully, the chances of either of these happening is minimal: it's much more common that the wrong settings will have been made in the BIOS. Fortunately, the BIOS is simple to use, and relatively easy to understand.

BIOSes have a limited amount of memory, which is used to store the settings. This memory keeps the settings – including the date and time – as long as the motherboard's battery has charge. However, despite huge advances in almost every other aspect of a computer, the BIOS has remained virtually unchanged in the way it looks and works for around 25 years.

There are only a few major BIOS makers, including Award and Phoenix, and most BIOSes look very similar. However, you need to bear in mind that yours may have different options to those shown over the next few pages. So, while the following steps may not match up with the options you have, it shouldn't be difficult to work out how to modify our instructions to apply them to what you see on your screen.

Initially, you may find that you don't need to make many changes to get to a stage where you can install your operating system. Here, we'll show you what all the options are for, so you can come back later and tweak everything to your liking.

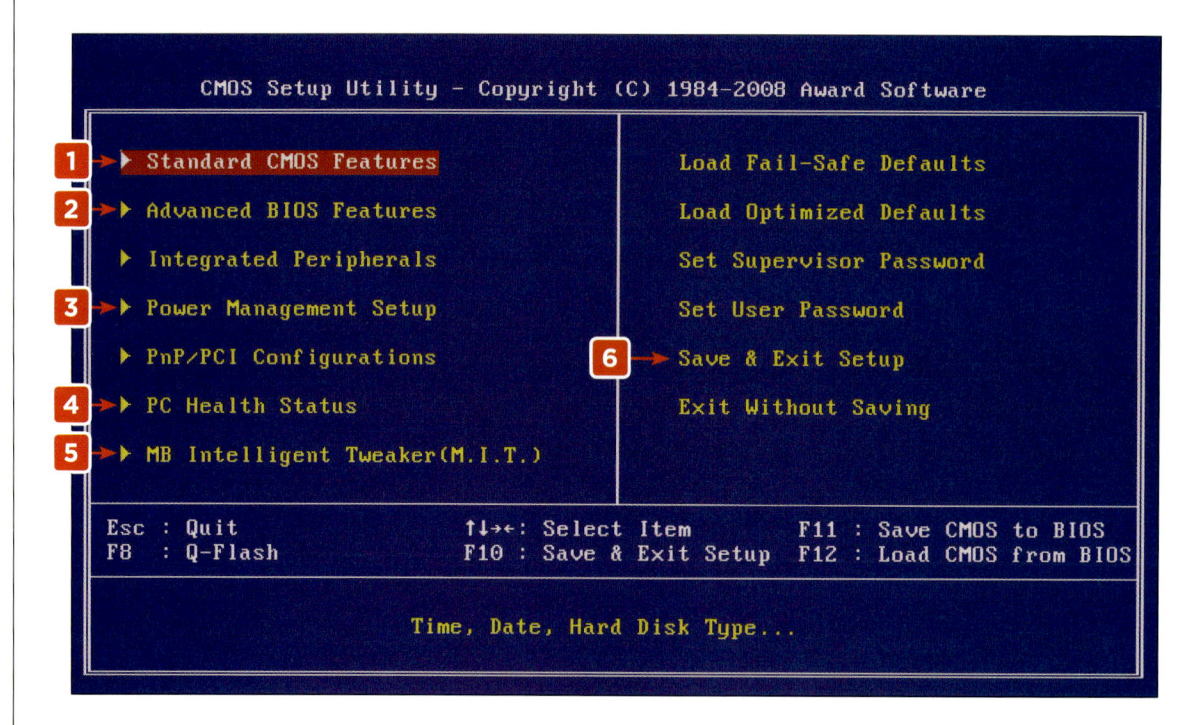

1 Contains settings for date, time, hard disks, optical and floppy drives

2 Here you can set the boot order, passwords and processor features

3 Head for power settings, including sleep mode and devices that can wake up the PC

4 Information on temperatures, fans and voltages

5 Here is the place to make advanced processor and memory settings

6 When you've made changes, choose this option to save and reboot

82   BUILD A BETTER PC

HOW TO...
Edit the BIOS

1. GET INTO THE BIOS
Many of the latest motherboards feature graphic splash screens, which hide the traditional black and white text. We've used a Gigabyte motherboard here. As with most other boards, you press the Delete key to access the BIOS. While a minority of BIOSes use alternative keys, such as F1, F2 or F10, it should be easy to spot which you need to use, as it will be shown somewhere obvious onscreen. Push the power button, wait for the POST (Power-On Self Test) screen to appear and press the appropriate key to enter the BIOS. If you miss the POST screen, press Ctrl-Alt-Del to restart the computer.

2. THE MAIN SCREEN
The main BIOS screen will now appear. Even if yours doesn't look like this, the menu options should be similar. To navigate around, use the cursor keys. On most BIOSes, you can select an option by pressing Enter or the right cursor key. Pressing Esc will return you to the POST screen, while F10 jumps to the Save & Exit confirmation prompt.

3. SET DATE AND TIME
Let's work through the main menu options in order. One of the first things you need to do is to set the correct date and time, as Windows uses this information. Standard CMOS Features should already be selected – it's highlighted in red – so you simply need to press Enter.

Again, you navigate through the settings using the cursor keys. All changeable settings are shown in yellow, while those that aren't are in light blue. Set the correct time and date by highlighting the part you want to change, and alter its value by pressing the + or – key. Alternatively, you can use the Page Up and Page Down keys.

4. CONFIGURE HARD DISK
In the IDE listing, you should see your hard disk and optical drive. Most motherboards don't differentiate between PATA and SATA drives, simply referring to them as IDE. All the entries marked None are the PATA and SATA ports, which no drives are connected to. During the POST, all of these are checked to see if there's anything connected, but to save a few seconds of boot time you can disable the unused channels.

To do this, highlight a channel, press Enter, then select the name of the channel in the screen that appears – in this case IDE Channel 0 Slave. Press Enter again and a window will appear with the options None, Auto or Manual. Change the setting

TIP
If you make a mistake or your settings aren't working, use the Load Fail-Safe Defaults option to reset the BIOS.

BUILD A BETTER PC   83

CHAPTER 6
POWER ON

from Auto to None, and this channel will no longer be checked at boot time. If you ever want to connect a drive to this channel, remember to re-enable it by changing it back to Auto.

5 CONFIGURE FLOPPY DISK

Press Enter to accept the change and return to the Standard CMOS Features menu. It's unlikely that you'll have fitted a floppy drive in your PC, so highlight Drive A and press Enter. This will open a window where you can select the type of floppy drive. Here, you can see proof that the BIOS hasn't changed for a long time, as there are entries for 5¼in floppy disk drives, despite the fact that this motherboard was brand new in summer 2008. Select None or 1.44M, 3.5" if you've installed a drive, and press Enter to Accept.

On the right-hand side of the Standard CMOS Features screen, you'll see contextual help, which provides terse information on the setting you've highlighted. Usually, this is fairly unhelpful, so it's a good idea to have your motherboard's manual handy in case you need to refer to it.

6 SET UP BOOT DEVICE

Press Esc to return to the main BIOS menu, and go to the second heading: Advanced BIOS Features. Depending on your particular BIOS, you may find processor and memory settings here, but we'll get to those in Step 13, as they're under a different heading in our BIOS. The most important settings in this menu are the Boot Device options. You need to ensure that the first boot device is set to CD-ROM, since the operating system is most likely to be on a CD. The BIOS doesn't differentiate between types of optical drive, so CD-ROM refers to all types, including DVD and Blu-ray drives. Press Enter to accept your choice, and then ensure that the second boot device is set to hard disk. This is necessary since, once you've installed an operating system, the hard disk becomes the bootable device.

7 MORE ADVANCED FEATURES

The rest of the Advanced BIOS Features vary from motherboard to motherboard, but you may want to check the rest of the options to make sure you're happy with their default values. The CPU Thermal Monitor, for example, can be disabled if you don't want the BIOS to keep tabs on the processor's temperature. However, it's advisable to enable this to prevent overheating and possible damage to your processor.

Other options include the ability to disable the POST splash screen, and also which graphics card is initialised first – either an integrated chip or a graphics card in the PCI Express slot.

8 CONFIGURE PORTS

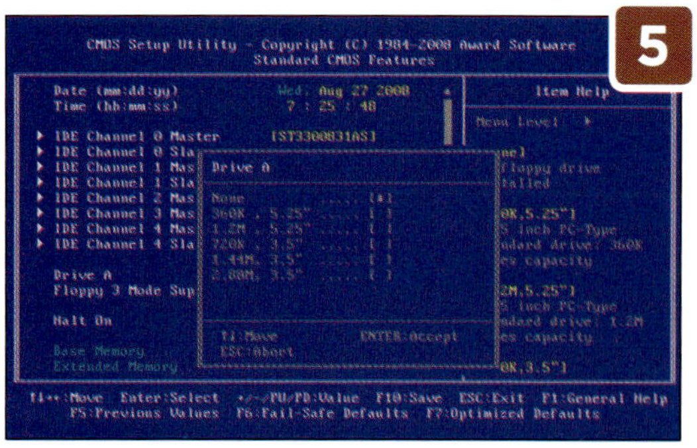

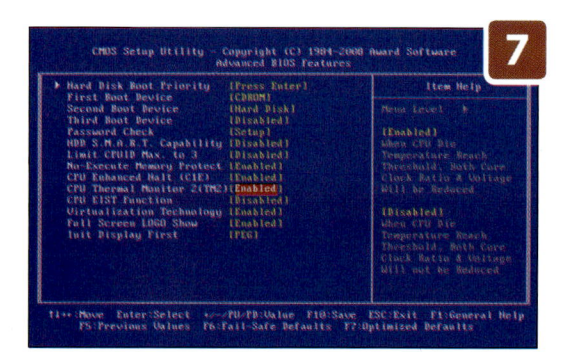

Press Esc to return to the main menu, then choose Integrated Peripherals. This will show a list of the main components on your motherboard, including SATA and RAID ports, USB ports, audio, FireWire, network adaptors and legacy ports such as serial and parallel. It's good practice to disable anything you know you're not going to use. Notable here is that, like many modern motherboards with Intel chipsets, the audio chip is somewhat mysteriously called Azalia Codec – this is a case where the motherboard manual may be useful.

9 POWER MANAGEMENT

Next, go into Power Management Setup. It's crucial that you make the right choice for ACPI Suspend Type, as this will determine whether Windows' Sleep mode works correctly or not. Usually, you'll see two options: S1 and S3. You want S3, which is the Suspend-to-RAM option.

S1 provides little in the way of power saving, and doesn't power down all the main components. S3, by contrast, turns off everything apart from the memory, so the processor, graphics card and other power-hungry components are switched off.

When you tell Windows to go into Sleep mode, the current state of open programs is saved to memory, enabling Windows to restart in just a few seconds when you push the power button.

10 POWER ON CONTROL

Other settings in Power Management Setup include Soft-Off by PWR-BTTN. This sets how long you have to hold down the PC's power button before it switches off. The options usually range from instant to four seconds. We'd advise setting this to the latter to avoid losing work if you accidentally knock the power button.

Other options include Resume by Alarm, which lets you specify when you want your PC to switch on either every day, on weekdays or at weekends. Usually, you can choose only one option and can't set a different power-on time for weekdays and weekends.

Finally, there are options that determine which devices can wake up the computer, including the mouse, keyboard and network adaptor. The latter is often called Power On by Ring.

11 PC HEALTH

Return to the main menu and then choose PC Health Status. This is where you can view voltages, temperatures and fan speeds. For most, voltages won't be of interest, but temperatures will be. There may be more than two, but you will certainly have at least CPU Temperature and System Temperature. The former will usually be quite a lot higher than the latter; 30°C to 60°C is a normal idle temperature for a processor. System temperature is the ambient temperature inside the computer's case, and if it's significantly higher than 30°C, you may want to install an extra case fan or two.

Fan speeds aren't particularly useful or interesting, but you might find Smart FAN options, which can be used to vary the fan speed according to temperature. Usually this leads to a quieter PC when you're not doing anything demanding.

12 MONITOR TEMPERATURES

One of the most useful settings in PC Health Status is the CPU Warning Temperature. Press Enter when this is highlighted and you'll see a

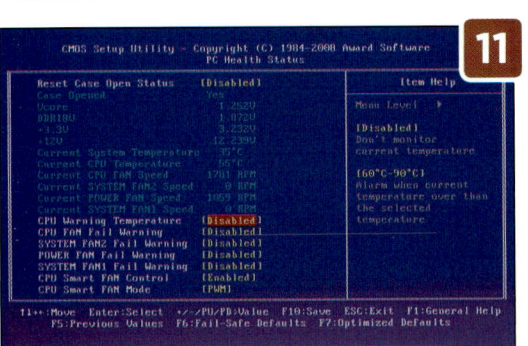

> **TIP**
> The temperature monitor can be useful in diagnosing problems with your computer: hot PCs will crash more often than cool ones.

BUILD A BETTER PC **85**

CHAPTER 6
POWER ON

window with a selection of temperatures. The one you choose will need to be based on the processor you have, as some run much cooler than others and you don't want a buzzer going off when it's running at a normal temperature. Our processor's idle temperature is around 55°C, so 80°C is a sensible warning temperature.

13 EXAMINE PROCESSOR SPEED
Somewhere in the main BIOS menu, there should be an item for processor and memory settings. Names vary, but it shouldn't be hard to find. Options for altering settings will also vary from those you see here, but the essential ones are always present. Check that your processor's speed is correctly set. Here, our Core 2 Duo E8500 is correctly showing under CPU Frequency as 3.16GHz (333x9.5). The part in brackets is the front side bus speed (also known as CPU Host Clock or Frequency) and the multiplier (also known as CPU Clock Ratio). Multiplying the two gives you the processor's speed. As long as you know the frequency your processor should run at and this figure matches what you see on this screen, you don't need to worry about the figures in brackets.

14 ADJUST PROCESSOR SPEED
If your processor's speed isn't showing correctly, set it manually by altering the CPU Host Frequency (MHz). Highlight this field, which represents the front side bus speed, and press Enter (you may first have to enable this field by choosing Enabled under CPU Host Clock Control).

Type in the speed, which will either be 333 or 400 for Intel processors, and 200MHz for AMD processors. If you're not sure, check the specification of your particular model. Press Enter and the change should be reflected in the CPU Frequency field.

15 ADJUST PROCESSOR MULTIPLIER
If the CPU Clock Ratio is showing the wrong value, you may be able to change it. Highlight this field and press Enter. You'll either see a list of the available multipliers, or a box in which to type the ratio number. Enter the right one for your processor. If the value you want isn't shown, your motherboard may not fully support the processor and run at a slower speed. It's worth noting that it isn't normally possible to alter the multiplier since most Intel and AMD processors have locked clock ratios. Only enthusiast processors such as AMD's Black Editions and Intel's Extreme Editions tend to have unlocked multipliers. Some Intel motherboards also force you to type an integer into the ratio box, and if you need a 0.5 multiplier, you have to select this in the next field down.

16 BIOS VERSION
You may be able to upgrade your BIOS to a newer version to add support for newer processors. Visit the website of your motherboard manufacturer to find out if there's a new version. This is often listed in the Downloads section under Firmware. To check which BIOS version your motherboard is currently running, save and exit the BIOS, and

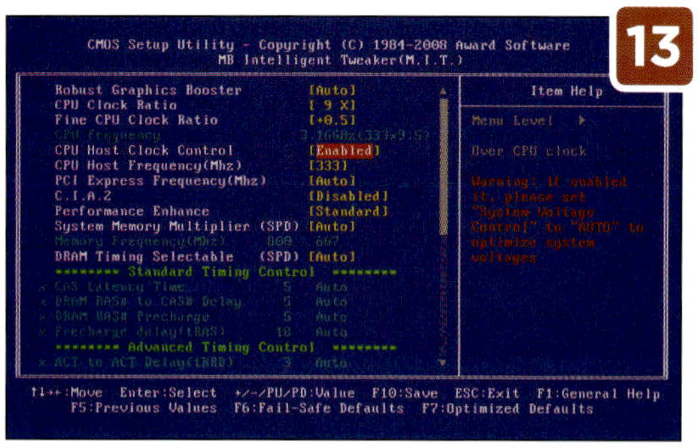

86 BUILD A BETTER PC

restart the PC. When the POST screen shows, look for a version number; it's usually at the top or bottom of the screen – we've highlighted it in the picture. Version numbers aren't shown on graphical splash screens, hit Tab to show the POST screen.

17 SET MEMORY SPEED

It's unlikely that you'll have a problem with your processor's speed being detected incorrectly. More common is that memory speeds are wrongly set. The BIOS usually defaults to Auto settings to ensure overall system reliability, but this can often lead to the memory running slower than it can. Memory has a headline speed figure, in MHz, such as 667, 800 or 1,066. But there are other speed ratings that can affect performance, including those shown here: CAS Latency; RAS-to-CAS Delay; RAS Precharge and Precharge Delay (tRAS).

18 SET MEMORY TIMINGS

Many memory modules have these timings printed in that order on stickers, so look to see what yours is rated at. It'll be something like 4-4-4-12 or 2-2-2-5. If the values in the BIOS are higher than these, change them manually. Highlight each in turn, press Enter and change it from Auto to the value you want. Higher numbers indicate slower performance, as they relate to times.

As with all advanced BIOS settings, we'd advise changing only one setting at a time and rebooting to see if everything is working correctly. If you make several changes and the PC doesn't boot, you won't know which one caused it.

19 OVERCLOCK YOUR PC

Scroll down the list of processor and memory options, and you should find voltage settings. We'd recommend leaving these at their default values, as changing them can damage your hardware. They're here for those that want to overclock some components, primarily the processor and memory. Overclocking makes components run faster than their stated speed, which can give extra performance for free, but it usually comes with the trade-off of reliability. When you overclock a component, you'll usually need to increase its voltage slightly to increase stability. Many motherboards have automatic overclocking options, so you don't need to change frequency and voltage settings yourself. Look for a menu that has options such as 2%, 5%, 10% or Standard, Turbo, Extreme.

20 SAVE YOUR SETTINGS

The rest of the options in the main menu are self-explanatory and let you set passwords – for the BIOS or the whole PC – and exit the BIOS having saved your settings. The other menu items are Load Fail-Safe Defaults and Load Optimized Defaults. The first sets all BIOS options to their original values, which should ensure that the PC will boot and avoid stability problems. You should use this option if you made changes to the BIOS that caused your PC to stop booting. Optimized Defaults loads settings to run the PC at optimal performance, but if you've followed these steps, you'll have the optimal setup.

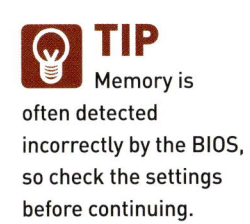

TIP
Memory is often detected incorrectly by the BIOS, so check the settings before continuing.

BUILD A BETTER PC **87**

CHAPTER 7
INSTALLING AN OPERATING SYSTEM

IT'S INCREDIBLY IMPORTANT **that** you install your PC's operating system and drivers correctly if you want a reliable and stable computer. Whether you've chosen Windows XP, Vista, Linux or you just want a Media Center PC for the living room, we'll show you how to install your PC's operating system.

IN THIS CHAPTER

Install Windows Vista	90
Improve Media Center	94
Install Windows XP	98
Install Ubuntu Linux	102

BUILD A BETTER PC **89**

CHAPTER 7
INSTALLING AN OPERATING SYSTEM

HOW TO...
Install Windows Vista

1 START YOUR COMPUTER
Turn your PC on and put the Windows Vista DVD into the optical drive. If you have a new hard disk, the Vista installation routine will load automatically, but if you're using an old hard disk with an operating system already on it, press any key when prompted. If you don't, your old operating system will start and you'll have to reset your PC to start the setup wizard.

Your computer will take a few minutes to start the installation routine, so don't worry if you've got a blank page to look at for a bit.

2 CHOOSE YOUR LANGUAGE OPTIONS
The first screen that appears will ask you to choose which language you want to use. Select English from the drop-down menu. Select English (United Kingdom) as the time and currency format. This should automatically change the keyboard or input method to UK. If it doesn't, select UK from the third drop-down menu. Click Next to continue.

3 INSTALL VISTA
On the next screen, click What to know before installing Windows if you want additional information about Windows Vista. The Repair your computer link only needs to be used if you've already installed Vista and are having problems with the installation. Everyone else should just click the Install now button.

4 ENTER YOUR PRODUCT KEY
Windows will prompt you to type your product key, which is inside the box that your copy of Windows came in. Leave the Automatically activate Windows when I'm online box ticked to let Windows activate itself when you connect to the internet. Unlike previous versions of Windows, you don't have to enter your product key now, and can proceed with the installation. However, after 30 days you'll be prompted for a key. If you don't enter one, you'll only be able to access a few of Vista's features. It's therefore easier to enter the key now. Click Next, and click the tickbox on the next screen to confirm that you've read the licence agreement and click Next.

5 CHOOSE TYPE OF INSTALLATION
You'll be asked to choose if you want to upgrade an old copy of Windows or run a new

90 BUILD A BETTER PC

Custom installation. As you're installing to a new PC, it's likely that the Upgrade option will be disabled. If you're using an old hard disk and a version of Windows that can be upgraded has been detected, select the Custom option. A clean installation of Vista is always the best bet and we don't recommend using the Upgrade option.

6 SELECT HARD DISK

Your hard disk should automatically be detected by Windows Vista. If it isn't, click on the Load Driver button and insert the CD, USB key or floppy disk with the relevant driver. You should need to do this only if you're using RAID or you have a brand new motherboard that Windows doesn't recognise.

From the list of disks, select the one on which you want Windows to be installed. This is usually Disk 0. If you click Next, Windows will format the entire disk automatically. However, it's best to create at least two partitions: one for Windows, and a smaller one for storing backups, drivers and other files you want to keep permanently.

Click Advanced options and then New to add a new partition. You have to select the size of the partition in megabytes (1,024MB = 1GB). Generally, we'd recommend leaving at least 40GB (40,960MB) for the second partition. So, subtract the size of second partition you want from the figure in the box, and enter this. Click Apply. Select Disk 0 Unallocated Space, click New and click Apply. You now have two partitions.

7 FORMAT DISKS

To make things easier once you've started Windows, you should format your partitions now. Select Partition 1 and click Format. Click OK in the warning box. You'll get an hourglass for a few moments while the disk is formatted. Repeat these steps for the second disk. When that has been formatted, click Next.

8 INSTALLING WINDOWS FILES

Next, Windows will automatically copy system files and install the necessary drivers to get your PC working on the first partition that you created. The process can take up to 30 minutes and your computer will restart several times during the operation. There's nothing for you to worry about at this point, and you can just sit back and

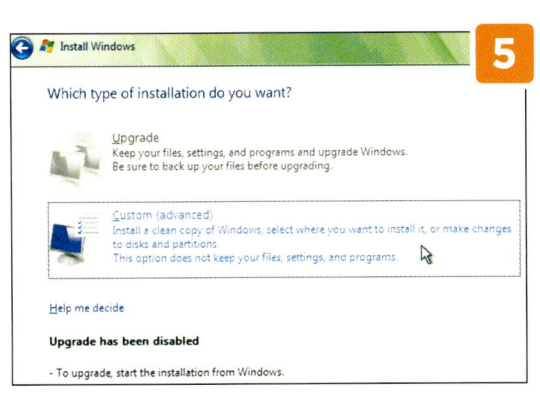

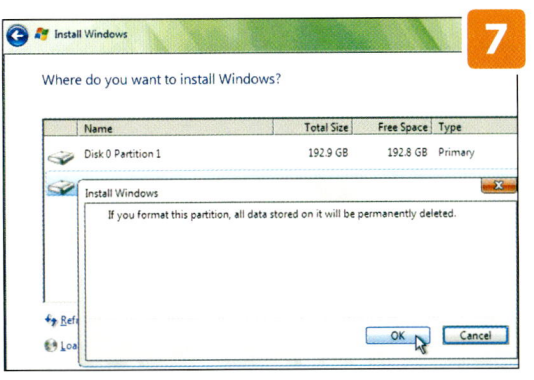

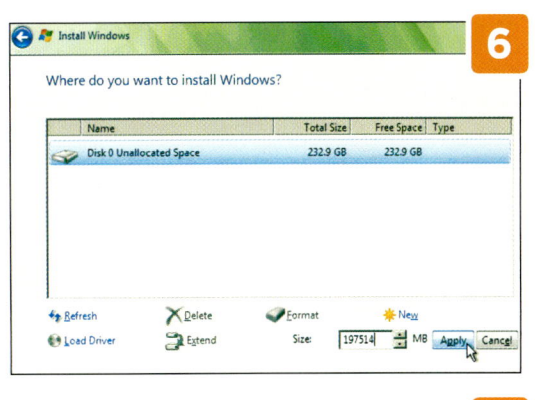

TIP
The blue arrow in the top-left of the installation screens allows you to go back to a previous step.

BUILD A BETTER PC **91**

CHAPTER 7
INSTALLING AN OPERATING SYSTEM

let Windows do its job until the operating system starts for the first time.

9 SET UP A USERNAME
When your computer starts Windows Vista for the first time, you'll be asked to type in a username and password. While the password is optional, if you want to protect your files from unwanted attention and ensure that only authorised users can access your PC, it's vital that you have one. So type in a username and password, and then click Next.

Give your computer a meaningful name and then choose which desktop background you'd like. Click Next to continue.

10 PROTECT WINDOWS
Windows now asks whether you want to turn on Windows Updates automatically. The best option is to select Use recommended settings. Click that box. Next, set the date and time of your computer. Make sure that your time zone has been set correctly. If you chose your location as the UK in the Windows installation routine, then the time zone will be set to GMT by default. Click Next and then Start to launch Windows.

11 START WINDOWS
Windows will now perform some tests on your computer's performance. These will take around five minutes to complete. Once it's finished, you'll be presented with the login screen. If you set a password, you'll have to enter it now and press Enter. Windows will prepare your desktop for its first use and log you on. You'll see the Welcome Center, which gives you quick access to information about Vista and also short cuts to common tasks, such as adding new users. The next time you start Windows, you'll see a box, which you can tick if you don't want to see the Welcome Center again. You can now remove the Windows Vista installation DVD.

12 INSTALL MOTHERBOARD DRIVERS
Although Windows is now working, you still need to install all the relevant drivers to make sure that everything will work smoothly. The first place to start is with your motherboard's drivers. If you downloaded these earlier, insert the USB key or disc you saved them to. If you couldn't do this, insert the driver disc and follow the onscreen instructions. You'll need to download the updated drivers later, and then follow these instructions.

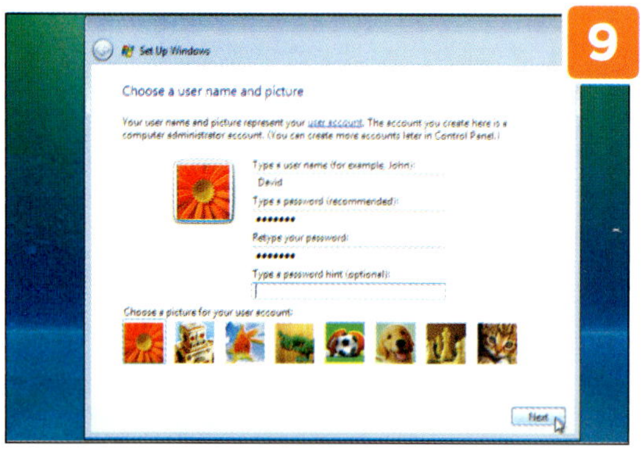

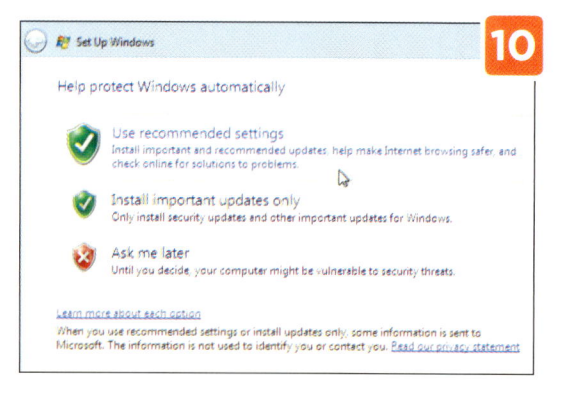

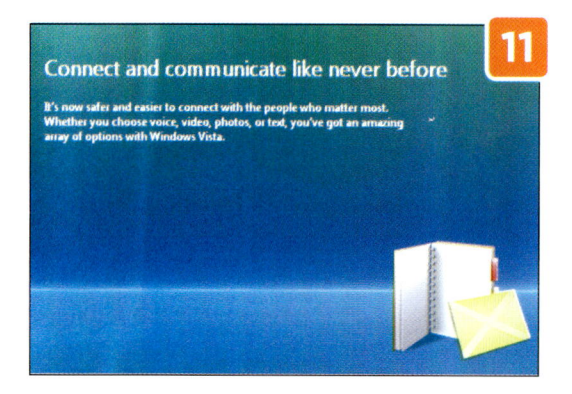

For each driver you downloaded, run the associated file. It's best to start with the chipset driver, but the order afterwards doesn't matter. If Windows displays any warning messages, just click OK. Be careful, as some files you download are actually just archive files that extract the actual driver files on to your hard disk. If this is the case, navigate to the folder the files were extracted to and run the Setup program that you find there. You'll probably need to restart your computer after each driver installation.

13 INSTALL GRAPHICS CARD DRIVERS
Windows will install its own graphics drivers for any onboard or dedicated cards that you have. These are good enough to run Windows, but you won't be able to play games properly. Instead, you need to install the graphics drivers.

Both ATI and Nvidia provide a single driver package. You simply have to run the file that you downloaded. If you couldn't download the drivers earlier, you need to insert the bundled CD, but remember to download newer drivers later on.

Restart your computer after the graphics drivers have been installed. Right-click on the desktop, select Personalize, then Display Properties and change your display resolution to match your monitor's native resolution.

14 INSTALL OTHER PERIPHERALS
You can now install the other peripherals that you've added to your PC. Install the relevant driver files for each device that's plugged into your motherboard. For USB devices, you need to install the driver file first and, when prompted, connect the device to a USB port. If you're in any doubt, you should read the manual that came with your peripheral. If you've installed a wireless adaptor, make sure that you connect it to your wireless network and follow the provided instructions.

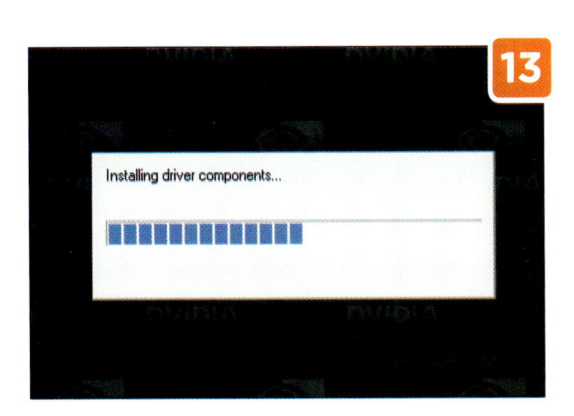

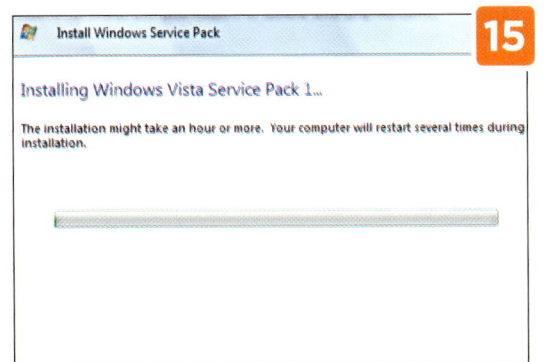

15 INSTALL SERVICE PACK 1
When everything else is installed, you should install Windows Vista Service Pack 1, unless the installation disc you used included this, in which case you can skip to the final step.

To install Service Pack 1, first connect to the internet. The easiest way to force it to install is to go to *http://tinyurl.com/vistaservicepack1*. Click Download and save the file to your hard disk. When it's finished, run the file and follow the wizard. Service Pack 1 will take around an hour to install and will restart your computer when necessary.

16 RUN WINDOWS UPDATE
Click on the Start menu, type Windows Update and click the entry that appears. Click the Check for Updates button, and Windows will connect to Microsoft's update server and detect which updates you need.

Click on View available updates and have a look at the list. There will be some that have been preselected as important updates, but there are also some optional ones, including even newer drivers for your hardware. Select what you'd like to update and then click Install.

When they've finished downloading and installing and your computer has restarted, you'll have a working copy of Windows Vista. You can now install our recommended free software (see page 108).

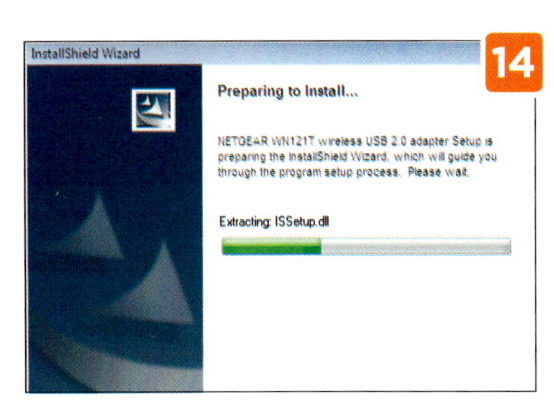

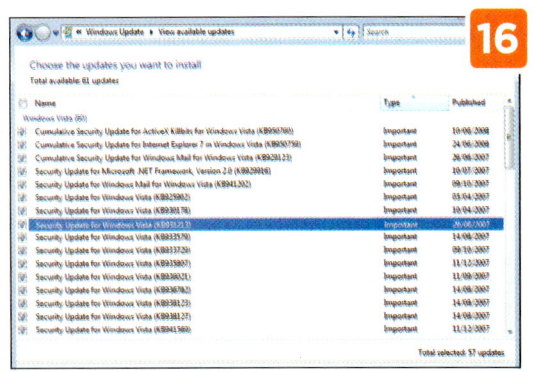

TIP
Windows Update is essential on all new computers, as it will make sure that you've got the latest patches and drivers.

BUILD A BETTER PC **93**

CHAPTER 7
INSTALLING AN OPERATING SYSTEM

HOW TO...
Improve Media Center

IF YOU'VE BUILT yourself a Media Center PC with Windows Vista Home Premium and a remote control, you may be excused for thinking that your job is done. However, Media Center isn't quite perfect and there are a few tweaks we'd strongly recommend to make it work better. For one, the support Vista offers for downloaded files, such as DivX and XviD, isn't very good. Even if you install the proper codec (the bit of software that decodes the video so that it can be played), you can't resume play, fast forward or rewind these files.

Fortunately, none of these problems is insurmountable. All the software we use here is free. This guide will also work with any PC running Windows Vista Home Premium or Vista Ultimate. The section about tweaking your remote control is written to work with non-Microsoft remote controls. If you're using a Microsoft remote, you can skip these steps, unless you're having problems.

1 First, you need to download and install the Vista Codec Package to enable support for additional video file types, such as XviD and DivX. Before you install it, though, you have to uninstall all the codecs already on your system, as these may conflict with the Codec Package. Go to the Windows Control Panel and, under Programs, click the Uninstall a program link. Select any codecs on your PC, such as DivX, XviD or RealPlayer, and click Uninstall/change to remove them.

Go to *http://shark007.testbox.dk*, scroll to the bottom of the page and choose a download location. This will take you to the download section of the relevant site, so download the program to your desktop and double-click it to run it. Select your language and click OK, click Next, then accept the terms of the licence agreement and click Next. In the next screen, you have a choice between a Complete and a Custom installation. Click the Complete button, then Next and finally Install. The Codec Package is designed to be fairly lean, so it won't put any more software on your PC than you need.

Once it's installed, open Windows Media Center and try to play an MPEG4 file, such as DivX, to make sure it's installed. You may have to restart your PC before the codecs will work. The files should now display thumbnails in Media Center and should play properly.

2 While Media Center will now play MPEG4 files, its support is limited. For example, unlike with WMV files, you can't fast forward or rewind files encoded with an MPEG4 codec.

To improve Media Center's handling of XviD files, you'll need to install a couple of extra programs. The first is the Media Control plug-in. This is a Media Center front-end for the ffdshow codec installed with the Vista Codec Package. Go to *http://damienbt.free.fr* and click the Download link. There are 32- and 64-bit versions available, so download the appropriate one for your Windows installation. If you're not sure which you have, click Start, right-click on Computer and select Properties. The System type field will show you whether you have a 32- or 64-bit installation.

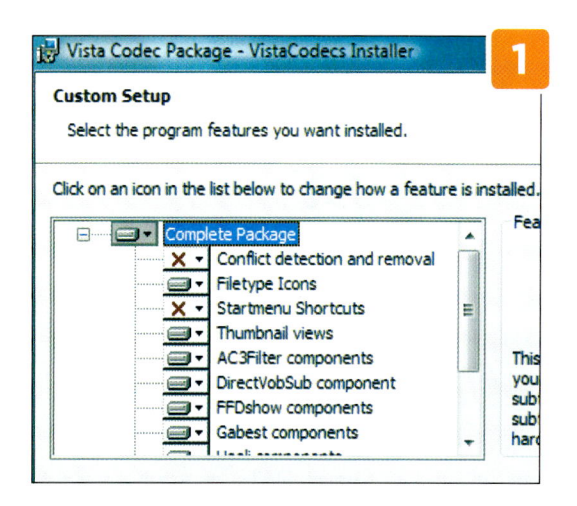

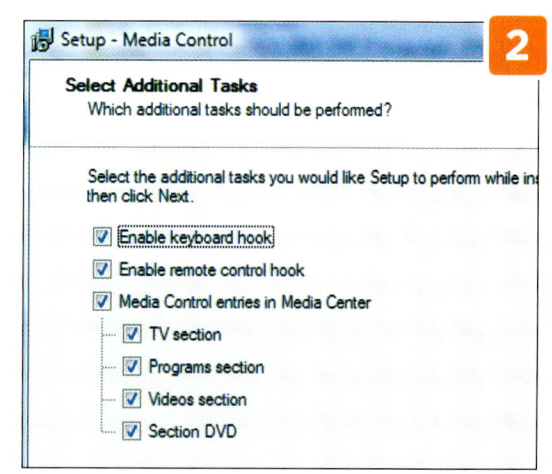

Save the Zip file to your hard disk, open it and then run the MediaControl_5.2.1.exe application. Most of the installation process is self-explanatory, but at one point you'll be asked which additional tasks you want to perform. They're all useful, so leave them all selected, click Next, Install and Finish. The program will run automatically.

3 You'll now be shown the Media Control Configuration window, which gives you a large amount of control over the plug-in. While this may look complicated, you can leave most of the options at their default settings for now. You just need to set up ffdshow to work with Media Center. Click the FFDShow configuration tab, click the Apply recommended configuration button and the Commit changes button. Now close the configuration tool.

The Windows firewall may block some of Media Control's functions, so you'll need to tell it to let the program through. To do this, run Media Center and then close it again. You should have a Windows Security Alert box on your desktop. Click Unblock. You may have more than one alert, so click Unblock for each one. Now run Media Center again, go to your videos section and select one of your MPEG4 videos.

When you stop playing a file and come back to it later, a window will appear asking if you want to resume playback where you left off. You should also now be able to use your remote's fast forward and rewind buttons to skip through your videos. There are three speeds, which you select by pressing the forward or rewind buttons once, twice or three times. If this doesn't work, you'll have to perform some additional changes, which are explained in Step 5.

4 Media Control also adds some extra functions to Media Center's video menu. If you press the Info button on your remote control or right-click when a video is playing, you'll bring up the Media Center menu. Click on the More… option to launch the Plug-in menu. Next click on the Media Control button, which will have a button for the Media Control plug-in to bring up a list of options that lets you select subtitles, adjust post-processing effects and adjust properties such as brightness and contrast, and adjust the image cropping.

One of the most useful functions is the Bookmarks feature. Clicking the Set Bookmark button will create a bookmark at the video's current position complete with a thumbnail, so you can skip to whichever point you want. This is particularly useful for bookmarking your home movies.

5 Depending on your remote, you may find that the forward and rewind buttons don't work, and the play button won't stop the video fast forwarding or rewinding. If this is the case, you'll need to use a piece of software called AutoHotkey to intercept commands from the remote and translate them into keyboard presses, which will be picked up by the Media Control plug-in to control your videos. This will work with any remote that's Human Interface Device (HID)-compliant. Most USB remotes will be HID-compliant, including CyberLink's popular and cheap remote.

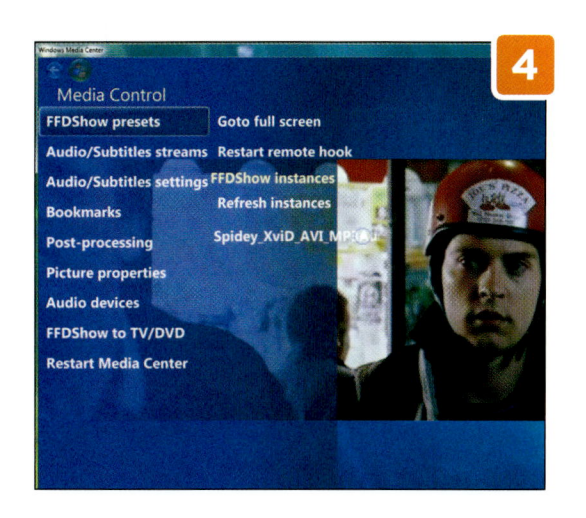

> **TIP**
> Nvidia and ATI's graphics control panels have dedicated settings for improving the quality of your video. Adjust them to get the best-quality image you can.

CHAPTER 7
INSTALLING AN OPERATING SYSTEM

To find out whether your remote control is HID-compliant, unplug it and go to the Device Manager by right-clicking on Computer in the Start menu and selecting Properties. Now click Device Manager in the left-hand pane. Find the HID category and click the + sign next to it. Make a note of the devices that are already there. The easy way to do this is to take a screenshot by pressing the Print Screen key, then paste the screenshot into an image-editing program such as Microsoft Paint. Now plug in your remote control's receiver. After the Device Manger refreshes, check if there's a new device in the list. If it's called something like HID-compliant consumer control device, then the remote is HID-compliant.

6 First, you need to set up the keyboard shortcuts for fast forward, rewind and resume playback in Media Control's configuration. Load the Media Control Configuration program and click the Remote control & keyboard tab. Make sure that F is set as the key for Fast Forward and B is set for Fast Rewind, and that all the boxes for each are ticked. This will mean that the keyboard shortcuts for fast forward will be Ctrl-Alt-Shift F, and rewind will be Control-Alt-Shift B, which won't conflict with any shortcut keys already assigned on your PC.

To enable the Play key to continue a video at normal speed, click the Add command button, which will create a blank command at the bottom of the list. Click the arrow on the right of the command box, scroll down and select Stop Fast Forward/Rewind as the command. Select P from the Key box, and tick all the boxes. Now click Commit changes at the bottom.

7 Go to *www.autohotkey.com* and click the Download link. Download the program and follow the installation instructions, leaving the default options selected. You also need an AutoHotkey add-on to help you set up the remote. Go to *www.autohotkey.net/~Micha/HIDsupport/Autohotkey.html*. Click the Download the archive link, and save the file to your hard disk. Don't worry about what it says about XP, as the add-on also works with Vista. To extract the file, you'll need a program that can open RAR files, such as WinRAR from *www.rarsoft.com* or the free ExtractNow from *www.extractnow.com*. Extract the files to the AutoHotkey installation directory, which should be C:\Program Files\AutoHotkey. Now navigate to the AutoHotkey directory and run the AutoHotkeyRemoteControlDLL script.

8 The AutoHotkey HID Support window will appear. This is a program that helps you identify which HID device is your remote control, and what codes it sends out when you press certain keys. You'll need these when you edit the AutoHotkey script to support your remote control. The top window has a list of HID-compliant devices attached to your PC. The keyboard and mouse will be labelled, but the rest of the devices will just be called HID. To find out which is your remote, click on each of the HID devices in turn, click the Register button and press the fast forward, rewind or play buttons on your remote. If you have the right one selected, response codes will appear in the bottom window.

Make a note of the UsagePage and Usage numbers, which are in the box under the device list box. The CyberLink remote should be UsagePage 12 and Usage 1. Now press the rewind, fast forward and play keys on your remote, and make a note of the codes generated in the output window. These are displayed in four pairs of two numbers. For example, the CyberLink remote should have a code of 03000004 for the rewind button, 03000008 for the fast forward button and 03000040 for the play button.

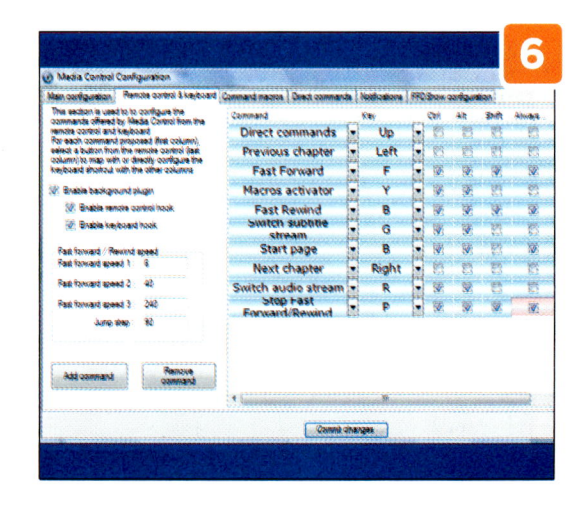

9 Close the HID-Support window. In the AutoHotkey folder there's an AutoHotkey script file called RemoteControl. Right-click on the file and select Edit Script. This will open the script in Notepad for editing. The AutoHotkey script tells AutoHotkey what to do when you press certain buttons on your remote. It looks daunting at first, but many of the settings should already be correct for your CyberLink remote.

First, find the Register my device and Register another device lines. One of these should have EditUsage and EditUsagePage values that match the values you noted from the HID-Support program. If you can't find the matching line, edit the values under Register another device.

Next, scroll down to find the ifequal commands. This is a list of remote control commands and the subroutines that each will call when the corresponding button is pressed. Delete the msgbox %vals% line, and remove all the ifequal lines apart from the three ending in Play, REV and FWD. Now compare the codes in the middle with those you noted down from the HID-Support program. Make sure the codes for Play, REV and FWD match the codes for your remote's play, rewind and fast forward buttons, and alter them if necessary.

The next set of commands in the script file are the subroutines that are called when you press the buttons on your remote. Delete all of them apart from Play, REV and FWD, but make sure you leave the cleanup: line. Now change the commands to the following:

Play:
Send +^!p
return

REV:
Send +^!b
return

FWD:
Send +^!f
return

The symbol for Shift is +, ^ is Control and ! is Alt, so the commands match the key shortcuts you set up in Media Control's configuration. Now save the script and close it. Double-click on the RemoteControl script to run it – you'll see a green H appear in your System Tray. Now when you load Media Center and play your MPEG4 video, you'll find that the fast forward, rewind and play buttons work as they should. To make the RemoteControl script run automatically every time you start Windows, drag it into the Startup folder in your Start menu.

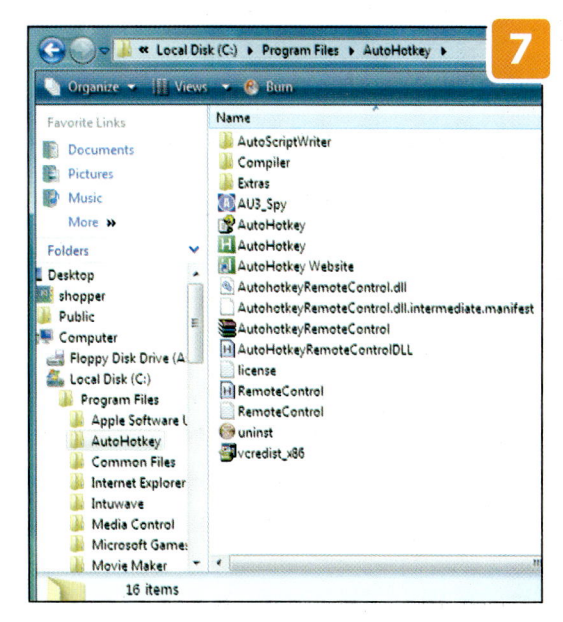

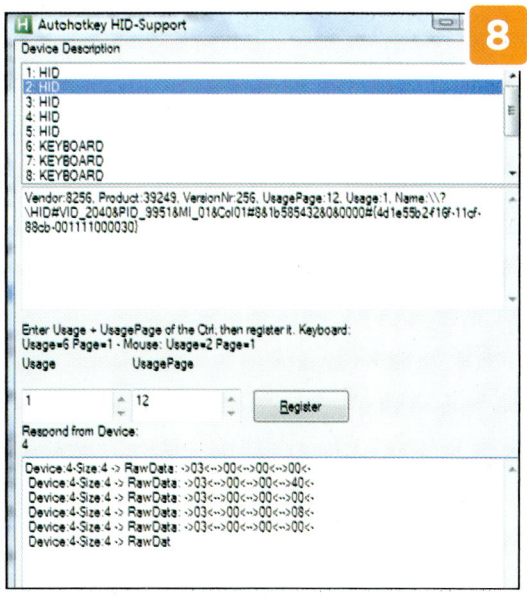

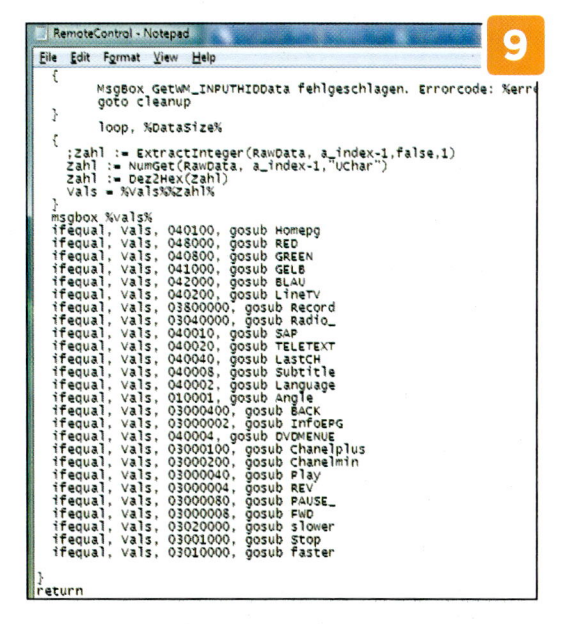

TIP
You can use the instructions for AutoHotkey to make your remote control run practically any command on your PC.

BUILD A BETTER PC **97**

CHAPTER 7
INSTALLING AN OPERATING SYSTEM

HOW TO...
Install Windows XP

1 START YOUR COMPUTER
Turn your PC on and put the Windows XP CD into your optical drive. If you're using a brand new hard disk, the XP installation routine will load automatically. If you're using an old hard disk that already has an operating system on it, you need to press any key when prompted onscreen. If you don't, your old operating system will start and you'll have to reset your PC to load the installer.

Your computer will take a few minutes to start the installation routine properly, so don't worry if you've got a blank page to look at for a bit.

2 ADD ADDITIONAL DRIVES
If you've got a RAID controller or hard disk that's not detected (you'll discover this later on and may need to restart the installation routine), you need to add additional drivers. When prompted, press F6. Windows will continue copying files, but after a couple of minutes, a screen will ask what drivers you want to add. Press S to specify additional devices. You'll need to have the files on a floppy disk and a floppy disk drive, as Windows XP can't read additional drivers from CD or USB drives like Vista can. When you're done, press Enter.

3 SELECT HARD DISKS
On the next screen, press Enter to install a fresh copy of Windows XP. Press F8 to accept the licence agreement. You'll now be able to partition your hard disks. From the list of disks, select the one on which you want Windows to be installed. This is usually MB Disk 0.

Press C to Create a new partition. You have to select the size of the partition in megabytes (1,024MB = 1GB). Generally, we'd recommend leaving at least 40GB (40,960MB) for the second partition, which you can use for backups and storing files that you don't want to overwrite during a fresh operating system installation. Subtract the size of second partition you want from the figure in the box and enter this. Press Enter to Apply. Select Unpartitioned Space and press C. Press Enter to create the partition. Don't worry if you've got a tiny amount of unpartitioned space left, as the way XP deals with disks means that this space can't be used. Select C: and press Enter to install.

4 FORMAT HARD DISK
The installation routine has to format the hard disk before it can copy the Windows XP files

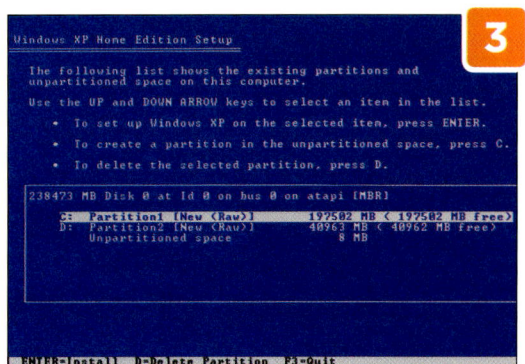

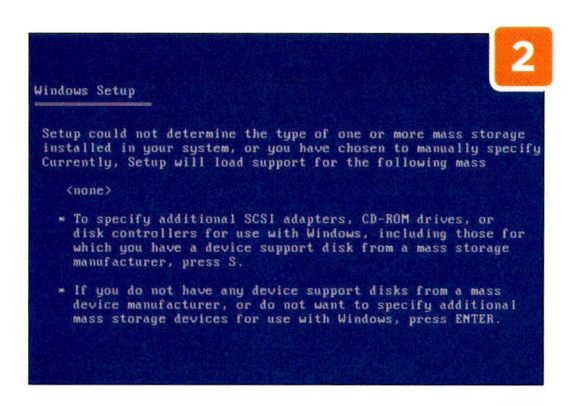

98 BUILD A BETTER PC

to it. Select Format NTFS and press Enter. While Vista has a speedy format option, XP's takes quite a while, and you may have to wait 30 minutes or more for it to complete.

Once the disk has been formatted, Windows files are copied to the disk. Your computer will reboot automatically once this is done and continue the installation using a graphical tool.

5 CHANGE REGIONAL SETTINGS

The first choice you get is to choose which language you want. Click Customize and change Standards and formats to United Kingdom. Change Location to United Kingdom, too. Click on the Languages tab and click on the Details button. Click Add, select United Kingdom as the input language and click OK.

Select US in the Installed services window and click Remove and then OK. You'll get a warning telling you it can't remove the US language because it's in use, but that it will be removed the next time you reboot your PC. Click OK on this message. Click on the Advanced tab and choose English (United Kingdom) from the drop-down menu. Click OK to apply these settings, then Next.

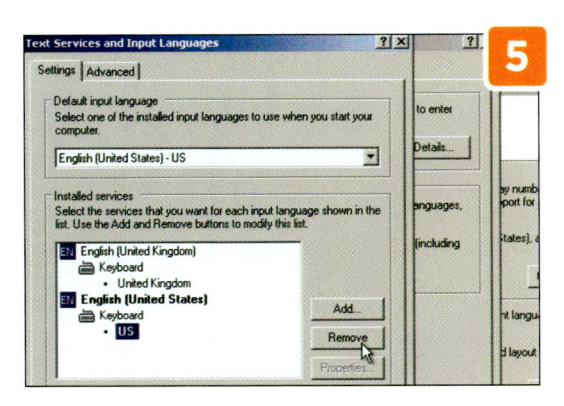

6 ENTER YOUR PRODUCT KEY

Enter your name in the next box, though you can leave the Organization field blank. Click Next. Enter your product key, which will be printed inside the box that your copy of Windows XP came in. On the next screen, give your PC a more meaningful name than the one that Windows gives it and click Next.

7 SET DATE AND TIME

Even though you told Windows in every setting that you're in the UK, it still sets itself to US time. Change the Time Zone option to GMT. Select the current date and time, and click Next.

Windows will next install the network drivers for your onboard network card. When prompted leave the network setting as Typical settings and click Next. Windows will finish copying files and finalise the installation.

8 RUN WINDOWS FOR THE FIRST TIME

When Windows starts for the first time, click OK when the dialog box appears to tell you the screen resolution will be automatically changed. Click OK again to confirm that the new resolution

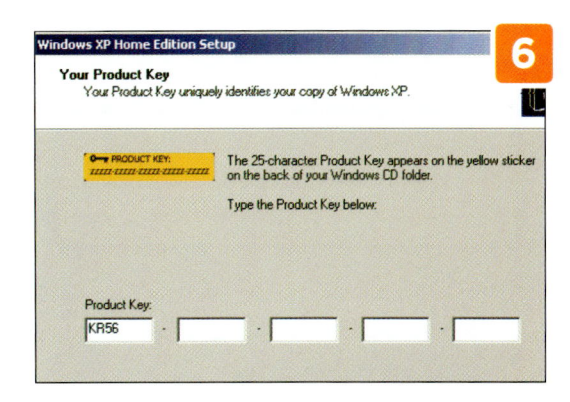

TIP
Make your choices carefully in the blue setup screens, as you can't go back once you've made a choice.

BUILD A BETTER PC **99**

CHAPTER 7
INSTALLING AN OPERATING SYSTEM

has worked. On the next screen, select Help protect my PC by turning on Automatic Updates now and click Next. Enter your name on the next screen, and anyone else that will be using your computer. Click Next and then Finish. You can now remove the Windows XP installation CD.

9 INSTALL MOTHERBOARD DRIVERS

Although Windows is now working, you still need to install all the relevant drivers to make sure that everything will work smoothly. The first place to start is with the motherboard drivers. If you downloaded the drivers earlier, insert the USB key or disc you saved them to: if you can't do this, insert the driver disc and follow the onscreen instructions. You'll need to download the updated drivers later, and then follow these instructions.

For every driver you downloaded, run the associated file. It's best to start with the chipset driver, but the order afterwards doesn't matter. If Windows displays any warning messages, just click OK. Some files you download are just archive files that extract the real driver files on to your hard disk. If this is the case, navigate to the folder the files were extracted to and run the Setup program you'll find there. You'll probably need to restart your PC after each driver installation.

10 INSTALL GRAPHICS CARD DRIVERS

Windows will install its own graphics drivers for any onboard or dedicated cards that you have. These are good enough to run Windows, but you won't be able to play games properly. Instead, you need to install the graphics drivers.

Both ATI and Nvidia provide a single driver package, so all you have to do is run the file you downloaded. If you couldn't download the drivers earlier, you need to insert the bundled CD, but remember to download newer drivers later on.

Restart your computer after the graphics drivers have been installed. Right-click on the desktop, select Properties, then the Settings tab and change your display resolution to match your monitor's native resolution.

11 INSTALL OTHER PERIPHERALS

You can now install the other peripherals that you've added to your PC. Install the relevant driver files for each device that's plugged into your motherboard. For USB devices, you need to install the driver file first and, when prompted, connect the device to a USB port. If you're in any doubt, you should read the manual that came with your peripheral. If you've installed a wireless adaptor, make sure that you connect to your wireless network, following the provided instructions.

12 INSTALL SERVICE PACK 3

When everything is installed, you should install Windows XP Service Pack 3, unless the installation disc you used included it, in which case you can skip to the final step.

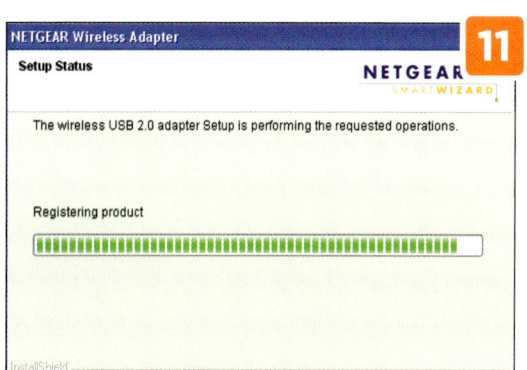

To install Service Pack 3, you should first connect to the internet. The easiest way to force it to install is to go to *http://tinyurl.com/XPservicepack*. Click Download and save the file to your hard disk. When it's finished, run the file you downloaded. Follow the wizard through. Service Pack 3 will take up to an hour to install, restarting your computer when necessary.

13 RUN WINDOWS UPDATE

Visit *www.windowsupdate.com* and click on the Custom button. Windows Update will then prompt you to download the Windows Genuine Advantage Tool in order to use the service. Click the Download and Install Now button and follow the wizard through. Click Continue until you get back to the first screen and then click the Custom button again. Windows Update will then search for the latest updates for your computer. When the list comes back, select the updates that you want, click Review and install updates, and then Install Updates to install them.

14 ACTIVATE

If your computer wasn't connected to the internet while you were installing Windows XP, it won't yet be activated. Unlike Vista, which doesn't bother you about activation until you need to do it, XP puts a permanent icon in the Notification Area that displays regular messages warning you about activation. It's worth getting rid of this annoyance now. Double-click the icon that looks like two keys. In the next dialog box, select Yes, activate Windows over the internet now and click Next. Choose whether you want to register with Microsoft and click Next. Within a few seconds, you should get a message saying that you've activated Windows. Click OK. If this didn't work, you may need to activate your copy over the phone following the onscreen instructions.

15 USER SETTINGS

Your PC and its users are not password-protected by default. If you'd like to add some security to your PC, you can change this. Click on the Start menu and select the Control Panel. Click on User Accounts, select your user and click on Create a password. Enter your new password and click Create Password. On the next screen click Yes, Make Private to ensure your files and folders remain private. Repeat these steps for every user you want to be password-protected.

16 FORMAT HARD DISK

The Windows setup wizard only formats the disk partition on which Windows is installed. If you created a separate partition, you won't be able to use it yet, as it's not formatted. Click on the Start menu, My Computer, right-click the D: drive and select Format. Click OK, make sure that NTFS is selected and then click Format. You can now install our recommended free software (see page 108).

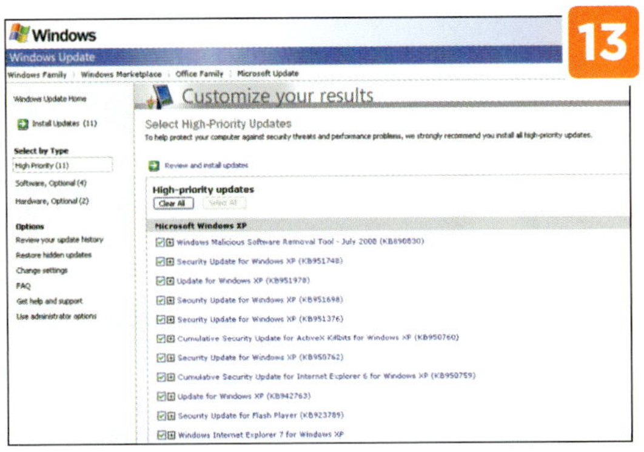

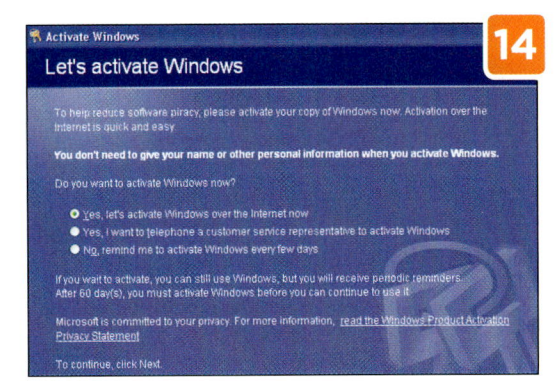

TIP

It's essential that you run Windows Update after an installation to get the latest updates and security patches.

CHAPTER 7
INSTALLING AN OPERATING SYSTEM

HOW TO...
Install Ubuntu Linux

1 DOWNLOAD UBUNTU
First, download Ubuntu Desktop Edition from *www.ubuntu.com/getubuntu*. The download (ubuntu-8.04.1-desktop-i386.iso, at the time of writing) is 694MB and is an ISO file that needs to be burned to CD before you can use it. Nero Burning Rom and Roxio Creator have built-in tools for letting you do this, but you can also use the free ISO Recorder (*http://isorecorder.alexfeinman.com/isorecorder.htm*). Version 2 is for Windows XP and Version 3 is for Vista, so make sure that you get the right version. Simply use Explorer to find the ISO file you downloaded, right-click it and select copy to CD.

Put a blank CD into your optical drive and click Next to copy the file to disc. If you don't have a CD writer, you can request a free copy of Ubuntu on CD, but the delivery time may mean that you're better off asking a friend to burn a disc for you.

2 BOOT FROM THE CD
Put the Ubuntu CD that you just created into your new computer's optical drive. Keep an eye out for the Press any key to boot from CD message. If you miss this, you'll have to restart your computer to load the Ubuntu installation routine. The first Ubuntu install screen should appear very quickly and you just need to select the installation language.

3 START INSTALLATION
You're then presented with an installation menu and a handful of options. The default installation option is to try Ubuntu without making any changes to your computer. This simply loads Ubuntu from the CD and doesn't write any files to your hard disk, and is a good way to try out Linux before making any commitments and filling up your hard disk. If you're still not sure about Linux, this is the safest option. To install Ubuntu properly, select the Install Ubuntu option.

The first thing you'll see is the Ubuntu loading screen, which looks a little like that for Windows. It can take a while for Ubuntu to chug through this part of its installation, so don't panic if the orange bar appears to freeze for a spell.

4 SELECT LANGUAGE
Eventually, you'll see the Ubuntu wallpaper and a welcome screen. Hopefully, this is in a

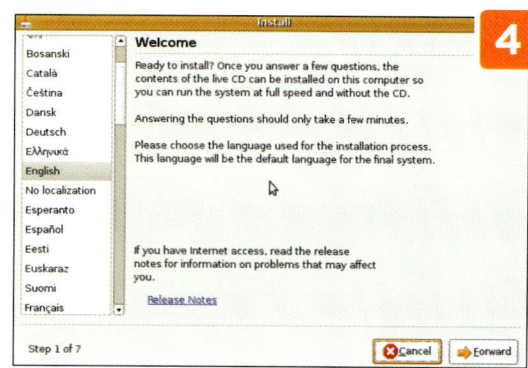

102 BUILD A BETTER PC

language you can understand; if not, select English from the list on the left.

If your computer is plugged into the internet via a wired connection, you can click the Release Notes link to find out more information on problems that may affect you. When you've finished, click the Forward button to continue.

5 SELECT LOCATION
Now select your location using the drop-down menu. UK cities are grouped under Europe towards the end of the list. Selecting a location in the UK should automatically select the correct time zone. If it doesn't, select the right one using the drop-down menu.

When you've chosen the correct settings, click Forward to continue. Your keyboard layout should be set to United Kingdom; if it's not, select this from the menu and click Forward.

6 SET UP HARD DISKS
By default, Ubuntu uses a simple partitioning system on your PC's hard disk. While perfectly adequate, this is worth tweaking to alter where files are stored. This will let you choose where your user files (My Documents in Windows) are kept, as well as create separate partitions for program files and virtual memory.

Linux stores user files in the /home folder, and moving this to its own partition is easy. Unfortunately, if you opt to set up one partition manually, you have to set them all up this way, so we'll need to take a slight detour to complete this process. If you just want to stick with Ubuntu's default partition scheme, just leave the Guided option selected, click Forward and move on to step 12.

7 DELETE EXISTING PARTITIONS
Select the Manual option on the Prepare disk space screen and click Forward. The installer will then scan your hard disk and display the disk partitioning tool. The first step is to delete all existing partitions on the hard disk, so select each one in the list and click the Delete partition button.

8 SET BOOT PARTITION
You should now just have free space listed under /dev/sda (Linux's name for the hard disk on the primary IDE channel). Since we're creating

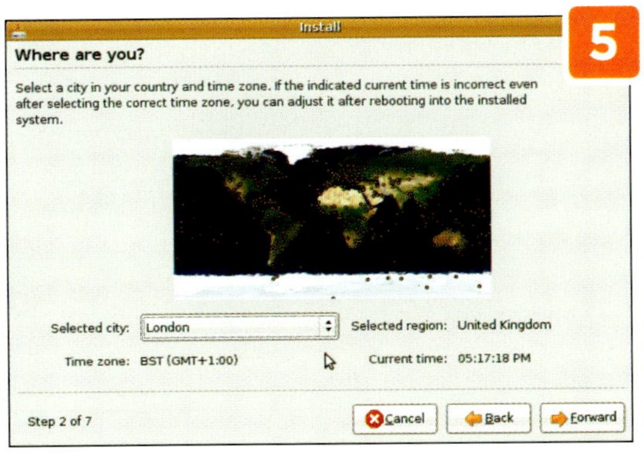

TIP
You can try Ubuntu without installing it. Simply boot off the CD and explore the desktop. When you're ready to proceed you just need to run the installer.

CHAPTER 7
INSTALLING AN OPERATING SYSTEM

partitions by hand, we need to create all the partitions Linux requires, starting with the /boot partition. Select free space in the list of partitions and click New partition. Enter a size of 50 (we're working in MB here) and select /boot as the Mount point. Click OK.

9 SET SWAP PARTITION
Linux also needs a /swap partition, which is the equivalent of Windows' swap file used for virtual memory. When your PC's real memory fills up, Ubuntu will swap bits of the memory that aren't currently being used (inactive applications, for example) to the hard disk. This gives the impression that your computer has more memory than it does, so you can run more applications.

Create another new partition in the free space and enter a size equal to the amount of RAM in the computer in megabytes (1GB = 1,024MB). Select Swap area from the Use as drop-down list, leave the other settings at their defaults and then click OK.

10 SET HOME PARTITION
Next is the /home partition, where user files are kept. This is the equivalent of Windows' My Documents folder, but kept on a separate partition.

The advantage of this method is that you can reinstall Linux and your documents won't be overwritten. Make this partition as large as you like, remembering to leave a few gigabytes free for the final /root partition. Select /home as the Mount point before clicking OK.

11 SET ROOT PARTITION
Last is the root or / partition. This is where Ubuntu is installed and it will use all of the remaining space. Set the Mount point as / and click OK.

You can see the final partition structure from the screenshot below, so click Forward when you're ready to continue. That's the end of the custom partitioning.

12 SET A USERNAME AND A PASSWORD
You now need to tell Ubuntu who you are. Type your name into the What is your name? box. This will automatically generate a username for you in the What name do you want to use to log in? box, but you can change this if you like. Type in a password to protect your account and prevent unauthorised users from logging on to your PC.

Finally, your computer will automatically have been given a name based on your name in the

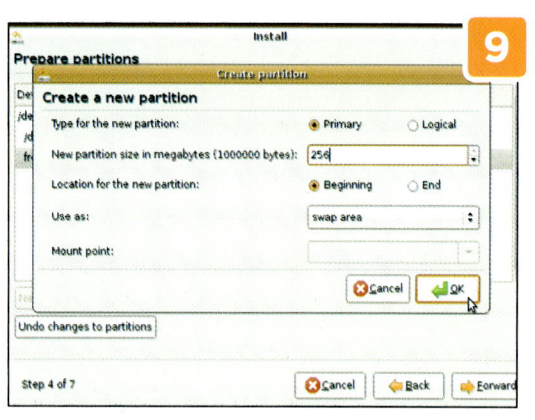

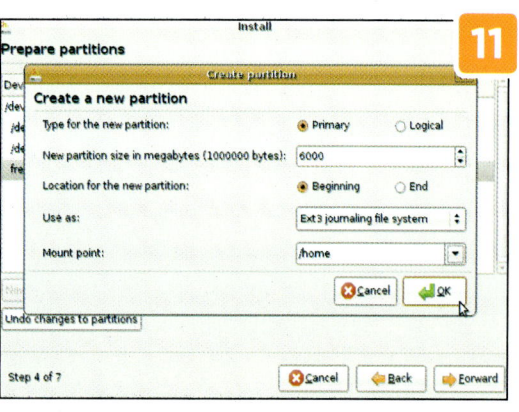

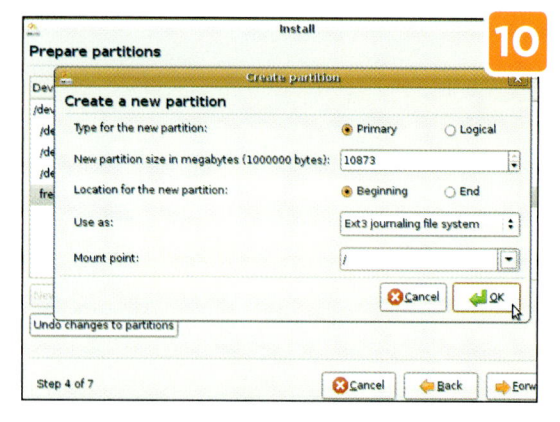

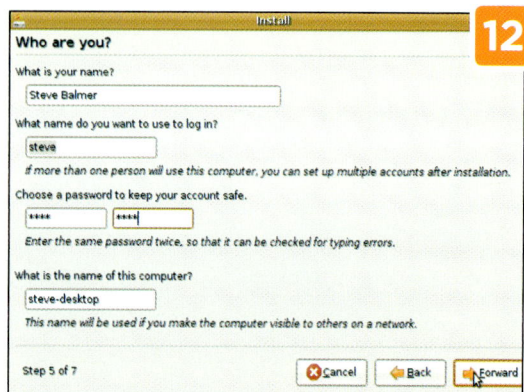

104 BUILD A BETTER PC

What is the name of this computer? box. You can change this to anything you like, if you prefer. Click Forward when you've finished.

13 INSTALL LINUX
So far, no files have been written to your hard disk, so this is the last chance you've got to back out of the installation. When you're ready to continue, click Install.

Ubuntu will now copy the necessary files to the hard disk partitions you created. This process will take a few minutes, so sit back and let it do its job.

14 START UBUNTU FOR THE FIRST TIME
Once the installation is complete, the Gnome desktop will load. This is very similar to the Windows desktop, and it's where the bulk of your interaction with Linux will take place. You'll find that a whole range of applications have already been installed and you can access them through the Applications menu at the top-left of the screen.

The applications that come bundled with Linux vary, but at the very least you can expect to find an office suite of some description, a web browser and an email client – Ubuntu comes with OpenOffice.org, Firefox and Thunderbird. Applications can be found in the Applications menu at the top-left of the screen.

15 INSTALL NEW APPLICATIONS
Ubuntu also simplifies the process of finding and installing new programs. Its Add/Remove Applications utility (available in the Applications menu) works in a similar way to its Windows namesake, with the added advantage of offering new applications to install, as well as old ones to remove. New programs are downloaded from the internet and any additional components that are required (known as dependencies) are automatically downloaded, too, which goes a long way to making Linux more user-friendly.

16 INSTALL UPDATES
Just as you would do with Windows, Ubuntu needs to have the latest security patches installed. Its rising popularity means that it's attracting increased interest from malicious hackers.

Fortunately, Ubuntu has its own update manager and will periodically check for updates. When new updates are ready to be installed, you'll see a warning on the application bar. Click the warning to bring up a list of available updates, and click the Install Updates button to install them.

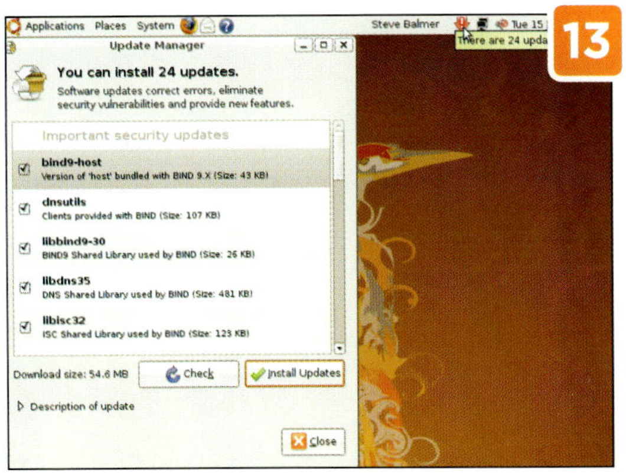

TIP
Finding drivers for all your hardware can be difficult, but a Google search should bring up some forums that may be able to help you get your hardware working.

BUILD A BETTER PC **105**

CHAPTER 8
NEW PC ESSENTIALS

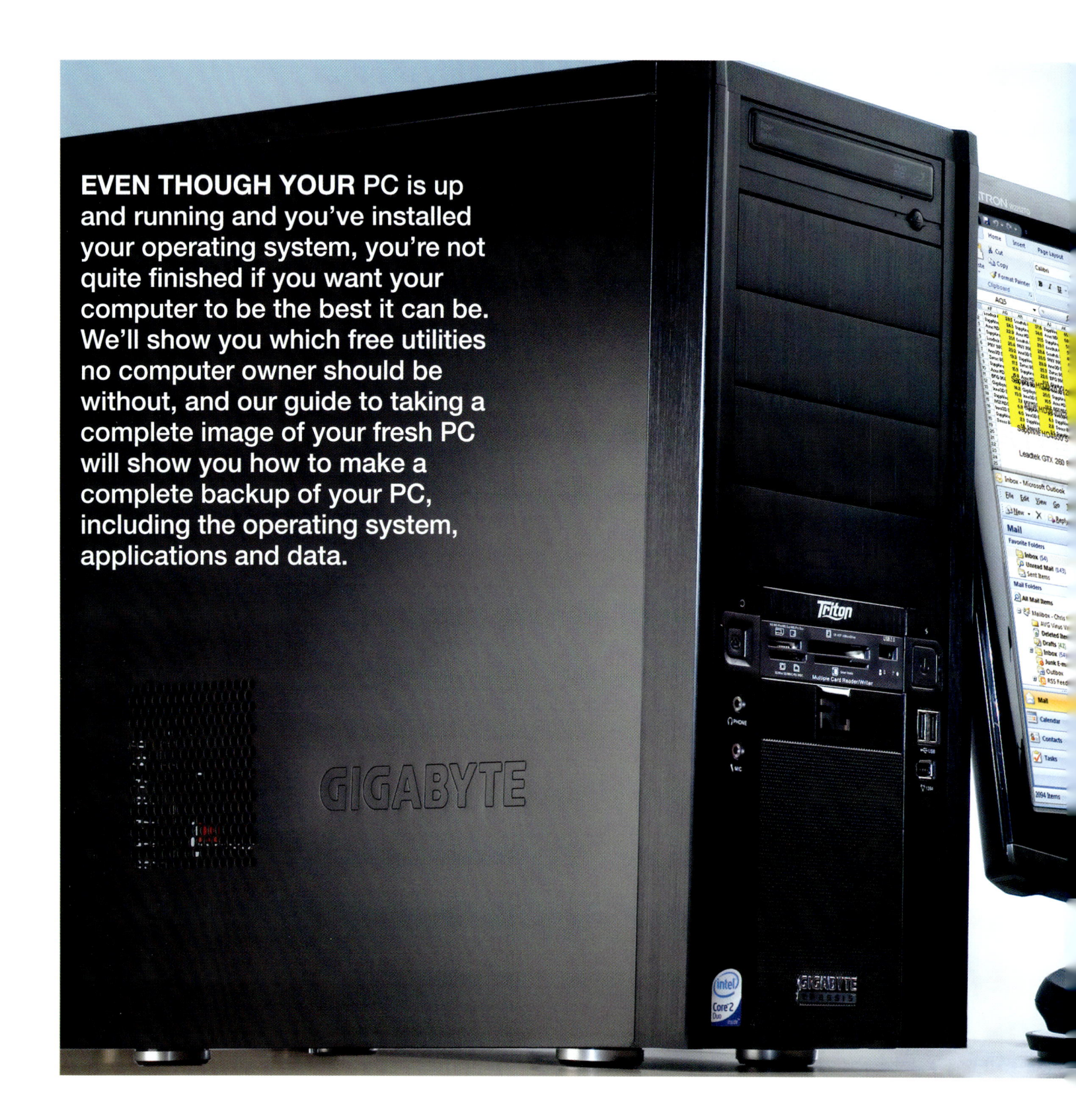

EVEN THOUGH YOUR PC is up and running and you've installed your operating system, you're not quite finished if you want your computer to be the best it can be. We'll show you which free utilities no computer owner should be without, and our guide to taking a complete image of your fresh PC will show you how to make a complete backup of your PC, including the operating system, applications and data.

106 BUILD A BETTER PC

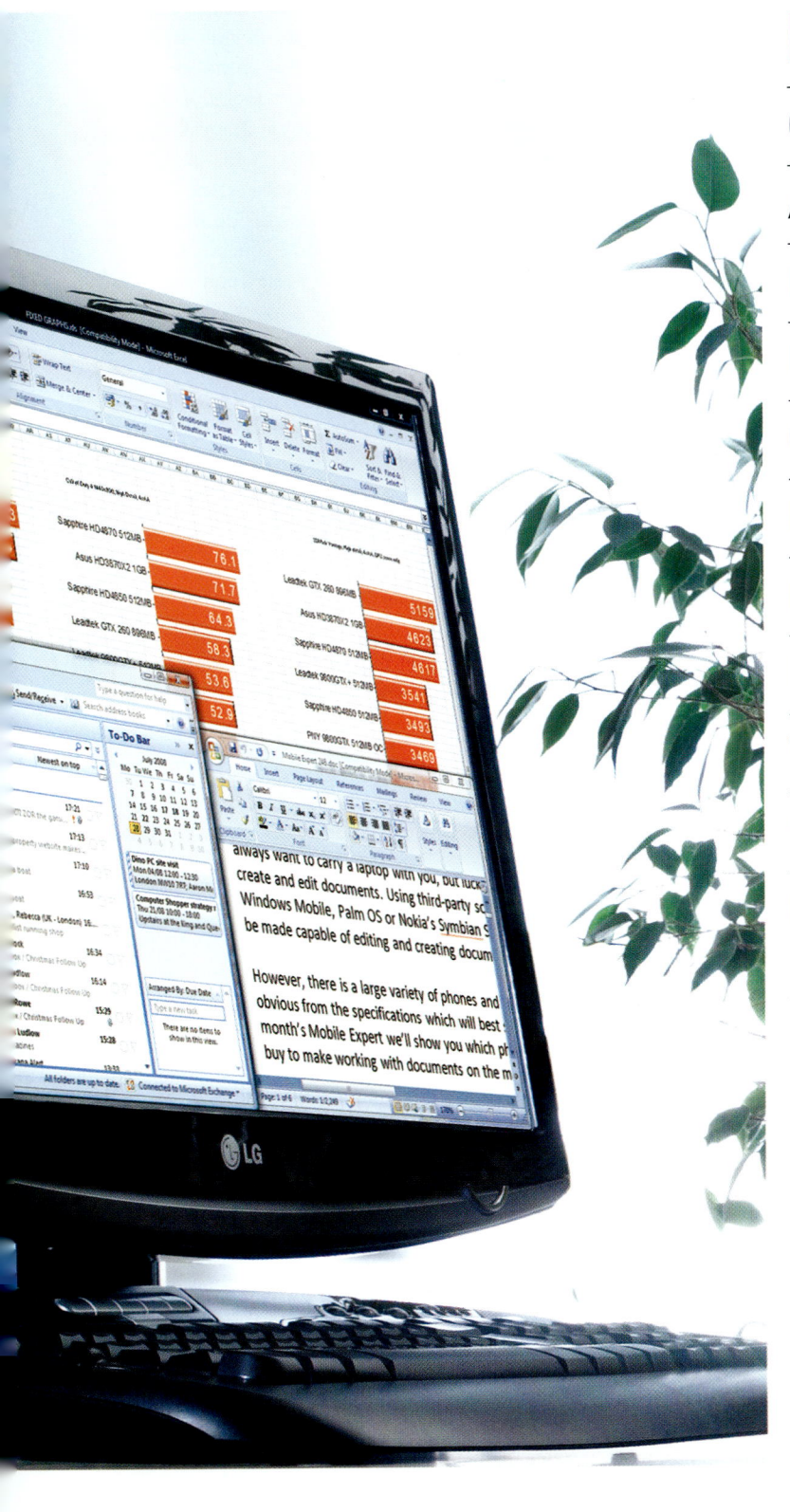

IN THIS CHAPTER

OpenOffice.org 3	108
AVG Anti-Virus Free Edition	109
Paint.NET	109
Picasa 3	110
CDBurnerXP	110
Free Download Manager	111
Freebyte Backup	111
ExtractNow	111
VLC media player	111
Saving power with your new PC	112
Making an image of your hard disk	118

CHAPTER 8
NEW PC ESSENTIALS

Essential tools

ONCE YOU'VE BUILT your PC and everything is working perfectly, you may feel that your computing experience isn't quite complete. This is because, unlike a Mac OS installation, very little extra software is installed with Windows XP or Vista. You get a primitive word processor called WordPad, an image program called Microsoft Paint, which has barely changed since 1992, and very little else. There's no way to create complicated word-processing documents, do your accounts in a spreadsheet or edit photos. As Windows doesn't come with a virus scanner, you're left wide open to all kinds of internet threats. Windows XP can't even burn files to DVD, and Vista's disc-authoring capabilities leave much to be desired. Both versions also lack a credible alternative to Apple's iPhoto image organiser.

■ Microsoft Office 2007 looks great and is very powerful, but it's expensive and most people won't touch half its features. OpenOffice is compatible with Office file formats, and is a credible and free alternative

In the not too distant past, you had to splash out on products such as Microsoft Office, Adobe Photoshop Elements, Norton Internet Security and Roxio Easy Media Creator to make your PC usable. Recently, though, a few software packages have emerged that offer the same features for free. As you'll see, OpenOffice is an impressive office suite, Paint.NET is a powerful image editor, AVG Anti-Virus will keep you safe online and CDBurnerXP lets you burn discs to your heart's content. Furthermore, Google's Picasa will let you organise your photos and share them online.

We've also covered some smaller free utilities that will make your new system easier and more fun to use, as well as keeping your data secure. Read on to find out about the essential free software to install on any new PC.

OFFICE SOFTWARE
Openoffice.org
OpenOffice.org 3

DOWNLOAD DETAILS **www.openoffice.org**
FILE SIZE **130MB**

As far as office software is concerned, a clean installation of Windows will come with an unimpressive word processor and nothing else. Fortunately, you don't have to splash out on the full version of Microsoft Office to give yourself powerful word processor and spreadsheet applications.

OpenOffice.org includes both of these essentials, as well as a presentation program, the Draw vector drawing package and the Base database application. The Writer word processing, Calc spreadsheet and Impress presentation applications are all compatible with Office file formats up to Office 2003, and can open and save documents either in Microsoft's formats or in the suite's OpenDocument format.

There's very little missing from the applications, and most are easy to use. Writer has a spellcheck, and a selection of styles and fonts, as well as word count and table of contents generation features. We can't really see anything missing from what Calc can do, as it supports all the functions and formulas we've ever needed. It even handles charts better than Excel 2007. Impress looks like an older version of PowerPoint, and comes with a couple of different templates

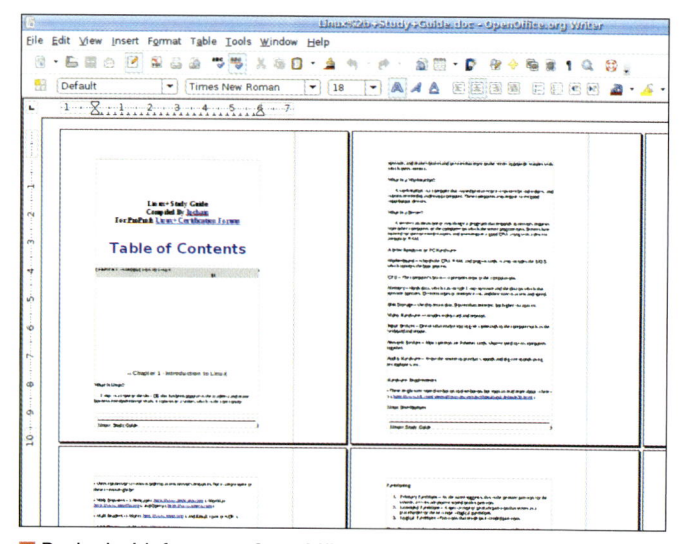

■ Packed with features, OpenOffice.org is an essential download

to get you started. The last two applications are more niche, but are reasonable. Draw is a fair program, but we found it the most fiddly part of the suite to use and took a while to master. Base is a powerful SQL-compatible database, which lets you create searchable linked data tables.

OpenOffice.org may not look as flashy as Microsoft Office 2007, but there's little missing in the way of features and it's free rather than £167. It's an essential download for every new PC.

108 BUILD A BETTER PC

SECURITY | **SOFTWARE**

AVG Technologies
AVG Anti-Virus Free Edition

DOWNLOAD DETAILS http://free.avg.com
FILE SIZE **47MB**

Even though Microsoft claims that Vista is more secure than any other Windows operating system, you'd be mad to go online without security software installed on your PC. A good security suite will protect you against viruses, but will also spot other malware, such as spyware and adware, which can lead to anything from a few annoying pop-ups to your banking logon details being passed on to unscrupulous criminals.

As new viruses and spyware programs are discovered all the time, your security suite needs to be continually updated to maintain the appropriate level of protection. Most security software companies make you pay a subscription to receive the updates, but AVG offers both its software and the subscription for free for non-commercial use. There's no catch, either.

The AVG software includes a virus scanner, which can be set to scan your hard disk at regular intervals, a resident shield that lives in your computer's memory and detects viruses as they appear, an email scanner and a program, which scans links

■ AVG's anti-virus application will help protect your computer

in search engine results to check whether or not they lead to malicious websites. Recently, AVG also added a spyware resident shield, so you're protected against all the threats the internet has to offer.

If you're seriously worried about security threats, consider a paid-for program, such as Kaspersky Internet Security 2009, but AVG Free is certainly a credible home alternative.

IMAGE EDITING | **SOFTWARE**

Rick Brewster/Ed Harvey
Paint.NET

DOWNLOAD DETAILS www.getpaint.net
FILE SIZE **1.5MB**

While Windows XP and Vista have reasonable image viewers as standard, Microsoft Paint is laughable as an image editor. Adobe Photoshop Elements is our favourite image-editing program, and, at £50, is fair value. However, a good free alternative is Paint.NET. It's not the only free image-editing application for Windows, as you can also download GIMP from *www.gimp.org*. GIMP's user interface may make your head hurt, though, which is why we prefer Paint.NET.

The program is a tiny download of just 1.5MB, though if you have Windows XP, you'll also need to install Microsoft's .NET framework, which is a free download from *www.microsoft.com*. It has a clean interface that's reminiscent of Photoshop, with floating palettes and information windows. The package supports all the usual image-editing functions, such as layers, cropping and levels and curves adjustments. It also has several image effects as standard. You can save images in most standard formats, including JPEG, BMP, GIF and TIFF, and compressed image settings are handled with a clear preview to show you what your saved image will look like.

It does have a couple of omissions, most notably an Unsharp Mask feature, which is a popular method to sharpen an image.

■ Paint.NET's clean user interface is reminiscent of Photoshop's

However, the application has an active user community producing plug-ins to use with the software, including an Unsharp Mask plug-in. You will have to search through the forums to find what you need, though.

Paint.NET is astonishing for a free program, and has the advantage of being a small download. It may take you a bit of work and research to add all the features you will need, but it's well worth the effort.

CHAPTER 8
NEW PC ESSENTIALS

PHOTO ORGANISING SOFTWARE

Google
Picasa 3

DOWNLOAD DETAILS http://picasa.google.com
FILE SIZE **6MB**

Picasa 3 is a fantastic photo organisation and editing program from Google. It's a relatively small download, and is easy to install and set up. You should be careful when installing the program that you select the options you want, as by default it'll add shortcuts to your desktop, Quick Launch and System Tray, and set Google as your default search engine.

Picasa will scan your PC for any images when you first run it, read the time data encoded in each photo and arrange your pictures by date. The Library view displays all your photos as thumbnails, and double-clicking on a picture takes you into the editing view. This gives you most of the editing options you'll need to make your photos presentable, such as cropping, red-eye reduction, straightening and contrast and colour adjustment. There are also several effects, including Sharpen, Sepia, Black and White and Soft Focus.

Once you're happy with your pictures, you can view them as a slideshow, with a lovely fade effect between each photo. The best thing about Picasa, though, is its online storage. To use this you'll need a Google Mail account, which you can get at *http://mail.google.com*. Once you have an account, you simply

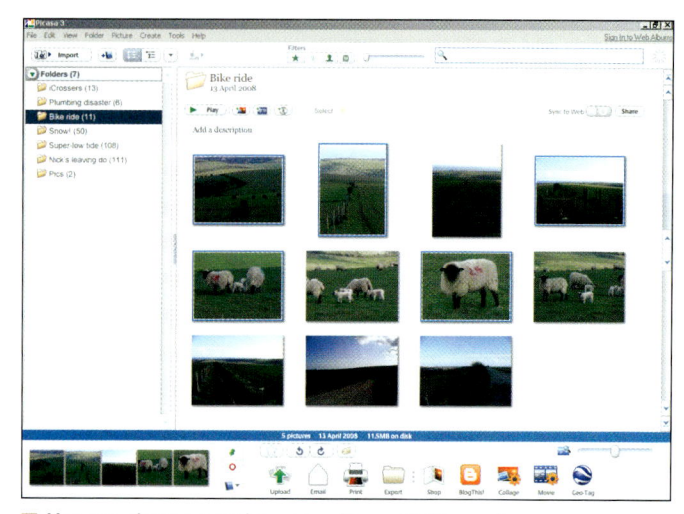

■ You can share your pictures online with Picasa 3

select the pictures you want to upload and click the Web Album button. You can upload photos in a quality suitable for viewing in a web browser, or upload bigger files that are good enough to print. Once your photos are online, you can make the album publicly available, or restrict it to only the people you invite to view your pictures. Google gives you 1GB of storage for free, which is enough for around 5,000 photos at web-quality settings. Vista users should try the built-in Windows Photo Gallery first before downloading Picasa, though.

CD/DVD BURNING SOFTWARE

Canneverbe Limited
CDBurnerXP

DOWNLOAD DETAILS http://cdburnerxp.se
FILE SIZE **2.9MB**

Both Windows XP and Vista have built-in CD-burning capabilities, and the latter can also burn DVDs, but both applications are fairly primitive and not particularly easy to use. CDBurnerXP is a powerful free program that makes it easy to burn data files to disc, turn audio files into a music CD and create CD and DVD images.

As with Paint.NET (page 109), if you're running Windows XP, you'll need to download and install the .NET Framework to use CDBurnerXP. The program itself is only a small download, and is simple to install.

The main interface will be familiar to anyone who's used a CD-burning program such as Nero. To create a CD, you just need to drag and drop files from the folder view at the top of the screen into your disc compilation at the bottom. You don't have to choose which type of disc you want to burn before you start your compilation, as CDBurnerXP automatically chooses the right file system depending on which type of disc is in the drive.

Once you've created your compilation, you just click the Burn icon to create your disc. You can also select Save

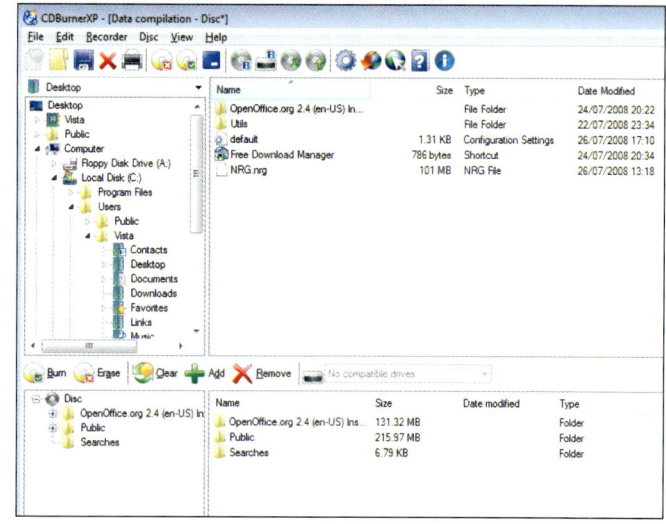

■ CDBurnerXP makes it easy to burn data files to CD

compilation as ISO file from the File menu to create a disc image to burn later. Usefully, the program also has the option to convert NRG and BIN image files, as used by Nero and some other CD-burning programs, to the more compatible ISO format.

Commercial applications such as Nero and Easy Media Creator have some impressive video disc-authoring features, but for most people CDBurnerXP will be the only disc-burning program they'll need.

110 BUILD A BETTER PC

DOWNLOAD MANAGER | SOFTWARE
Free Download Manager
Free Download Manager
DOWNLOAD DETAILS www.freedownloadmanager.org
FILE SIZE **5.6MB**

Essentially, Free Download Manager makes downloading files faster. When you start to download a file, the program splits the file into blocks and downloads all of them simultaneously. We found downloads were often four times faster using this program. You can also pause and resume downloading most files.

The application also has some other powerful features. You can use it to download movies from various video-sharing sites, such as YouTube and Google Video, and you can automatically convert these from the FLV format to more compatible formats such as MPEG4. Free Download Manager can also be used as a BitTorrent client, so is the only program you need to install to take care of all your downloads.

■ You can download video from sites such as YouTube

BACKUP | SOFTWARE
Freebyte.com
Freebyte Backup
DOWNLOAD DETAILS www.freebyte.com/fbbackup
FILE SIZE **785KB**

Freebyte Backup is a simple program that lets you back up the contents of your PC's hard disk to an external hard disk. To make a backup, you simply add the drives and directories to be included, then specify any files you want to exclude from the backup, either by the date they were created or by file type. You then just click the Start button and the files you specified will be backed up.

Once you've made your first backup, you can set the software to copy only files that are new or have been changed since the last time you backed up your PC, which cuts down drastically the amount of time the process takes. Automatic backups can be scheduled using the Windows Task Scheduler, although this can be tricky to configure.

■ Back up your data with Freebyte

ARCHIVE EXTRACTING | SOFTWARE
Nathan Moinvaziri
ExtractNow
DOWNLOAD DETAILS www.extractnow.com
FILE SIZE **940KB**

Even though Windows-supported ZIP files are the most common form of archive, there are many other kinds. ExtractNow can extract the majority of archives, including the popular RAR format, and CD and DVD image ISO files.

The program is particularly useful for extracting batches of archives. You just have to drag files into its window, click Extract and the program will extract each archive's contents into the folder where the archive is situated.

You can also associate archive file types with the program, so it will open automatically when you double-click on an archive in Windows. ExtractNow is an easy way to deal with different types of archive without having to install multiple programs, and it's a tiny download. The only thing that it doesn't let you do is create files, but Windows has this functionality built in.

■ ExtractNow can deal with different types of archive

MEDIA PLAYING | SOFTWARE
VideoLAN
VLC media player
DOWNLOAD DETAILS www.videolan.org
FILE SIZE **9.3MB**

Playing back audio and video files on a PC can be tricky. Even though all PCs come with Windows Media Player, there are many types of file that it doesn't support, so you'll need to install specific audio and video codecs to play them. Windows XP doesn't even have support for DVD movies as standard.

Finding out which codec is missing from your system can be a tricky business, but VLC takes much of the pain out of this process. It will play most types of audio and video files, including DVDs. It's simple to install, and will launch automatically when you double-click on a compatible file type. It can even play files that are incomplete. With built-in support for DVDs, it's one of the most comprehensive media players and it's completely free. VLC is the simplest way to play back media files.

■ VLC lets you play DVDs as well as most other media files

BUILD A BETTER PC **111**

CHAPTER 8
NEW PC ESSENTIALS

Saving power with your new PC

THE RISING COSTS of electricity and increasing concerns over the environment are two very good reasons to consider ways of cutting down on power consumption. PCs are one of the worst offenders in the home, but other devices connected to them, such as printers, monitors and external hard disks, all have their part to play.

Fortunately, there are several things you can do to save power and make your computer more efficient. We'll show you how much power your devices really use, how much it costs you to run them and how to save money by putting your devices into standby mode.

COST OF LIVING
First, it's worth explaining how costs are calculated. Every electrical device draws power, measured in watts (volts x amps). This is the figure used to describe light bulbs – a 100W bulb draws 100W of power. Over an hour this would be a watt hour. Electricity companies then charge your consumption based on the number of kilowatt hours (kWh) you're using. As a kilowatt is 1,000W, you first have to convert the wattage of any measured product into kilowatts by dividing by 1,000. So, a 100W light bulb uses 0.1kW. Over an hour, this would be 0.1kWh. If your electricity company charges you 11p per kWh, your 100W light bulb would cost you 1.1p per hour to run. In reality, most electricity companies use a two-tier system of charging. A fairly common tariff is 14p per kWh for the first 728 kWh per year and then 12p for each kWh thereafter.

For our calculations we've assumed the higher figure of 14kWh. While this means that we've ended up with higher costs overall, it gives us a fair comparison between each device. You can try our Google Docs spreadsheet for calculating running costs by visiting *http://tinyurl.com/powersaver*. You'll need a Google account to access it, but can

■ Devices left on can use a huge amount of power, which will cost you a small fortune

■ Devices such as the Intelliplug can help you save power

DEVICE	POWER WHEN ON	STANDBY POWER	TYPICAL COST PER YEAR*
PC	129W	3W	£40
Laptop	32W	3W	£17
LCD monitor	29W	2W	£8
Inkjet printer	Varies**	3W	£2
Network storage	41W	1W	£34
LCD TV	158W	3W	£33

*We've assumed a typical day's use for each product (eight hours a day for PCs, four hours a day for TVs), using standby modes where appropriate and being turned off at the plug when not in use

**Inkjet printers typically use between 10W and 30W to print a page of paper, but this is for a short amount of time, so the standby power is the biggest factor

sign up for a free one on that web page. Once you've accessed the spreadsheet, select Copy spreadsheet from the File menu to edit it in your own account. All you need to do is set your kWh cost and, for each device, type in its power usage figures, the number of hours a day it's on, off (at the socket) and in standby mode and the sheet will work out the rest.

MEASURING YOUR DEVICES

Measuring electrical devices is easy. All you need is a plug-in power monitor, such as the Plug-In Mains Power and Energy Monitor (£28, www.maplin.co.uk). This plugs into your wall socket, and then you just plug the electrical device you want to test into it. The reading on the screen tells you how many watts your device is drawing. Using the calculations above, you can work out how much a device will cost you each year.

You'll be quite surprised at the results. For example, a typical PC uses around 120W when on, while an LCD monitor will use around 29W (149W in total). If you were to leave both on all day every day for a year, you'd be using 1,305kWh per annum, which would cost a staggering £183 a year. However, putting a PC into standby mode means that it uses only around 3W, which is similar to an LCD monitor's 2W in standby mode. Turning them off at the plug when you're not using them would save more money, as you're not drawing any power.

Typically, a computer that's on eight hours a day with no standby modes turned on would cost around £61 a year to run. If you were to set the PC to go into standby mode when not in use for, say, three hours a day, it would cost £47 per annum to run – a saving of around £14 every year. The same can be said of every device that you use. The table (above) shows typical usage figures for electrical devices you have in your home.

COMBATTING THE PROBLEM

To save money, devices need to use less electricity. For PCs this means following our advice over the next two pages to adjust Windows Vista's power-saving settings. For other devices, you need to power them down when they're not in use. Ideally, you should switch devices off at the plug, because many still draw power when they're in standby mode. For example, the average LCD TV draws 3W when in standby mode. If this was to be left on all year, it would cost you £3.67 every year. Not a huge amount of money, guaranteed, but multiply this sum for every device you own and it adds up to a small fortune. For computer devices, such as printers, switch them off when you're not using them.

If the thought of having to switch off a plug under a desk sounds like too much hassle, then consider buying a product such as OneClick's Intelliplug (£17, www.oneclickpower.co.uk). This has a master socket for your PC and two slave sockets that only get power when your PC is turned on. It's ideal for your monitor and printer, as they'll only be on when your computer is.

You can try other power-saving techniques, too. For example, if you've got network storage, check to see if there's a sleep mode. Setting your storage to shut down overnight when you won't be using it can save you money every year. Follow this advice for all your electrical kit and you could knock more than £100 every year off your electricity bills.

■ Measuring how much power your devices use could be a real shock

BUILD A BETTER PC   113

EASY STEP-BY-STEP WORKSHOPS

BUILD A BETTER WEBSITE

YOUR COMPLETE GUIDE TO WEB DESIGN

FREE ONLINE RESOURCES

BUILD A SITE IN 30 MINUTES

£7.99

ISBN 1-906372-19-5

FROM THE EXPERTS AT **COMPUTER SHOPPER** **PC**

with images

Perfecting your site's navigation

Uploading your site

Finding inspiration

View your FREE sample at www.computershopperbooks.co.uk

ON SALE NOW*

WHSmith

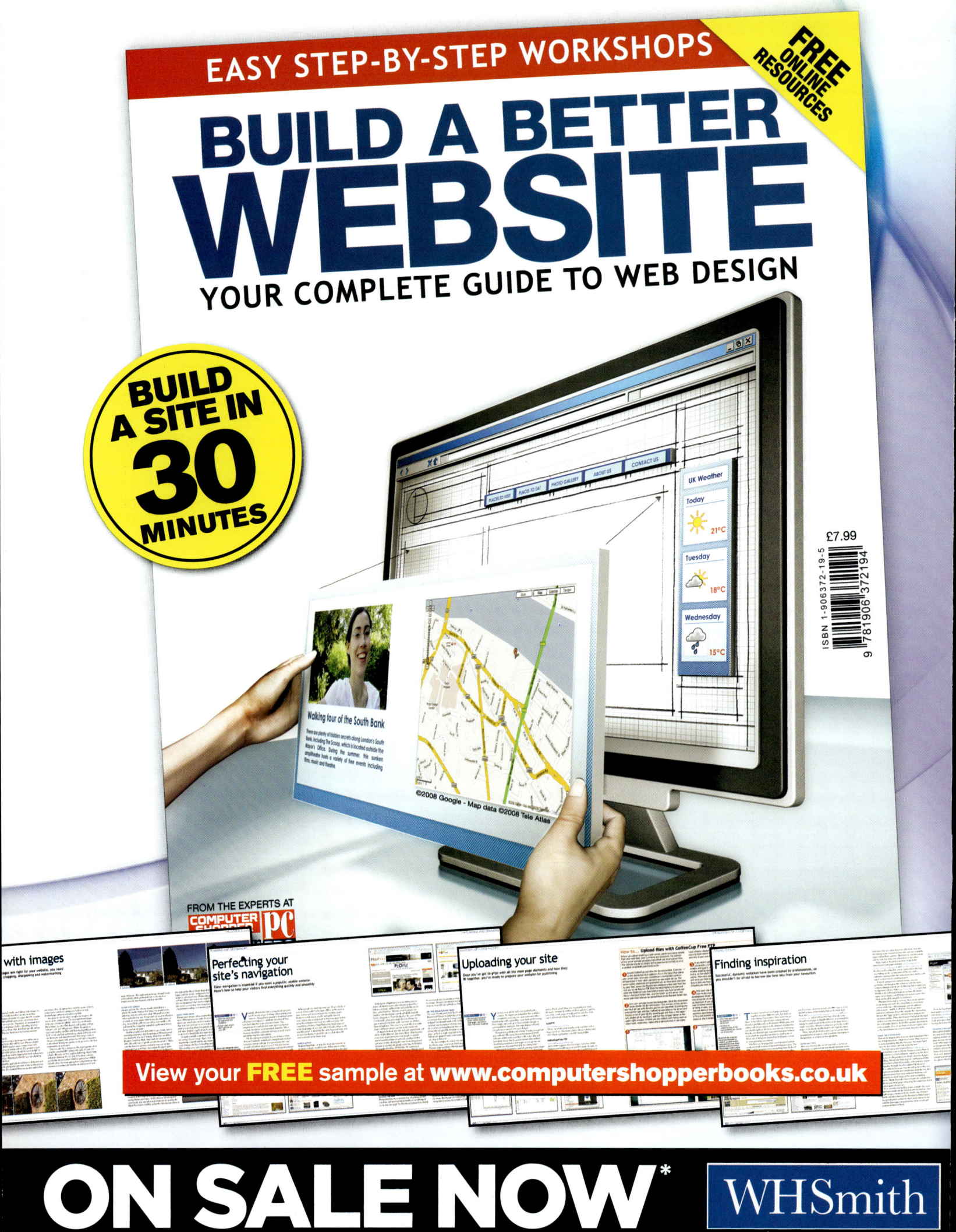

To order direct call **0844 844 0053** or visit **www.computershopper.co.uk/buildawebsite**

*Available at WHSmith, Tesco, Sainsbury's, Borders, ASDA and Amazon

CHAPTER 8
NEW PC ESSENTIALS

HOW TO...
Save power with Vista

1 CREATE YOUR OWN CUSTOM PLAN
Open the Control Panel from the Start menu and select System and Maintenance and then Power Options. Vista has three built-in power plans, but it's best to make your own. Click Create power plan, type in a name for your plan and click Next. On the next screen choose how long Windows should wait before turning off your monitor (10 minutes is reasonable). You can also set how long your PC should wait before it goes into Sleep mode (30 to 45 minutes is recommended). It takes only a few seconds to exit Sleep mode and Vista will save your data to hard disk, protecting unsaved work. Click Create when you're done.

2 PUT THE HARD DISK TO SLEEP
To change other settings, you need to click Change plan settings under the plan you created. Click Change advanced power settings.

First, expand the Hard disk setting and set Turn off hard disk after to 20 minutes. If you've got a wireless adaptor, you can set the Wireless Adapter Settings to power off when it's not in use. There are three options: Lower Power Saving; Medium Power Saving and Maximum Power Saving. The difference is how long your PC waits before shutting down the adaptor. This can cause problems with some wireless routers. If you're having trouble, adjust this setting to Maximum Performance.

3 SLEEP
We've already set the system Sleep time in Step 1, but Vista can also automatically go into Hibernation mode, where it saves your current state to hard disk and powers down the computer completely. To do this, expand the Sleep section and the Hibernate after section and set the time in minutes that you want to wait before your PC hibernates. We recommend two hours.

4 OTHER SETTINGS
There are some other settings that you can consider changing. First, under Search and Indexing, change the Power Savings Mode to Power Saver. This will stop Vista from thrashing your hard disk while it indexes your files. Next, your computer might not go into Sleep mode if you're sharing media files. To change this, expand the Multimedia Settings section and set When sharing media to Allow the computer to sleep. Click OK to apply.

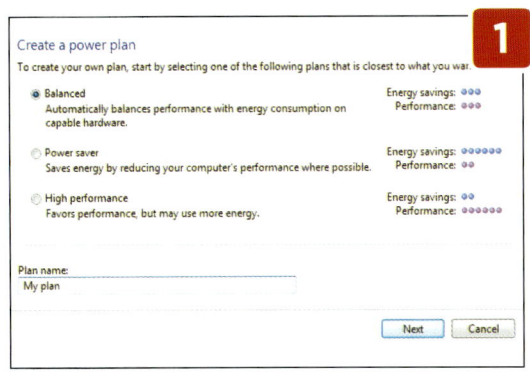

TIP
Turn your devices off at the plug to save money by not using power for standby.

BUILD A BETTER PC   115

CHAPTER 8
NEW PC ESSENTIALS

HOW TO...
Save power with XP

1 ENABLE HIBERNATION
Click on the Start menu and click on Control Panel. Click on Performance and Maintenance, and then Power Options to bring up the controls for power management. Click on the Hibernate tab and tick the box called Enable hibernation. This will let Windows save the current state of your computer to hard disk, including the current status of all your applications and all your open windows. Not only is it handy for power saving, as we'll show, but it's great if you've got lots of documents open but want to power down your computer for the night.

2 SET INITIAL POWER SCHEMES
Click on the Power Schemes tab. Windows has several default schemes, but it's best to edit the default Home/Office Desk instead. The default scheme turns the monitor off after 20 minutes, but this is probably too generous. Set the monitor to turn off after 10 minutes.

The default scheme doesn't turn the hard disks off at all, but you should do so to reduce power. Setting the hard disks to power down after 20 minutes should do the job.

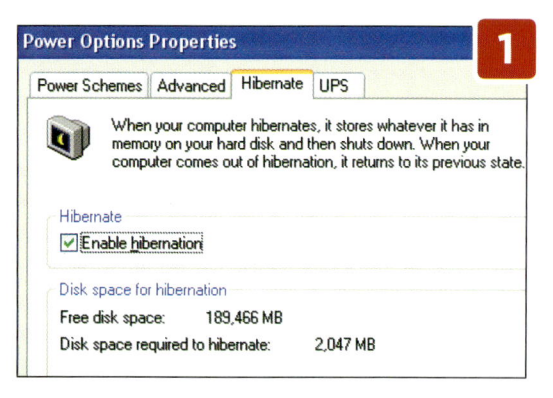

3 STANDBY AND HIBERNATION
Now standby has been enabled, you can set Windows to hibernate automatically if the PC hasn't been used in a while. First, it's best to set the System standby time. This puts your PC into a low-power state, where it uses just a few watts of power (the S3 setting that you used in the BIOS). Generally, we'd say that if you haven't used your PC for 30 to 45 minutes, then it's good to put it into Standby. Finally, set your PC to hibernate after two hours.

4 ADVANCED SETTINGS
Click on the Advanced tab for more control. By default, your PC will ask you for a password when it resumes from standby or hibernation, but you can remove this tab if you'd prefer. You can also control what the power button and sleep button (if you have one) do. By default, the power button is set to Shut down, but you can change this to Hibernate if you'd rather save your current system state. You can also ask Windows to prompt you every time you push the power button, in a similar way to when you click Turn Off Computer in the Start menu.

> **TIP**
> Windows XP's Sleep mode doesn't back up data to the hard disk, so Hibernate is a safer option.

www.scan.co.uk

t: 0871-472-4747 Celebrating 21 years in business! SCAN COMPUTERS

Each SCAN order contains

3XS SYSTEMS — systems built by enthusiasts

- Stock Availability 100%
- Great Pricing 100%
- Technical Support 100%
- Customer Service 100%
- Customer Satisfaction 100%

www.scan.co.uk

27-28 Enterprise Park • Middlebrook • Horwich • Bolton • Lancs BL6 6PE • Tel: 0870-755 4747

of a customers online shopping expectations

Custom PC Reader Award For Best Retailer Awards 2004 | *PC Pro Highly Commended Awards 2005* | *Custom PC Reader Award For Best Manufacturer Support Awards 2005* | *Custom PC Reader Award For Best Retailer Awards 2006* | *Custom PC Reader Award For Best Retailer Awards 2007* | *Custom PC Best Retailer Awards 2007* | *Custom PC Dream PC Award Awards 2007*

Scan Platinum Partners

NVIDIA® GeForce®. The Force Within.
NVIDIA® PhysX™ is the next big thing in gaming! Enjoy destructible worlds, life-like characters and cloth that tears naturally. Available now on NVIDIA® 8, 9 and GTX series GeForce GPUs.

PhysX™ by NVIDIA | XFX play hard.

XMS2 DOMINATOR™ DDR3 Performance Memory (CORSAIR)
Featuring Dual-path Heat Xchange (DHX) and Enhanced Performance Profiles (EPP) technologies.

Intel® Core™2 Extreme Quad-Core processor QX9770
The Intel® Core™2 Extreme processor QX9770 running at 3.0 GHz delivers the best possible experience for today's most demanding users.

SF Scan Finance — More sense than money... Buy now, pay in 9 months and pay no interest*.

*Example 1: Buy Now Pay Later (9 months) This is a Buy Now Pay Later agreement. Customers will initially only have to pay a 10% deposit, with the original loan amount payable in the 9th month, in order to incur no interest charges. Cash price: £1,000.00 Deposit: £100.00 Balance Before Charges: £900.00 Charge For Credit: £646.86 Amount Payable(Cash Price + Charge For Credit): £1646.86 Balance Payable (Total Monthly Payments): £1546.86 Total 48 Monthly Instalments of: £36.83 APR: 29.8% Option Period: 10 months If the balance of £900.00 is paid in or before the 9th month no charges for credit will be incurred. Terms and Conditions apply.

CHAPTER 8
NEW PC ESSENTIALS

Making an image of your hard disk

NOW YOU'VE FINISHED building your PC, installed Windows and downloaded all the drivers and extra software you need, you'll understand just how much work is needed to get a computer up and running from scratch. Beyond simply getting it working, there's all the additional hassle associated with ensuring that Windows looks and feels right, setting up all your applications the way you like them, and organising all your favourites and home page in your web browser.

It's hours of work, so imagine how you'd feel if your PC suddenly shut down, taking your hard disk with it. Thankfully, this is very unlikely, but a more probable scenario is that as time goes on Windows will become increasingly bloated. Over the years, you will install and uninstall any number of extra applications and additional hardware, which will leave a large number of extra files and services on your hard disk. These will slow your PC down to a crawl, and reinstalling everything from scratch isn't a huge amount of fun.

This is where using a disk-imaging program can save you a world of trouble. It will take a complete copy of your hard disk, including the operating system, your applications, all of your settings and every file on your hard disk.

NO MORE REINSTALLING
When restored, the image will take your computer back to the day that the image was made. Instead of having to reinstall Windows when it's no longer working the way you want it, you can just flash the image back and return to when you first installed Windows, complete with all your original settings and applications. So instead of hours of work, with a disk-imaging application it only takes a fraction of the time.

The best thing is that you're not just limited to taking one image. With the right software, you can also schedule images to occur regularly, so that you're constantly making a backup. If you should suffer a problem, you simply restore your computer back to the last good image – a little bit like a super System Restore.

Disk-imaging applications also include standard file backup options, so you can take less regular images, which use a lot of disk space, but still protect all your data.

HARD DISK
Ideally, you should store images on an external hard drive so you won't lose them if your main hard disk fails. This also means that you can restore the image to your old hard disk (or to a new one in the case of a major problem), getting up and running again in a short period of time. You could also back up to a secondary partition on your primary hard disk.

NORTON GHOST
We can't stress the importance of using disk-imaging software enough, particularly when you build a new PC, as you can create an amazing recovery disc just like the one you'd get with a new computer from a manufacturer. Over the next few pages, we'll show you how to image your PC using the best application on the market: Norton Ghost 14. We used the download version of Ghost, which costs £40 and is available from *www.symantec.co.uk* (click on the online store). This is identical to the boxed version, although the installation steps may differ very slightly. You'll also have to download the recovery CD image file, which we'll show you how to use later.

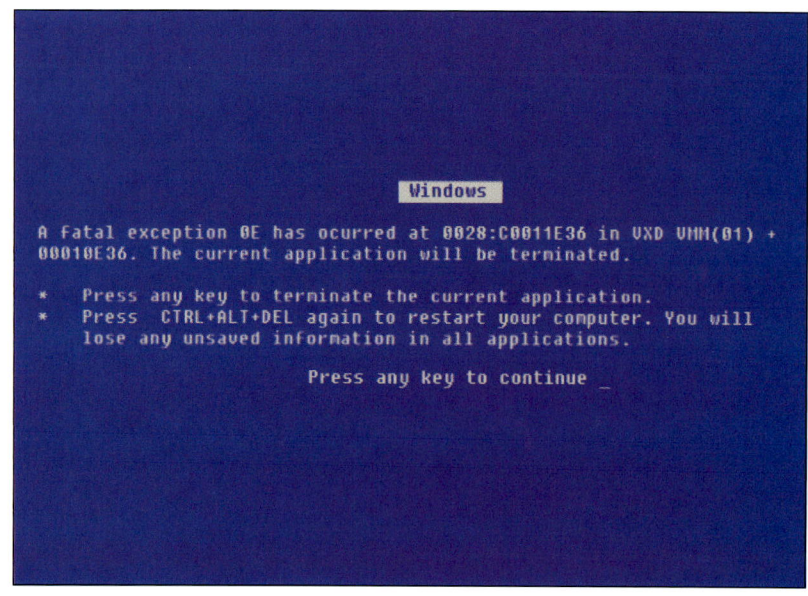

■ To recover from a system error quickly, you need a disk image of your hard disk

HOW TO...
Make a hard disk image

1 INSTALL GHOST
Run the Ghost installation program and follow the wizard. The software should install quickly and automatically, without asking you any questions. When it's finished, you'll be prompted to restart your computer. Do this and wait for your PC to load Windows again. When prompted, enter the product key that you were provided with when you bought the application, click Next, and then click Next again to run LiveUpdate and to download the latest version of the software. Restart you computer again if prompted.

2 CHANGE SCHEDULE
After LiveUpdate has finished, the Easy Setup application starts. This automatically sets up a scheduled imaging job and a scheduled file backup job. These tend to be a bit extreme, though, so you should change some settings.

First, under My Computer Backup, click the box next to Schedule to specify when you want a backup taken. The default is set for every Sunday and Thursday, but once a week should be sufficient. These backups only record the changes to files since the last image to save on disk space.

Ghost is also set to create a full new image set, which takes up a lot of disk space, once every three months. This should be fine for most people.

3 ADD TRIGGERS
You can also set Ghost to run a backup when certain triggers are detected. Click on the General link under Event Triggers, and select the options you want – Any application is installed, for example. Be warned that using any of these options will increase the amount of disk space you'll need for backups, so use them carefully. When you're happy with your settings click OK.

4 MANAGE FILES
Ghost will also take regular file backups. It's set by default to back up the Documents, My Video, My Pictures and My Music folders, Internet Explorer favorites and your desktop settings. Click on the blue text to the right of Select at the top of the screen to add more options. Click OK when you're done. You can now change the schedule for this backup in the same way as in Step 3.

Finally, Norton Ghost tries to pick a suitable backup destination, such as an external hard disk.

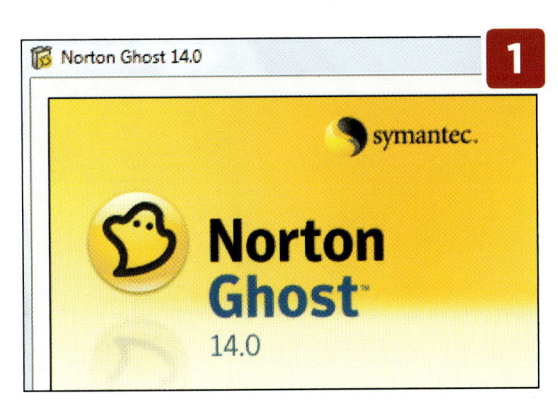

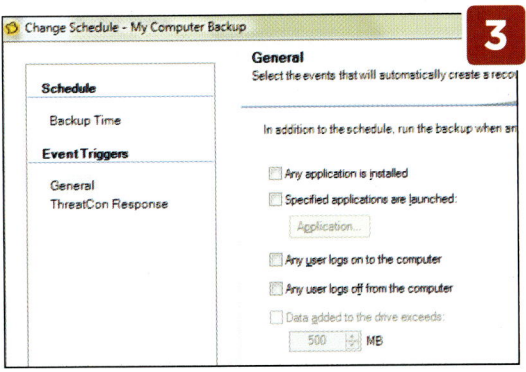

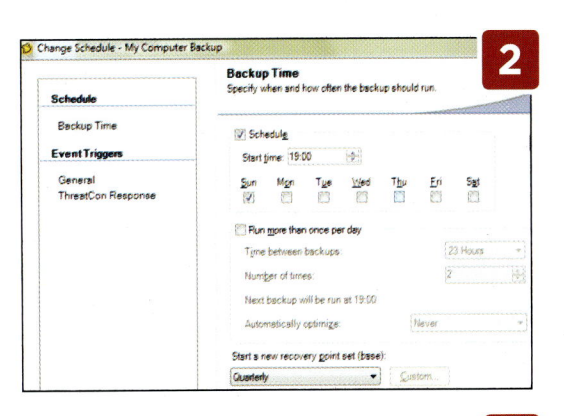

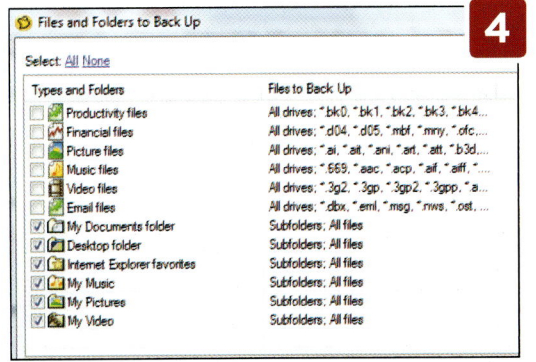

TIP
A second physical hard disk or external disk are the best places for backups, as they won't be affected if your main hard disk fails.

BUILD A BETTER PC 119

CHAPTER 8
NEW PC ESSENTIALS

You can also back up to a separate partition, like the one we created when we installed Windows in Chapter 7. This will be safe from Windows crashes, but not hard disk faults, so an external hard disk is the safest option. Use the secondary partition if you don't have an external disk. Click OK, select Run first backup now and click OK again.

5 MANAGE BACKUPS
While your backups will run to the schedule you set, you can modify this or choose to start a backup manually if, for example, you've just saved a lot of new files or made a major system change. Start Norton Ghost and select Run or Manage Backups. The next window will display your current jobs. Select one and click Run Now to run it. You can Change schedules and edit what's being backed up by clicking Edit Settings. With the default My Documents Backup, you can now add your own custom files and folders.

6 RECOVER FILES
If you want to recover individual files, click Recover My Files from Ghost's main screen. You can search for a specific file or click Search to find all backed up files. Right-clicking a file or folder lets you view the different backup versions and recover the one you want. You can also restore files from an image. Click Recovery Point, select the backup you want and choose Explore from Tasks. You can browse the image like a regular folder and drag files to your computer.

7 RECOVER A HARD DISK
You can restore an image to a hard disk by selecting the Recover My Computer link from Ghost's Welcome page. Select the Recovery point you want and click Recover now. Provided the Recovery point isn't for your boot partition (the one with Windows on it), Ghost will restore the image. If it is for your boot hard disk, Ghost can't recover it while Windows is running. Instead, you need to follow Steps 8 to 12 to create a recover CD.

8 CREATE A RECOVERY CD
If you bought the download version of Ghost, you should have also downloaded the recovery CD image file. This needs to be recorded to a CD. You can do this with CD-writing software such as CDBurnerXP (see page 110). If you don't have CDBurnerXP, you can download ISO Recorder from *http://isorecorder.alexfeinman.com*. Version 2 is for Windows XP and version 3 is for Vista, so make sure that you get the right one. Install the software.

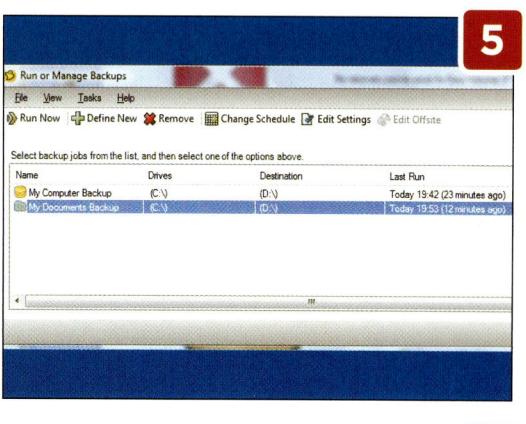

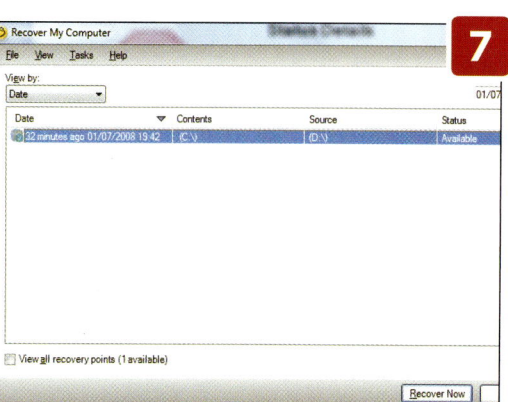

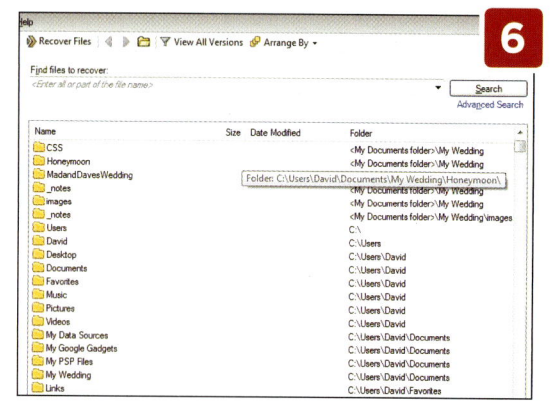

Browse to the directory to which you downloaded Norton Ghost and look for the ZIP file (NGH140_AllWin_EnlishEMEA_SrdOnly.zip). Open this by right-clicking on it and selecting Extract. Right-click on the resulting ISO file and select Copy image to CD. Click Next and then Finish when the operation is done. You now have a bootable restore CD.

9 BOOT FROM YOUR RESTORE DISC
Make sure that your BIOS is set to boot from your optical drive (see page 84) and then restart your PC. You'll be prompted to hit a key to boot off the CD, so make sure you're ready. When the Windows loading screen starts, click Accept to accept the Norton Ghost licence agreement.

There are several options on the next screen. Click on Analyze to perform system tests, and Check Hard Disk for Errors to run a system scan on your hard disk. The Virus scanner is useful only if you've also got Symantec Anti-Virus, otherwise the definitions will be too old. You can also click on Explore your hard disk.

10 ADD DRIVERS
While this recovery disk will recognise most hard disks, it can't identify them all, particularly if you're running RAID. If the image you want to restore is saved on a networked hard disk, then you may have to install a driver for the network adaptor, too. To do this, click on Utilities and then Load drivers. You need to use the Explorer-like window to navigate to a folder with the relevant driver in it. You can plug in USB drives or use a CD, so adding extra drivers shouldn't be hard. You should also have them available if you had to add extra drivers when installing Windows.

11 RECOVER YOUR COMPUTER
Click on Home and Recover my Computer. Select the recovery point you want to restore (if the list is blank, select View by filename and click Browse to find it) and click Next. Click Finish and then Yes to start recovering your PC. The files will then be restored to your computer. Once it's completed, you can reboot your computer and it will be back to the exact state at which you made the recovery point.

12 RECOVER FILES
Alternatively, you can use this interface to recover individual files from a restore point. Select Recover from the main screen and then Recover My Files. Navigate to a recovery point, select it and click OK. You'll then be presented with the Symantec Recovery Point Browser.

You can navigate through this like an ordinary disk. When you find the file or files that you want to recover, you just have to select them and click Recover Files. You can then choose where to restore the files to, such as another disk or drive.

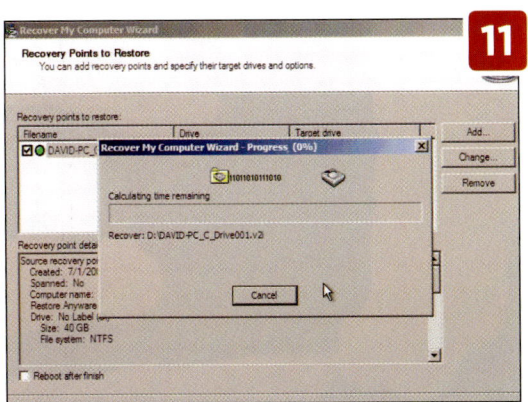

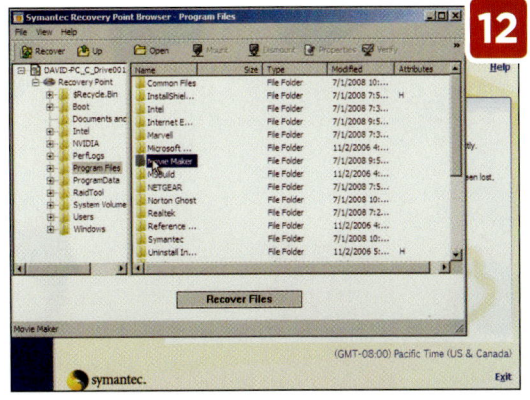

TIP
You should run a hard disk scan before recovering your files to make sure there's nothing wrong with your disk.

BUILD A BETTER PC **121**

CHAPTER 9
TROUBLESHOOTING

HOPEFULLY THIS BOOK has given you everything you need to build the perfect PC. However, you may have run into problems along the way or simply haven't understood some of the terms we've used. Don't worry – we haven't abandoned you. In the next few pages, we'll give you some essential troubleshooting and problem-solving tips. There's also a useful glossary, so you can look up any terms you don't know.

IN THIS CHAPTER

Troubleshooting hardware problems	**124**
Troubleshooting Windows	**128**
Testing memory	**134**
Testing your hard disk	**136**
Testing your new PC for heat	**138**
Testing your processor	**140**

CHAPTER 9
TROUBLESHOOTING

Troubleshooting hardware problems

PCs ARE FINICKY beasts that seem to thrive on causing their owners trouble by not working properly. If you've followed our instructions all the way through but are still not happy with the way your computer works, don't panic.

The vast majority of problems are best solved by trying one fix at a time. After each attempted fix, try and run your PC again to see if the problem has been solved. This is better than trying several things at once, as you'll be able to track down what the problem is, which could be useful if your computer has similar difficulties later on. The other thing to remember is that a lot of problems are caused by something simple, such as cables being plugged in the wrong way round, so check the simple stuff first before you start taking your computer apart.

We'll go through all the common problems that might affect your PC and suggest fixes that should get your system running. Before we start, though, you should never rule out simple problems, such as a blown fuse or faulty cables. Changing power or internal cables can often solve a problem quickly and with much less hassle.

While our suggestions are general, if you get a specific error message, you should make a note of it. From another computer, either yours or a friend's, type this message into a search engine. This should help you narrow down the problem. *Computer Shopper* magazine also offers a regular computer clinic, which you can read every month and contact by emailing helpfile@computershopper.co.uk.

Finally, if your PC stops working just after you install a new bit of hardware, remove it and turn your computer back on. If this fixes the problem, you can try and reinstall the device again. If you still don't have any luck, then your new hardware probably doesn't work and you should ask for a refund or replacement.

TIP Try one fix at a time so that when you get your computer working again you'll know what caused the problem.

■ Make sure the power switch is connected to the motherboard

PC WON'T TURN ON

One of the most frustrating problems you can have after building your PC is that it won't turn on. At this point, it can feel as though all your hard work was for nothing, but this problem is usually easily fixed. First, check that you've got the power cable plugged in all the way and that the wall socket and power switch on the power supply are turned on. If that doesn't fix the problem, you'll need to open up your PC and have a look inside.

First, check that the case's power button is connected to the motherboard's power switch jumper. You'll need to check your board's manual to find the exact pins to which it's supposed to be connected. The other main reason that a computer won't start is because the power cables haven't been connected to the motherboard correctly. Make sure that the ATX power connector (the large 24-pin connector) is plugged into its socket and the secondary power connector is also connected (see page 54).

If you're still not having any luck, reseat the processor (page 58), check that the memory is in the right slots and connected properly (page 60), and, if fitted, the graphics card (page 68). Finally, remove any expansion cards you've fitted. If your computer still won't turn on, try removing the graphics card and the memory. If your PC turns on it will now beep at you (see the next section for more information) to warn you that there's a problem. Refit the memory and try again.

If you still haven't found the source of the trouble, try using one stick of memory at a time to find out if one of them is causing the problem. You could also try removing the graphics card and all other expansion cards one at time.

TURNS ON BUT BEEPS

A more usual scenario is that your computer will turn on, but you'll either get a blank screen or some beeps. The number of beeps is designed to tell you what the problem is. Unfortunately, your motherboard's manual won't decipher these codes. Instead, go to *www.pchell.com/hardware/beepcodes.shtml* for a list of the common codes, and the problems they relate to. This site also contains some helpful troubleshooting information,

■ Resetting the CMOS can fix loads of hardware errors. The jumper pins are highlighted

so we recommend printing out the page and keeping a copy in a handy location. The site covers BIOSes manufactured by AMI, Phoenix and IBM. Phoenix is the most popular BIOS, followed by AMI; you're unlikely to have an IBM BIOS. The manual for your motherboard should tell you which company manufactures the BIOS you're using.

The beeps can give you an idea of what's causing the problem, and you may think that the solution will probably entail replacing a faulty part in your computer. In our experience, however, this is rarely the case, and the fault is normally caused by devices not being connected properly. You should always check that your memory, processor, hard disk, optical drive and power connectors are all in place before you start worrying about getting a replacement. Try installing one stick of memory at time, in case you've got a faulty module causing problems.

Sometimes faults are caused by the motherboard not detecting your hardware correctly, particularly the processor. The easiest way to get it to do this is to reset the CMOS, which wipes the BIOS back to its default state. This should force it to detect your hardware correctly and can solve a lot of problems. Your board's manual will tell you how to do this.

In general, most motherboards have a jumper that has to be placed over two pins to reset the CMOS. To do it, you need to change the jumper and turn the PC on. Then, turn the computer off and put the jumper back to its original setting. Some motherboards designed for overclocking have a dedicated button on the back. Hold this

CHAPTER 9
TROUBLESHOOTING

in and press the power button. Turn your PC off, take your finger off the button and turn your computer back on.

When you reset your CMOS, you'll be prompted to hit F1 when your PC starts, as a warning messages tells you the CMOS has been reset. This will reset all of the BIOS settings back to default. You'll now be able to follow our instructions on page 82 to configure your BIOS properly.

ERROR MESSAGE BEFORE PC STARTS
When computers are first turned on they run a Power On Self Test (POST) to check that hardware is working correctly. This will identify if your processor isn't working, the keyboard isn't connected or memory isn't working.

Read any message carefully and then check the component that's at fault to make sure it's plugged in correctly. In the case of memory, you can try installing one stick of RAM at a time to make sure that there's not a fault in one of the modules.

DRIVE TROUBLE
If your optical drive isn't being detected, make that sure it's connected properly. This is easy for SATA drives, as you just need to check the cable. For IDE drives, check the cable and the jumpers on the back. If you've only got one optical drive, it should be set to Master; if you've got two, one should be set to master and one to slave.

You should also check that the IDE cable is inserted the right way round on both the drive and the motherboard. If your cable doesn't have a notch in it, then the red cable needs to be next to the power connector on the drive; on the motherboard, the red cable needs to be plugged into pin 1 (this will be marked on the board or, at least, in the motherboard's manual).

For hard disks, make sure you've got the cable connected properly. The easiest first step is to go into your computer's BIOS and restore it back to its default settings. To do this, you need to access your BIOS by pressing a certain key (usually Delete or F2) when your computer boots. Your motherboard's manual will explain how to do this, but look out for an onscreen message that will tell you which key to press when you first turn your computer on. Check the manual to find out how to access the hard disk screen. Our guide to the BIOS on page 82 tells you how to configure your disks correctly.

If your hard disk still isn't being detected, make sure it's plugged into the right SATA port and not one for RAID. After that, you may have a broken hard disk. Put your ear to the disk when it turns on – if you repeatedly hear a clunking noise, then it's probably broken.

If your hard disk is detected in the BIOS but can't be seen by Windows, you'll need to install a driver for your computer's hard disk controller. For

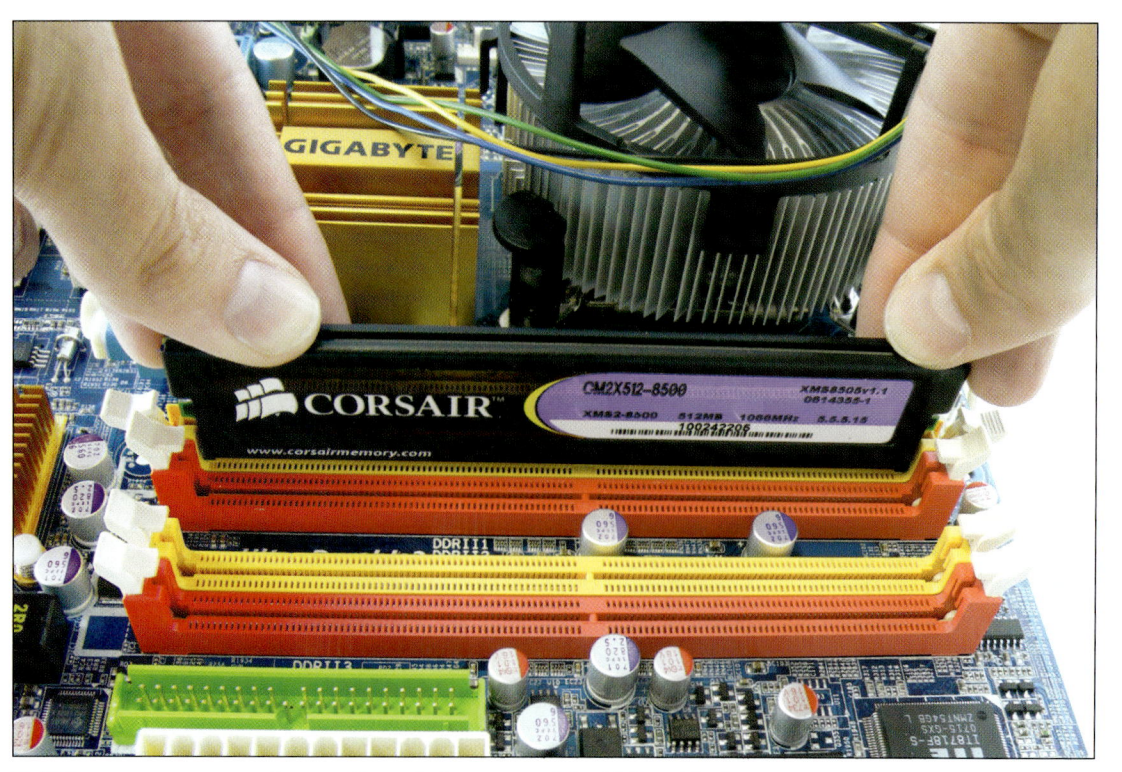

> **TIP**
> Make changes one at time so you can identify the problem easily.

■ Make sure your memory is correctly seated, or you could get intermittent errors

XP (page 98) this involves getting a floppy disk with the driver on it, while Vista (page 90) is more forgiving and lets you use optical drives, floppy disks and USB drives to store the driver.

CRASHES WHEN INSTALLING

Perhaps the most frustrating problem is when your PC turns on correctly and recognises all your hardware, but crashes without warning when you try and install an operating system. We've seen this happen on lots of computers before, and the fix is to check your hardware methodically. The first step is to go into your BIOS and reset it back to default values. When you get into your BIOS, you need to find the section that lets you load default values. Quite often this is under the Exit menu, but this differs between manufacturers, so check your manual. Given the choice, try and load the Optimal default first, and the Fail-Safe default second. If you don't have these options, the basic default setting is best. Select Exit Saving Changes and your computer will restart. You may need to set your BIOS up the way you want it again by following our advice on page 82.

Typically, these kinds of problems are usually caused by just a few components. Overheating is one of the big causes, especially in the case of the processor. It's worth checking that your processor cooler is fitted properly (page 58). This is particularly true of Intel processors, as the four push-in feet don't always go in smoothly. It's easy to miss one and end up with the cooler not making proper contact with the processor. Also check that the processor has an adequate covering of thermal paste, applying more where necessary.

If that doesn't do the job, the memory could be the culprit. Running an application such as Memtest86+ (see page 135) can help you test your memory and find any errors. If this application won't run, then it's worth manually checking your memory. First, make sure all the modules are seated properly in the correct sockets (page 60). If you're still having trouble, then it may be that one stick of memory is causing the problem. Remove all but one stick and try it again. Swap the stick of memory for another one and try your computer again. By a process of elimination, you should be able to work out which stick of memory, if any, is damaged.

Other bits of hardware can also cause problems, so it's worth checking that your optical drive (page 66) and hard disk (page 64) are connected properly. For the hard disk, make sure that it's connected to the right SATA port of your computer by checking your motherboard's manual. Some boards have ports that are reserved

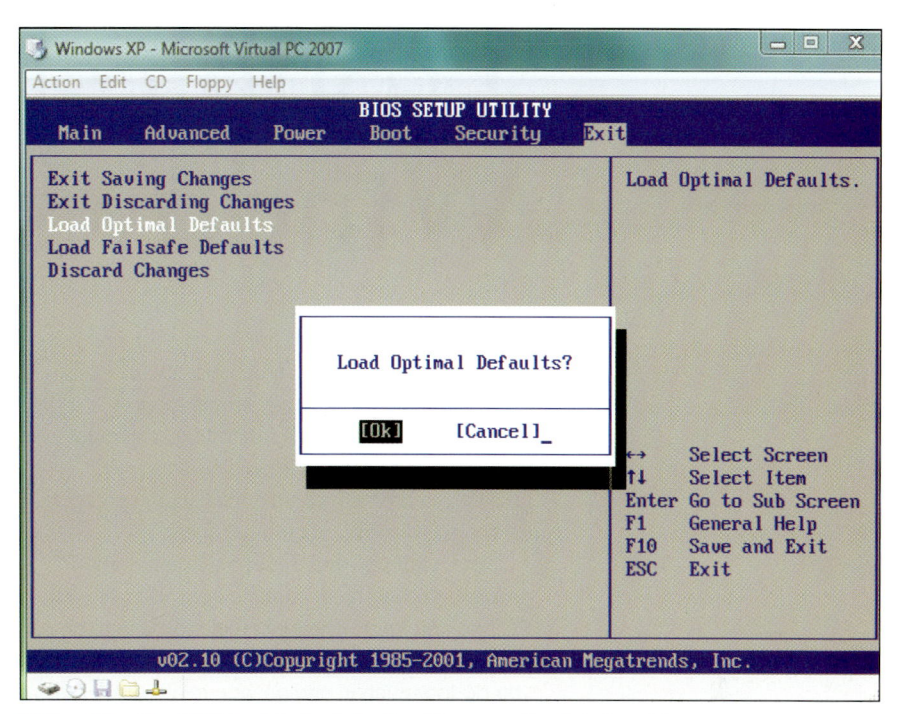

■ Resetting the BIOS back to its default settings can fix a lot of problems

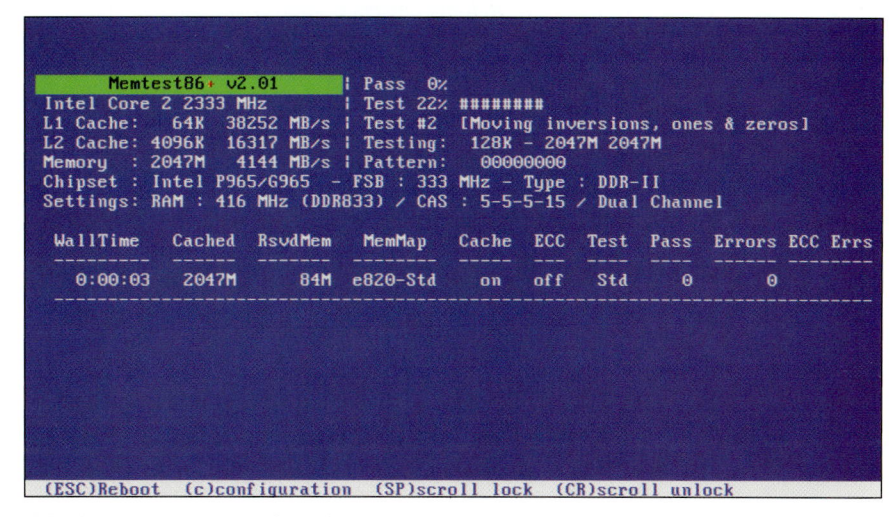

■ Bad memory can cause lots of problems in PCs, including random Windows crashes. Memtest can help you track down the problem by running diagnostic tests on your RAM

for RAID. It may be worth disconnecting your hard disk entirely and trying the install process again. We've seen damaged hard disks before that have caused the Windows installation to crash. If removing the hard disk lets the installer work, it's worth running Hitachi's free Drive Fitness Test (page 137) to see if you can identify a fault with the hard disk. You can also try connecting the hard disk to a different SATA port. Finally, remove all non-essential hardware such as wireless adaptors and TV tuners one at a time to see if this fixes your problems. If you get Windows to install, you should reinstall the removed hardware.

CHAPTER 9
TROUBLESHOOTING

Troubleshooting Windows

WHILE WINDOWS HAS improved a lot since its early days, there are still times when it will give you a headache and simply refuse to work properly. This this can be frustrating, particularly if you've just spent hours building a new PC. Luckily, the problems aren't usually fatal and can be solved with a bit of perseverance.

Here, we'll talk you through some common problem-solving techniques to help you get your PC back on track. The main thing to do is to be methodical and rule out one problem at a time. If you do too much in one go, you might solve the problem, but you'll never know its source, which could cause trouble further down the line.

In most cases, problems with getting peripherals or other hardware to work are usually caused by the drivers you've installed. Most of the time, simply using Add/remove programs to delete the offending driver and installing a new one will fix your woes. In other cases, downloading the latest drivers from the device manufacturer's website will fix the problem.

UNSTABLE WINDOWS CRASHES
If you find that your computer's not very stable and keeps crashing, and you've made sure that your hardware isn't getting too hot (see page 138), then the problem is likely down to one of two things: hardware compatibility or software compatibility.

In both cases, note down the error message that appears. If you type the exact phrase into a search engine, there's a good chance you'll find a website that will tell you what caused the error and how to fix it. Look for tell-tale signs in the error message, as Windows will usually say which bit of software or hardware has caused the problem. You can then look for support from the relevant manufacturer.

If your machine just crashes or the error message isn't particularly helpful, remember what you were doing when your computer crashed. If it always occurs when you open a particular application, then it's probably that piece of software causing the problem. This is especially likely to be the case if you're installing an old application that you used in an earlier version of Windows.

Fortunately, most manufacturers carry updates for software on their website, so visit the site and look for a new update. If there isn't one, you may need to upgrade to a newer version of the application that is compatible with your version of Windows. Look for upgrade offers, as these usually provide you with the latest version of the software at a reduced price.

HARDWARE
If your PC crashes randomly and not always when you're using a particular bit of software, then it's probably a piece of hardware that's misbehaving or hasn't been properly detected. Don't worry, as this is easy to check.

First, right-click Computer in the Start menu (My Computer in Windows XP) and select Properties. This will display System Information windows, which will tell you which processor you've got installed and how much memory you've got. If this information doesn't match up with what you put in your PC, then you've probably got a problem. You should try and reseat the memory and processor, and reread the section on setting up your BIOS (see page 82) to find out how to get your computer to detect your hardware properly.

■ Device Manager shows you if any of your hardware isn't installed properly

128 BUILD A BETTER PC

If everything is detected properly here, then it could be another bit of hardware that's causing the problem. To see if this is the case, you need to check Device Manager. In Vista, right-click on Computer and select Properties. Click on the Device Manager link on the right-hand side of the screen. In XP, right-click on My Computer, select Properties, click on the hardware tab and select Device Manager.

If any devices aren't installed properly, a yellow warning triangle containing an exclamation mark will be displayed. This is Windows' way of highlighting that there's a problem. If the warning icon is next to an Unknown Device, then the problem is probably that you haven't installed all the necessary drivers. Go back through your list of downloaded drivers and make sure that you installed everything. If you did, then you should check your device manufacturers' websites to make sure that you downloaded everything you were supposed to. The motherboard manufacturer's site is worth checking, as it's easy to miss a driver download.

If the warning triangle is next to a known device, then its driver is not working properly. First, try and reinstall the driver. If that doesn't work, you may have an incompatible driver and should check the manufacturer's website for an updated version. You should also look for compatibility information online to make sure that the device is compatible with your operating system.

■ Software manufacturers routinely release patches for their software, which can fix bugs and introduce compatibility for newer operating systems

■ Windows' System Information screen tells you what hardware has been detected

SPECIFIC HARDWARE DOESN'T WORK
The steps above give you information on specific hardware problems, but just because a device is listed correctly in Device Manager, this doesn't mean it's working properly. Here we'll examine some of the most common bits of hardware and take you through some troubleshooting techniques for them.

KEYBOARDS AND MICE
Windows has built-in drivers, so any keyboard or mouse that you plug in will work automatically. However, while you'll get all the basic functions if you've got a keyboard with extra controls, such as buttons to control volume and media playback, or a mouse with programmable buttons, you'll still need to install the manufacturer's software.

This will be easy to find by visiting the manufacturer's website and searching the support section for your product. Once you have downloaded and installed the recommended software, you should find that all your buttons will start working correctly.

AUDIO
If you're using a dedicated sound card, you should read its manual for full instructions on how to install it, as well as troubleshooting advice.

TIP
Check the manufacturer's support forums for help on a specific problem. The chances are that if you're having a problem, someone else will have already encountered it and has a solution.

BUILD A BETTER PC **129**

CHAPTER 9
TROUBLESHOOTING

Windows will automatically install sound drivers for your onboard sound, but they're not as good as the real drivers. If you're having problems, make sure that you've installed the proper ones from your manufacturer.

If you can't get the sound working at all, there are several things you can check. With most onboard sound, you should notice an icon in the Notification Area (to the left of the time), which looks like a speaker. Double-click this to bring up the audio management software. Your speaker configuration should be set to match the number of speakers that you have. It's worth checking at this point that your speakers or headphones are connected to the right ports on your motherboard. Check your board's manual for full details.

You can also test your sound inside Windows' Control Panel. In Vista, open the Control Panel from the Start menu and select Hardware and Sound, Manage Audio Devices. Right-click the audio device you want to use and select Test. This will play a sound through each of your speakers. If you only hear it through some of the speakers, you've either got a faulty connection somewhere – in which case you should plug all the cables in again – or you haven't told Windows the correct speaker setup you're using.

Finally, the sound output you're using should have a tick next to it. If it doesn't, it's not the default device. Right-click it and select Set as default device. Click on OK to apply the settings.

In XP, select Sounds, Speech and Audio Devices, Sounds and Audio Devices from the Control Panel. Click Advanced under Speaker settings to choose your speaker setup. Click on Audio to choose your default playback device. There's no way to test your speakers, as with Vista, so play an MP3 file to test your audio output.

GRAPHICS CARDS

In order for you to be able to see the desktop before you've had a chance to install the proper graphics card drivers, Windows can use a generic display driver that works with all cards. So, just because you can see something onscreen, it doesn't mean your graphics card is set up properly.

In Device Manager, expand the Display adaptors section and see what's listed. If the full name of your graphics card isn't there and it says something like Generic VGA adaptor, your drivers aren't installed properly. For onboard graphics cards, download the drivers from the motherboard manufacturer's website.

For graphics cards, make sure you've got the latest driver from Nvidia's or ATI's website. With both of these, it's important to fill out the request forms properly, as doing so will take you to the latest driver for your card. Not all downloads contain information for all cards, though. The latest Nvidia driver, for example, may not have drivers for a GeForce 8800 GTS graphics card, so trying to install from that will display an error message.

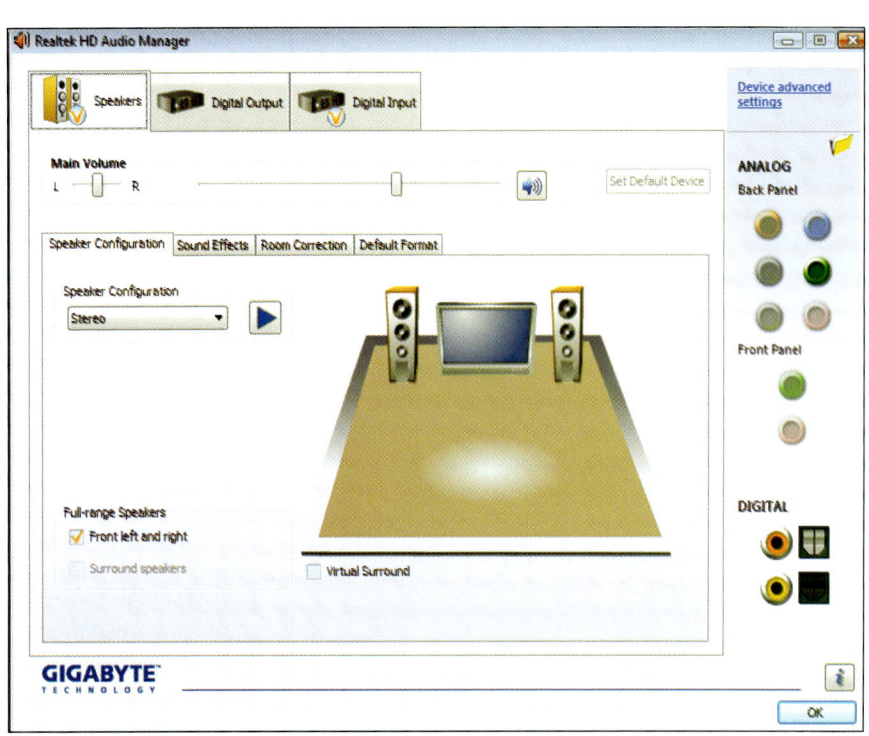

■ Your sound card should have a control panel where you can test the audio

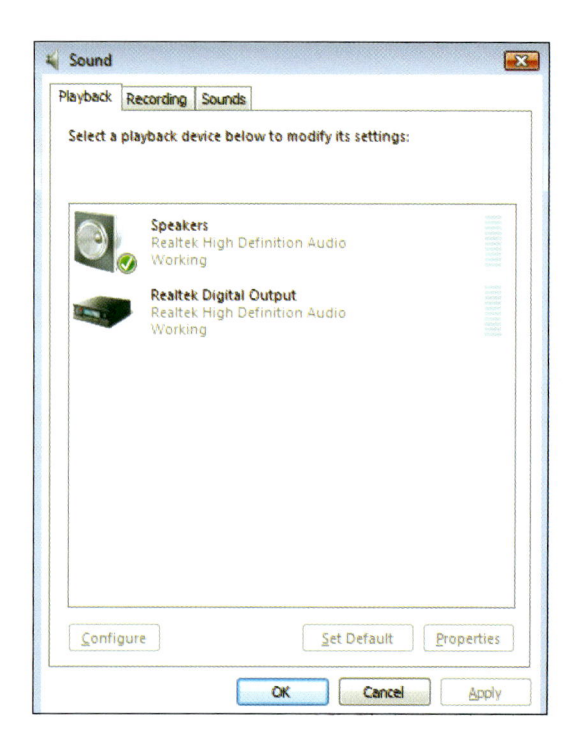

■ Windows can help you choose which audio device you want to use for sound

130 BUILD A BETTER PC

Includes laptop upgrades

The Complete PC Upgrades Handbook 2009

Your step-by-step guide to upgrading *any* PC

144 PAGES Brand new! Fully updated

£7.99

ISBN 1-906372-33-0

View your **FREE** sample at
www.computershopperbooks.co.uk

ON SALE NOW AT WHSmith

Or to order direct call 0844 844 0053 or visit www.computershopper.co.uk/upgrades

CHAPTER 9
TROUBLESHOOTING

Once your graphics card is correctly installed, you can check that it's working by pressing Windows-R, typing dxdiag and pressing Enter. This will show you details of your hardware and let you know which version of DirectX (required for playing games) you're running. Those of you running Vista will be using DirectX 10, while XP owners should be running DirectX 9.0c. If dxdiag doesn't work in XP or you're running an older version of it, update to version 9.0c on Microsoft's website (*http://tinyurl.com/directxinstall*).

If you're running Vista and find that you can't use some of the new features, such as Flip3D (this turns all open windows into a 3D slideshow, and is accessed by pressing the Windows key), then it's because Aero has been turned off. Aero is the new Windows manager, and is only turned on when a graphics card that supports its features is detected. All too often, though, Windows can't properly detect a dedicated graphics card at installation, and so turns this feature off. To turn it back on, right-click on the desktop and select Personalize. Select Windows Color and Appearance, choose Windows Aero from the list and click OK.

WIRELESS NETWORK ADAPTORS

If you're using wireless networking and have installed your network adaptor, you may find that Windows' wireless network configuration tool can't see any networks. In all likelihood, this is because your wireless adaptor has installed its own management software. You can use this application to control access to wireless networks, but often this software isn't very good. You'll also have to turn to the wireless adaptor's manual to find out how to use it.

A better way is to force Windows to take control over a network adaptor. This can be done in several ways. First, a lot of client software can be turned off by right-clicking the icon in the Notification Area and selecting an option. This is usually along the lines of Let Windows manage this connection or Disable client software.

You may still have problems with Windows displaying a message that it can't manage a wireless connection, though. This can be easily fixed. In XP, right-click on the wireless icon in the Notification Area and select Open Network Connections. Double-click the wireless network connection, click Properties, click the wireless networks tab and select Use Windows to configure my wireless network settings.

In Vista, it's a little harder. Click on the Start menu and type cmd. Right-click on cmd.exe and select Run as administrator, selecting OK in the dialog boxes that appear. At the command line type netsh wlan show settings.

Make a note of the name of the interface on the final line (probably Wireless Network Connection). Type netsh wlan set autoconfig enabled=yes interface="name of the interface you noted down". This should let you manage your wireless card through Windows.

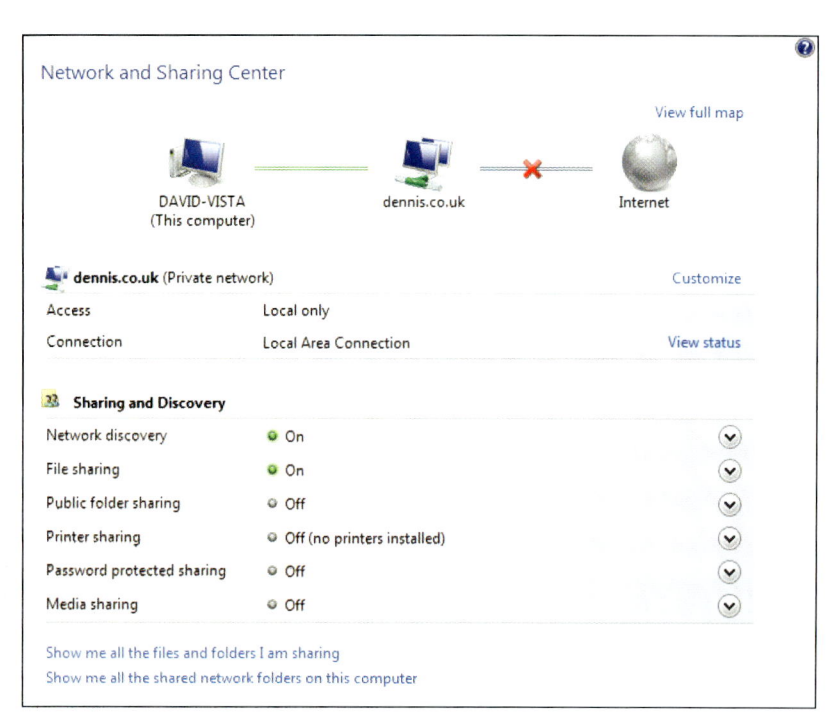

■ Vista's Network and Sharing Center is used to manage all your network settings

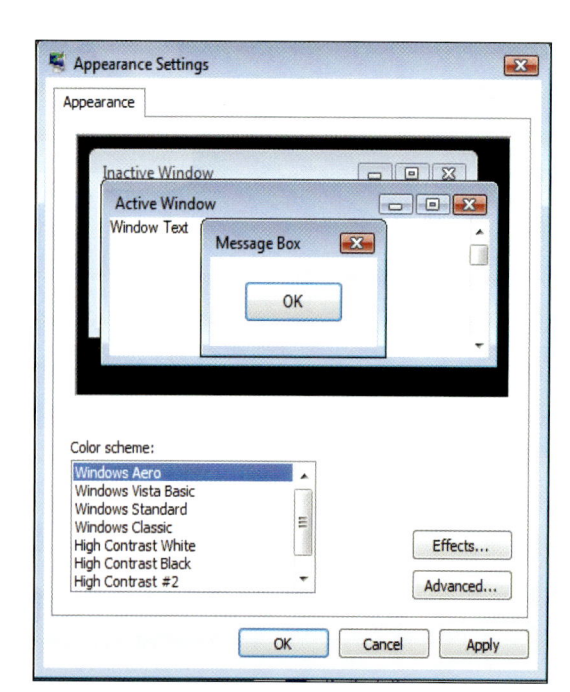

■ To use the new graphical features of Windows Vista, you need to enable Aero

132 BUILD A BETTER PC

TIPS & TRICKS EXPOSED

The independent UK guide to

eBay 2009

HOW TO MAKE SERIOUS MONEY ON EBAY

OVER 120 eBay ADD-ONS TESTED

NEW! UPDATED & EXPANDED

FROM THE MAKERS OF **COMPUTER SHOPPER** **PC PRO**

ISBN 1-906372-26-8
9 781906 372262
£7.99

THE ESSENTIAL GUIDE TO BUYING AND SELLING

ON SALE NOW*
To order direct call **0844 844 0053** or visit
www.computershopper.co.uk/ebay2009
*Available at WHSmith, Tesco, Sainsbury's, Borders, ASDA and Amazon

JUST £7.99 + FREE P&P

CHAPTER 9
TROUBLESHOOTING

Testing memory

MEMORY IS ONE of the most important components of your PC. It stores every aspect of the programs and data that you're currently running, from the window showing your holiday snaps to the spreadsheet with your accounts. Memory also holds important Windows data, such as device driver information and the core components of how Windows works.

A problem with memory can, therefore, be incredibly serious. For example, if your memory should corrupt a critical part of Windows, when the processor tries to use this data, it can end up causing a serious system crash. This can result in damage to Windows and the loss of any important data that you were working on.

To prevent this happening, it's worth running some diagnostic tests on your computer using the free Memtest86+ (*www.memtest.org*). This utility runs directly from a bootable CD before Windows has started and runs a series of tests on your system memory. Any problems reported here could lead to major problems in Windows. The step-by-step guide opposite shows you how to run the test, but here we'll explain what to do with the results.

ERRORS
An error doesn't automatically mean that you've got a major problem with your memory. First, try checking the BIOS to find out what speed your memory is running at (see page 82 for instructions on how to do this). If it's running faster than it's supposed to, then you could be pushing it too much. Our guide on testing for system heat (page 138) is also worth reading. If your system temperature is too high, then you could be suffering from its effects.

It's always worth checking the obvious things, too. If you didn't plug your memory all the way in, it may be detected but cause intermittent faults. Try unplugging your memory and reseating it. Once you've done this try, run the Memtest86+ program again to see if the problem has disappeared. If it hasn't, it's time to try a new tack.

SWITCH SLOTS
It could be that one of the memory slots is causing the problem. Try switching memory slots on your motherboard and rerunning the test. If you're getting the same error, there's probably something wrong with your memory. You can attempt to find out which stick of RAM is causing the problems by taking out all the memory bar one stick and running the tests again. By rotating the stick of installed memory, you'll be able to track down the offending stick.

As processors access memory through their own onboard caches, your processor could be causing the error. If you change your memory and the problem persists, you should change the processor or motherboard.

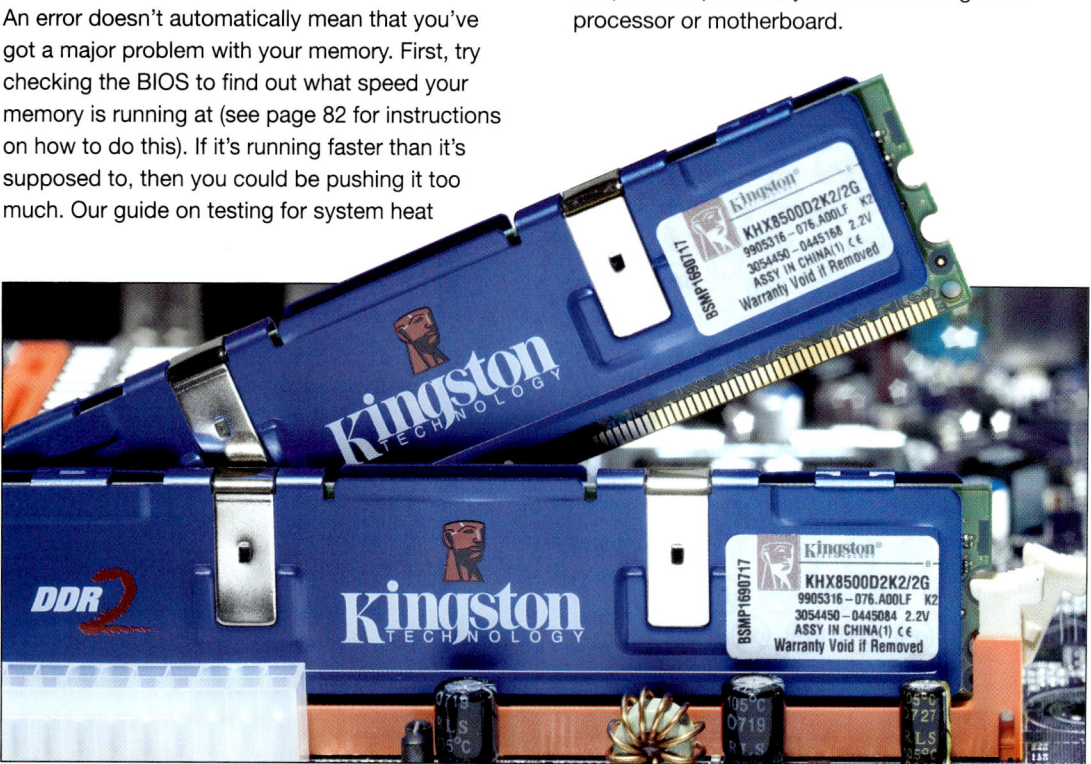

> **TIP**
> Often, only one stick of memory is at fault, so it's worth replacing each stick one by one to try and solve any problems.

■ A problem with your system memory can make your new computer frustrating to use

134 BUILD A BETTER PC

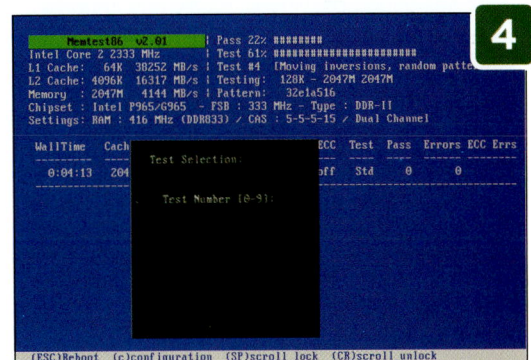

HOW TO...
Test your memory

1 CREATE BOOT DISK
Memtest86+ runs from a CD. Download the ISO file from *www.memtest.org* and save it to your hard disk. If you've already got a CD-burning utility such as CDBurnerXP, you can follow the instructions for writing the ISO file to CD. If you haven't, download the free ISO Recorder from *http://isorecorder.alexfeinman.com*. Version 2 is for XP and Version 3 is for Vista, so make sure you get the right one.

Once the software's installed, find the ISO file you downloaded, right-click it and select Copy image to CD. Put a blank disc in your optical drive and click Next.

2 BOOT FROM THE CD
Put the CD that you just created into your drive and restart the computer. Make sure that your BIOS is set to boot from the optical drive. The CD will automatically load the test environment and start running the tests.

On the screen, you'll see system information and the current test status. The test can take 20 minutes or more to run, so you should leave it running. When it finishes, you'll either get details of the errors discovered or a message saying that your memory has passed the test.

3 COMPARE DATA
The details on the screen show you the speed your memory is running at. This is displayed after the settings heading, in brackets after DDR. You should compare this to the speed that it's supposed to be running at. If the detected speed is faster than the memory's rated speed, you could have a problem. However, don't worry about small fluctuations in speed, such as a difference of around five per cent. It's common for the timings to be slightly wrong and components made to run a bit quicker than their rated speeds.

4 CONFIGURE TEST
If you want to configure which test to run, you need to press C while the initial test is running. You may need to reset your computer and boot from the CD you created to get this option. In the menu, press 1 to access the test selection. Press 3 to select the test you want to run, and then type a number from 0 to 9 to run that test. You can find a list of the tests on the Memtest website.

CHAPTER 9
TROUBLESHOOTING

Testing your hard disk

WE'VE ALL BECOME used to having masses of storage space, which most of us stuff full of gigabytes of photos, videos, music and important documents without a second thought. As wonderful as this all is, hard disks are mechanical and are, therefore, quite sensitive. They can fail rapidly and, even if they don't lock up completely, they can cause problems to some files.

Although you should make regular backups, it's also worth checking your hard disk after you've built your PC to make sure that it's reliable and won't cause you problems. Don't worry if you find a problem, as you can use the guide on taking an image of your PC (page 118) to save your installed operating system and restore this to a new hard disk. We'll show you how to test for free using Hitachi GST's Drive Fitness Test application (*www.hitachigst.com/hdd/support/download.htm*). Although it's made by Hitachi, it works on all brands of hard disks. It's run from a bootable CD, which we'll show you how to make.

■ Hard disks are mechanical devices that can malfunction in a number of different ways

HOW HARD DISKS WORK
The problem with hard disks is that they're mechanical, and are therefore prone to faults. Inside the sealed enclosure are a series of platters, which are disks stacked above each other. These platters, like floppy disks, store data magnetically, and are written to and read by heads that sit just above the surface. Hard disks are therefore very sensitive to movements, as sudden jerks can make the heads touch the platter and destroy any data that's stored on the disk.

If you get problems when you run Drive Fitness Test, make sure your hard disk is firmly attached inside the case and that your computer is standing on a level surface. We've known of a computer that was kept on an old wobbly desk constantly having problems with corrupted Windows files.

PROBLEM DETECTION
Other problems can affect a disk, including lots of bad areas on the disk (known as sectors). These might be detected in normal use only when you fill your disk up and your computer starts trying to access these areas. By running a system scan beforehand, you can detect these bad sectors now. These will be marked as bad by the hard disk, which prevents data being written to them, but you should replace the hard disk if you find that you get a large number of bad sectors.

Mechanical problems are also a big worry. A damaged disk can make a horrible, metallic clunking sound. While there's little that can be done to prevent this in the long term, running diagnostic tests that access the whole disk can warn you of potential mechanical failure in the future by giving the hard disk a good workout.

Heat, as for other components, can cause massive problems inside a hard disk, so make sure that the inside of your PC is kept cool, and add more cooling if necessary (see page 138 for more information).

Modern hard disks have built-in S.M.A.R.T. technology. This lets your BIOS and other applications talk to the disk and see if there are any problems. S.M.A.R.T. can also notify you of an impending disk failure before it happens.

Finally, the interface between the hard disk and your PC can cause problems if it's damaged. In this case, there's nothing you can do but replace the hard disk.

HOW TO...
Test your hard disk

1 CREATE BOOT DISC
Drive Fitness Test runs from a CD that you can create yourself. Download the ISO file from *www.hitachigst.com/hdd/support/download.htm* and save it to your hard disk. If you've already got a CD-burning utility, you can follow use that to write the ISO file to CD.

If you haven't, download the free ISO Recorder from *http://isorecorder.alexfeinman.com*. Version 2 is for Windows XP and Version 3 is for Windows Vista, so make sure you get the right one. Once the software's installed, find the ISO file you downloaded, right-click it and then select Copy image to CD. Put a blank CD into your optical drive and click Next.

2 BOOT FROM THE CD
Put the CD in your optical drive and restart your PC. Set the BIOS so that your optical drive is the first boot device. You'll be given a menu with a choice of two options. Select the second option and press Enter. Accept the licence agreement by selecting I Agree. The Drive Fitness Test program will then detect your hard disks, and ask for confirmation that this list is correct. Select Yes.

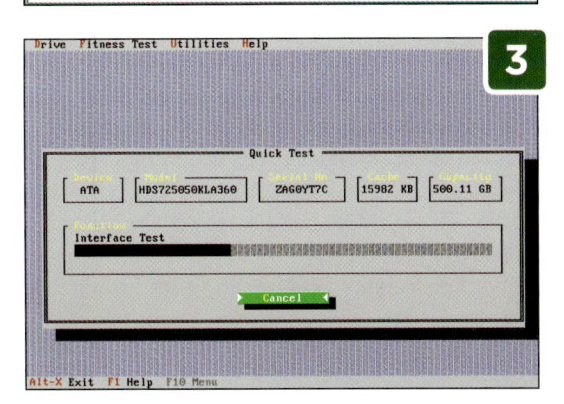

3 RUN A QUICK TEST
Select the hard disk you want to test and then choose Quick Test. On the next screen, click Start. Drive Fitness Test will now run a series of diagnostic tests on your hard disk to make sure it's working properly. If the software detects any errors, you'll be told at the end of the test; otherwise you'll get a green completion message. Click OK to accept it.

With a brand new disk this should be good enough to show that it's working correctly. If you're using a hard disk from an old computer, follow Step 4 for a more in-depth test.

4 ADVANCED TEST
The Quick Test doesn't give the drive a full workout. For this you need to run the Advanced Test. This will run more thorough tests and check the surface of the disk for errors.

As this involves checking every part of the disk, this test will take a lot longer to run than the Quick Test, but it's worth doing, particularly if you're using an old disk from an existing PC. It's also essential if you think that your hard disk could be causing problems.

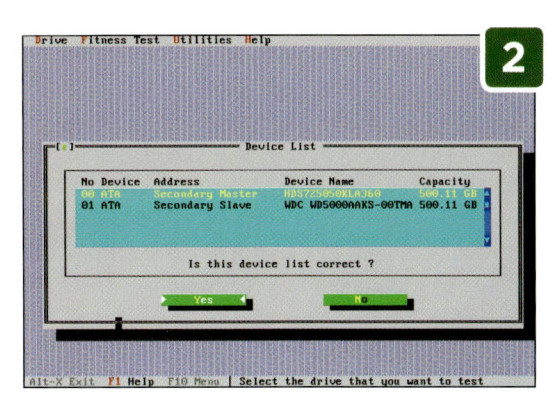

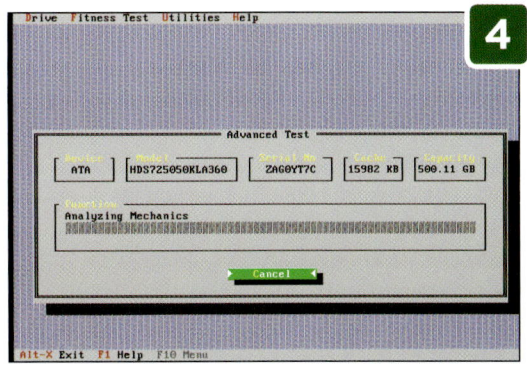

TIP
You should run Windows Check Disk on your hard disks regularly to find and fix faults before they become too serious.

BUILD A BETTER PC **137**

CHAPTER 9
TROUBLESHOOTING

Testing your new PC for heat

EVERYTHING INSIDE YOUR computer generates heat to some degree. It may seem obvious that your processor does – after all, it has a giant fan and heatsink on top of it – but all components produce a certain amount of heat. Memory, hard disks, graphics cards and even your optical drive all contribute to the overall internal temperature of your PC's case.

Heat is a big problem inside computers. If it's too hot, you'll find that your PC will crash more often, as the components shut themselves down to prevent damage. In the long term, the effects of heat inside your system can cause your components to have a shorter lifespan. In the case of your hard disk, this could see it failing before its time, taking some of your important data with it.

MONITOR AND MEASURE

It's really important, therefore, to make sure you've got a PC that's running at the right temperature. Keeping it cool will save you trouble and hassle down the line. Our step-by-step guide on the opposite page shows you how to monitor your computer's temperature with the free utility SpeedFan. You can download this from *www.almico.com/speedfan.php*. Click the download tab and click the link in the download section of the page. Once installed, it can monitor and help control the temperature inside your PC. Before you can set it properly, though, you need to know what should be expected from your system.

IDEAL TEMPERATURES

To get SpeedFan working properly, you'll have to set some maximum temperatures. These can be tricky to work out, but we've got some tips that should help. Hard disks, for example, shouldn't run any higher than 55°C, or they can be damaged. Overall system temperature inside the case should be kept below 50°C, but the lower the better.

Processors are harder to measure, as it depends on the type you're using. Generally speaking, AMD processors should have an external temperature of less than 40°C. Intel processors should have an external temperature of less than 55°C.

■ Keeping your PC cool will extend its lifespan

You may find that, depending on your system, your temperatures are either close to these figures or a lot lower. A lot of this depends on the temperature sensors in your PC. Motherboard manufacturers use different quality sensors placed in different locations, which can cause a lot of variance between boards. As long as you're running your computer at temperatures less than we've highlighted, it will be fine.

MORE FANS

If your PC is running really hot, there are some things you can try to lower the temperature. First, try reseating your processor cooler, making sure it has enough thermal paste on it to increase the efficiency of the heatsink. Make sure your case's fans aren't clogged up with dust. If you've got manual control over your fans, try turning them up.

Finally, if you haven't got any case fans or have enough space for more, then install some. They're easy to fit, and pretty much every case has mountings for them. Inspect your case's manual for full instructions on the size of fans you can install. Ideally, you want to get airflow moving through the case to extract hot air. So, if your fan at the rear is blowing out the back of the case, fit one in the front that blows into the case. This will bring in cool air from outside and help push the hot air out of the case. If you've got one hot component, such as a hard disk, then you need to try and fit fans near it to help cool it down.

> **TIP**
> Fans have arrows printed on them showing the direction of the airflow.

HOW TO...
Monitor system temperature

1 READINGS

SpeedFan automatically detects temperature sensors on the motherboard and displays their current readings. Unfortunately, it doesn't always give them very good names, so it can be hard to tell which one is your processor's temperature and which one is the system temperature. The easiest way to tell is to leave your system idle for a few minutes until the temperatures settle. Note down the temperatures, restart your computer and go into the BIOS. Its monitoring section will give you real names for the sensors – all you have to do is match the relative values you recorded.

SpeedFan places an icon next to each temperature reading, which is designed to show you the current status of your computer. A green tick means that everything's all right, arrows show whether the temperature is increasing or decreasing, while a fire means that it's too hot. However, SpeedFan doesn't always get the warnings right, so ignore them for now.

2 HDD AND CORE

As well as accessing the motherboard, SpeedFan can read the temperature of your hard disks using S.M.A.R.T.. Each disk in your PC will be numbered (HD0, HD1 and so on and have its own temperature). You can also get a report on your hard disk by clicking on the S.M.A.R.T. tab. The core temperatures are the readings directly from inside your processor.

3 CONFIGURE SETTINGS

Click on the Readings tab and then on Configure. You'll see the list of temperature sensors. Click to select one, wait a few seconds and then click again. You can now rename the sensor to match what you identified in Step 1. Press Enter to set the name. Single-click a sensor and you'll see two readings: desired and warning. The first is an ideal temperature, while the warning determines when a flame will be displayed. You only need to set the warning temperatures for hard disks and the external processor temperature, as defined by the limits we set above.

4 CHARTS

Click on the Charts tab and put ticks in the sensors that you want to measure. SpeedFan will then track temperatures over time. This is a good way to see how your system responds when you do different jobs. For example, if you play a lot of games and see that your temperature is running very high during this activity, you'll know that you need to get some extra cooling. This can also be useful when running burn-in tests, such as Hot CPU Tester (see page 141).

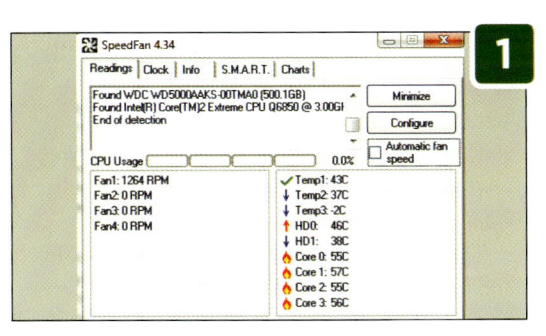

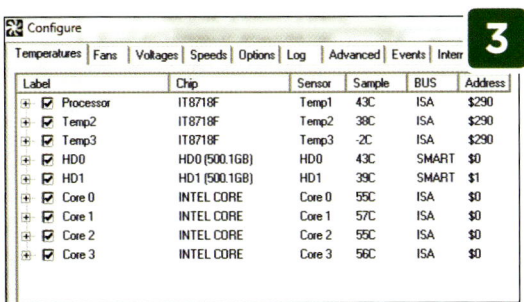

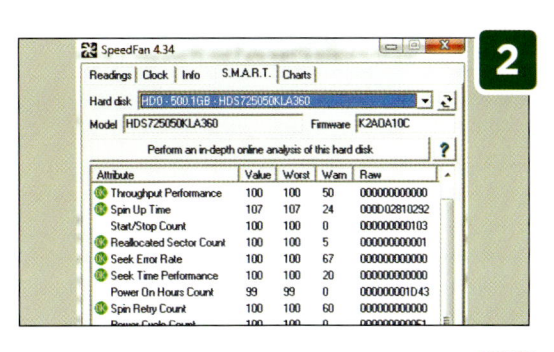

BUILD A BETTER PC

CHAPTER 9
TROUBLESHOOTING

Testing your processor

THE PROCESSOR IS just about the most important part of your PC. Without it, you'd just have a collection of components that wouldn't be able to do anything. The processor controls every single aspect of your computer, from loading and running the operating system to running the clever artificial intelligence in the latest games.

Processors are constantly being updated and are also becoming more complicated. These days, it's the norm for a single chip to house at least two processors (called cores in this context), but four cores are rapidly becoming more affordable. While this extra complexity means that computers today can storm through tough tasks such as video encoding quicker than ever, the result is that there's more that can go wrong. A processor crashing will immediately freeze your computer, losing any unsaved work in the process. If the hard disk was being accessed at the time with an important Windows system file open, a processor crash can even mean that you need to reinstall Windows. Here we'll show you how to test your computer for stability with the free Hot CPU Tester (*www.7byte.com*).

PROBLEM SOLVING
The free version of Hot CPU Tester doesn't run the full suite of diagnostics, like the Professional version. However, there's enough there to make sure that your processor is running properly. Using its Burn-in test, you can find out how effective your processor's cooling is.

The most common resaon for a processor to fail any of the diagnostic tests is heat. Processors are sensitive to heat, and can start causing errors when they get too hot. Intel's processors try and deal with the problem by slowing themselves down, which makes your computer very sluggish until the core temperature has dropped. Alternatively, processors can shut themselves down completely, meaning that you need to restart your computer.

COOL OFF
The essential thing with processors is to make sure that there's plenty of cooling. Follow our step-by-step advice opposite to work out how hot your processor is. If it exceeds the limits we set on page 138, you've got a problem. Take your PC apart and make sure that its fan is working and that there's decent contact between the processor and the cooler. You may need to reapply thermal paste.

If heat doesn't seem to be the problem, and your processor is still failing diagnostics checks, make sure you're running it at the intended speed in the BIOS (see page 82). Running the processor faster than it is meant to can cause errors.

Finally, try taking the processor out of its socket. In Intel LGA-775 sockets, look for any bent pins. If you see any, push them gently back into place with a jeweller's screwdriver. For AM2 and AM2+ processors, make sure that you haven't bent any pins on the processor. Inserting a credit card between the rows should let you bend them back into shape.

■ The most complicated part of your computer, the processor needs to be kept cool and stable if your new build is to be successful

HOW TO...
Test your processor

1. SET TEST DURATION
Install Hot CPU Tester (*www.7byte.com*) and run it when the installation has finished. Click OK to skip the message about upgrading to the new version. Before you start, click on the Options tab and select the Test Modules item. You'll see that the test duration is set to six hours. While this will give your PC a thorough workout, it's probably too much for most people. We'd recommend setting it to an hour or slightly under.

2. RUN TEST
Click on the Diagnostic button and click Run Test. Hot CPU Tester will then give your processor a thorough workout. It will run lots of mathematically complex tasks to stretch your processor to its limit. It will use every core in your PC, so you'll be unable to use your computer for anything else during this time.

Once the program has finished the test, you'll receive a report telling you if your processor failed any of the tests. If it didn't, you know it's working properly.

3. BURN IN
Click the Burn-in icon. This test will run your processor at 100 per cent load, and is useful for checking how temperature affects it. However, in the free version of Hot CPU Tester, which tests only a single core, you can only run a single thread. A workaround is to run Hot CPU Tester as many times as you have cores by double-clicking the program icon.

4. MEASURE
Before you start the Burn-in test, run SpeedFan (see page 139) in order to measure the temperature. Keep it somewhere onscreen where it will be visible. Start the Burn-in test on every open copy of Hot CPU Tester by clicking the Run CPU Burn-in button. SpeedFan may stop responding, as your processor is too busy to deal with it. Don't worry; just leave the test running for around 10 minutes and then stop all the Burn-in tests. When they're stopped, look at the temperature of the processor in SpeedFan. If it's exceeded the limits you set for it, you may have overheating problems.

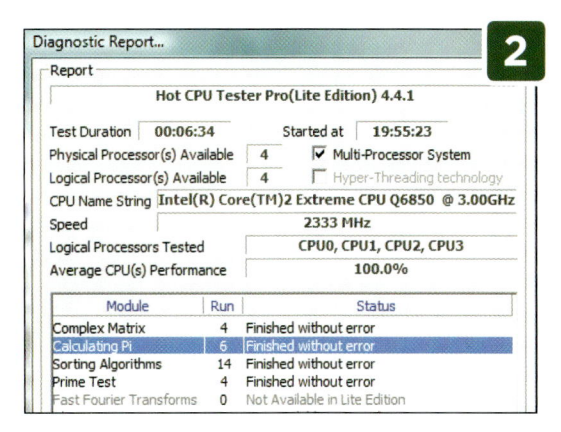

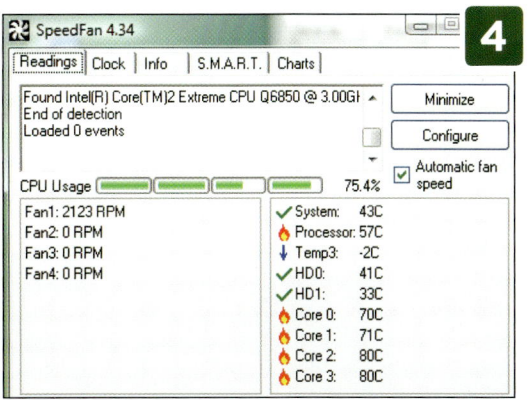

TIP
If you've got fan speed switches inside your case, try using them to increase fan speed to cool a hot processor down.

CHAPTER 10
JARGON BUSTER

Glossary

From ADSL to ZIF, we explain 100 key PC terms – with pictures

10/100Mbit/s See Ethernet.

10BASE-T See Ethernet.

64-BIT 64-bit processors have an extended instruction set, allowing them to process more data at once and access more memory. Only software that supports 64-bit extensions will benefit.

802.11b, 802.11g See WiFi.

ADSL Asymmetric digital subscriber line, the commonest form of broadband. It works over existing BT phone lines, provided that the local exchange is ADSL-enabled.

AGP Accelerated graphics port, a slot for graphics cards. Several versions of increasing speed and decreasing voltage were launched. Now superseded by PCI Express.

ATA AT attachment. See IDE.

ATAPI AT attachment packet interface. See IDE.

ATHLON 64 AMD's current mainstream processor. Has been made for Socket 754, Socket 939 and now Socket AM2.

ATX POWER CONNECTOR This PSU connector supplies the PC's motherboard. It was previously a 20-pin connector, but a 24-pin version started appearing on motherboards in 2005. A split connector is commonly provided to power either version.

ATX See Form Factor.

BIOS The basic input/output system configures your motherboard at startup and boots your PC. It's stored on a flash memory chip and keeps its settings in the CMOS.

BLANKING PLATE Used to cover unoccupied PC case cutouts. You must remove one to install a PCI, PCI Express or AGP expansion card.

BTX See Form Factor.

CARDBUS The 32-bit expansion slot most commonly found on laptop PCs, equivalent to the PCI slot on desktops. Is now being superseded by ExpressCard.

CAT5, CAT6 See Ethernet.

CELERON Intel's budget processor. Current models are cut-down Pentium 4s, available for Socket 478 and LGA775.

CLOCK SPEED All computer components work in time with a clock signal. Each has a maximum clock speed, shown in megahertz (MHz) or gigahertz (GHz), at which it's designed to run. Running the clock faster (overclocking) boosts performance, but can cause a PC to crash.

CMOS Battery-backed memory where the BIOS stores its settings. Can be cleared using a jumper.

COMPONENT VIDEO A high-quality analogue video connection using three cables.

COMPOSITE VIDEO A basic-quality video connection using a single cable.

CORE 2 Intel's newest processor, available for LGA775 in mainstream Duo and premium Extreme versions.

CPU Central processing unit, also known simply as a processor.

CROSSFIRE ATI's system for combining the power of two Radeon graphics cards in a single PC. Also see SLI.

CRT Cathode ray tube. Refers to a conventional glass-tube monitor.

DDR The type of memory used in most current PCs, called double data rate because it runs twice as fast as SDRAM of the same clock speed. Comes in several speeds, including PC1600, PC2100, PC2700 and PC3200. PC3200 DDR runs at 200MHz but is called 400MHz DDR because of its doubled effective speed.

DDR2 The type of memory used in the newest Pentium 4, Core 2 and Athlon 64 systems. Available in speeds from PC2-4200 (533MHz effective).

DHCP Dynamic host configuration protocol. This allows PCs on a network to obtain their network configuration automatically from a DHCP server, often running on a router.

DIMM Dual inline memory module, a common name for the similar physical packages in which SDRAM, DDR and DDR2 come, with 168 pins, 184 pins and 240 pins respectively.

DIRECTX Windows extensions from Microsoft that give games and other performance-hungry software fast access to hardware. Check that your PC has the latest version – currently 10 – installed.

D-SUB Analogue monitor-to-graphics-card connection, also known as a VGA cable.

DUAL-CHANNEL Capability of a processor or motherboard to access two DIMMs at once, improving performance.

DVB-T Digital Video Broadcasting – Terrestrial, a standard used by Freeview digital TV in the UK.

DVI Digital visual interface. A monitor-to-graphics-card connection that can include digital and/or analogue signals. The commonest form, DVI-I, has both.

ETHERNET Non-specific networking term, today used to refer to any networking hardware using RJ45 plugs and one of a number of compatible standards including 10BaseT, 100BaseT and Gigabit Ethernet (GbE). Older 10/100Mbit/s hardware supports only the two slower speeds, and runs reliably with the Category 5 (Cat5) grade of cable. The highest grade, Cat6, is a safe choice for Gigabit networks.

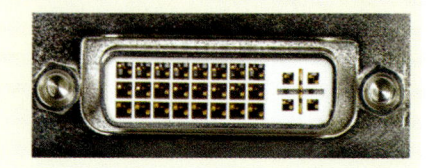

EXPRESSCARD Expansion slot found on new laptop PCs, equivalent to PCI Express on desktops. Incompatible with CardBus.

FAT32 See NTFS.

FIREWALL Software or hardware designed to protect networks from hackers or from software that they control.

FIREWIRE Also known as IEEE 1394 or i.Link. Fast data connection used by PCs, digital camcorders, external hard disks and more. The connector comes in four-pin and six-pin versions, the latter including pins to power one device from the other. A faster nine-pin version, known as FireWire 800, is backward-compatible.

FIRMWARE Software used by a hardware device and stored on a flash memory chip so that it can be upgraded, typically to improve compatibility.

FLASH A type of memory chip that stores data permanently unless it is deliberately overwritten, a process known as flashing.

> **FLOPPY POWER CONNECTOR**
> A compact four-pin power connector for floppy drives.

FORM FACTOR Motherboards adhere to standards called form factors that dictate size and layout. The commonest are ATX and its compact relative microATX. BTX is Intel's newest standard. Cases will support one or more form factors, telling you which motherboards can be fitted.

FSB The frontside bus connects the processor and other parts of the system. On all but the latest motherboards, the memory runs at the same speed as the FSB – typically 133MHz, 200MHz or 266MHz.

GIGABIT ETHERNET (GbE) See Ethernet.

> **HEADER** A group of pins on a motherboard where you can connect additional ports. USB and FireWire headers are the most common.

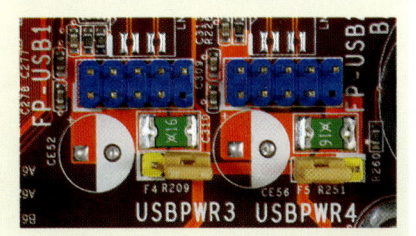

IDE A common name for the ATA disk connector, strictly called ATAPI in its modern form, which supports a variety of devices. All three are also known as PATA (Parallel ATA), to distinguish them from SATA (Serial ATA).

IEEE 1394 See FireWire.

JUMPER A plastic-enclosed metal contact used to connect two pins to configure a hardware device. For example, see Master.

LGA775 Intel's current processor socket, with pins rather than holes. Used by Pentium 4, Celeron and Core 2 processors.

LINE-IN Audio input for signal of standard 'line-level' volume (louder than microphone input). Usually light blue and takes a 3.5mm jack.

LINE-OUT Audio output of standard 'line-level' volume. Usually lime green, and takes a 3.5mm jack.

> **MASTER** Two IDE devices can share a single cable, provided that one is configured as a master and the other as a slave. This is done using jumpers on the devices.

MICROATX A compact mainstream motherboard form factor of maximum size 244x244mm.

MIMO Multiple-input, multiple-output: a way of improving the range and performance of wireless (WiFi) networks using multi-faceted antennas. A technology, not a standard. See Pre-N.

MOLEX Common name for the four-pin power connector used by hard disks and other drives. It has yellow (12V), red (5V) and two black (ground) wires.

NTFS Hard disk file system used by XP, Vista and other advanced versions of Windows. Replaces FAT32, as used by Windows 95, 98 and Me.

OEM Original equipment manufacturer. Used to describe products intended for PC manufacturers rather than end users. Typically these will have minimal packaging and manuals.

PATA See IDE.

PC100, PC133 See SDRAM.

PC1600, PC2100, PC2700, PC3200 See DDR.

PC2-4200 See DDR2.

PCI A motherboard expansion slot used for all kinds of upgrade cards except graphics cards. Internal modems, TV tuners and sound cards generally use PCI.

PCI EXPRESS (PCI-E) New expansion bus for all kinds of upgrades. Slots come in several lengths. Long, fast x16 slots are for graphics cards; short, slower x1 slots are for devices previously made for PCI. A slower card can be used in a faster slot.

PENTIUM 4 Intel's current mainstream processor.

PHENOM AMD's latest processor is designed for Socket AM2+ motherboards, but can work with some older Socket AM2 boards, too.

> **PHONO** Hi-fi style interconnect, correctly known as an RCA jack and used for various audio and video connections. Red and white plugs are used for right and left audio channels, yellow for composite video.

POST Power-on self-test, performed by PCs when switched on, generating the text output that you see before Windows loads.

PRE-N A term used for wireless networking equipment based on the draft 802.11n standard, which has not yet been finalised. Uses MIMO technology.

> **PRIMARY CHANNEL** Most motherboards provide at least two IDE connectors for hard disks and other drives. The PC will boot from the master disk on the connector marked as the primary channel. The secondary channel is typically used for CD and DVD drives.

PS/2 CONNECTOR Used for keyboards and mice, although these now often connect via USB.

PSU Power supply unit. Refers to the device inside a PC that converts mains electricity and distributes it to the system's components, and also to the external mains adaptors supplied with some peripherals.

BUILD A BETTER PC **143**

CHAPTER 10
JARGON BUSTER

RAID Redundant array of inexpensive disks: a way of storing data on several hard disks to improve performance, or to provide a backup if one disk fails, or both. Modern motherboards support RAID on their PATA or SATA ports.

RAMBUS The company responsible for the expensive RDRAM type of memory used for a few years in Pentium III and Pentium 4 systems. Now obsolete, RDRAM came in modules called RIMMs. If your PC needs it, try eBay.

RCA See Phono.

RDRAM See Rambus.

RF Radio frequency, referring to the coaxial cable connection of TV antennas. An RF signal carries many video channels, while S-video and composite carry only one.

RIMM See Rambus.

RJ45 Plug used for Ethernet network cables, with eight wires. Larger than, but often mistaken for, RJ11.

SATA The Serial ATA interface is used for modern hard disks because it's faster and neater than PATA (Parallel ATA). The original SATA ran at 150MB/s, but the current standard has a 300MB/s mode, compared to PATA's maximum of 133MB/s.

SDRAM The memory type used by most Pentium II and Pentium III PCs. Common speeds are PC100 (100MHz) and PC133 (133MHz).

SECONDARY CHANNEL See Primary Channel.

SERIAL PORT Old, slow port rarely used today but still present on many motherboards as a nine-pin connector.

SLAVE See Master.

SLI Nvidia's system for combining the power of two GeForce graphics cards in one PC. Also see CrossFire.

SOCKET 478 Intel's previous-generation processor socket, still supported by a handful of new motherboards and Pentium 4 and Celeron processors.

SOCKET 479 Socket for Intel's Pentium M and Core Duo mobile processors, the predecessors of Core 2.

SOCKET 754 Socket used by AMD's early Athlon 64 and current Sempron processors. Only supports processors with a single memory controller.

SOCKET 939 Socket used by AMD's Athlon 64 processors, including dual-core X2 versions. Supports processors with a dual memory controller.

SOCKET A Also known as Socket 462, used by AMD's old Duron, Athlon, Athlon XP and Sempron processors. Now obsolete.

SOCKET AM2 AMD's processor socket, which supports DDR2. Used by Athlon 64, Athlon FX and Sempron processors. Very similar to Socket 939 with one extra pinhole.

SOCKET AM2+ AMD's latest processor socket, which supports PC-8500 DDR2 memory and Phenom processors. Backward-compatible with older processors.

S-VIDEO An average-quality analogue video connection with a four-pin cable.

TV-OUT Generic analogue output used for connection to a TV. Includes S-video and composite.

USB Universal serial bus. These ports are used to connect all manner of external devices.

USB2 The latest version of USB, which supports the Hi-Speed 480Mbit/s mode as well as older USB 1.1 devices.

VIVO Video in, video out. A compound connector on graphics cards that combines video inputs and outputs. Usually has a breakout cable that maps the pins to standard S-video or composite video connectors.

WEP Wired equivalent privacy. An encryption standard used to secure wireless networks. Comes in various strengths up to 256-bit, all weaker than WPA.

WIFI Name used collectively for the IEEE 802.11 wireless networking standards, including the 11Mbit/s 802.11b and 54Mbit/s 802.11g standards.

WPA WiFi protected access. An encryption standard used to secure wireless networks more reliably than WEP.

ZIF Zero insertion force: a processor socket where the chip is clamped using a lever.

BUILD A BETTER PC

EDITORIAL
Editor
David Ludlow
david_ludlow@dennis.co.uk
Production
Steve Haines
Design and layout
Colin Mackleworth

CONTRIBUTORS
Chris Finnamore, David Ludlow, Jim Martin, Kevin Pocock

PHOTOGRAPHY
Danny Bird, Timo Hebditch, Andrew Ridge, Hugh Threlfall

ADVERTISING
Julie Price
ads.shopper@dennis.co.uk

INTERNATIONAL LICENSING
The content in this bookazine is available for international licensing overseas.
Contact Winnie Liesenfeld
+44 20 7907 6134, winnie_liesenfeld@dennis.co.uk

MANAGEMENT
Bookazine Manager
Dharmesh Mistry (020 7907 6100, dharmesh_mistry@dennis.co.uk)
Publishing Director
John Garewal
Operations Director
Robin Ryan
Group Advertising Director
Julian Lloyd-Evans
Circulation Director
Martin Belson

Finance Director
Brett Reynolds
Group Finance Director
Ian Leggett
Chief Executive
James Tye
Chairman
Felix Dennis

A DENNIS PUBLICATION
Dennis Publishing, 30 Cleveland St, London W1T 4JD. Company registered in England. All material © Dennis Publishing Limited, licensed by Felden 2008, and may not be reproduced in whole or part without the consent of the publishers. Dennis Publishing operates an efficient commercial reprints service. For more details, please call 020 7907 6640.

LIABILITY
While every care was taken during the production of this bookazine, the publishers cannot be held responsible for the accuracy of the information or any consequence arising from it. Dennis Publishing takes no responsibility for the companies featured in this bookazine.

Printed by BGP, Bicester.

The paper used within this bookazine is produced from sustainable fibre, manufactured by mills with a valid chain of custody.

ISBN 1-906372-53-5